PRAISE FOR

GOING TO THE CHAPEL

"If anyone is up to the task of creating a comprehensive wedding guide for black couples [it's] the editors of *Signature Bride* magazine. . . . *Going to the Chapel* serves as a one-stop resource for practically every aspect of planning a wedding."

—*Asbury Park Press*

"Discusses the basics of invitations, meal planning, music, and other practical details . . . as well as tips from black designers and other experts. Today's sophisticated bride can turn to *Going to the Chapel* for ways to plan a wedding across a spectrum of color and culture. Whether you want to walk down the aisle in a long gown with two hundred friends and family . . . or fly twenty of your nearest and dearest to Jamaica to witness the exchange of vows on the beach at sunset, *Going to the Chapel* has a wealth of information and will guide you from the planning stages to your wedding in style."

—*Amsterdam News*

"Refreshingly direct."

—*St. Petersburg Times*

"[Gives] no-nonsense, useful advice for couples about to tie the knot . . . does more than address Afrocentric wedding attire. It also lays out in detail African wedding rituals and deals with touchy subjects such as telling an ex-spouse about a new engagement and how interracial couples should talk to their respective parents."

—*The Des Moines Register*

Going to the Chapel

From Traditional to African-Inspired,
and Everything in Between—The Ultimate
Wedding Guide for Today's
Black Couple

The Editors of *Signature Bride* Magazine
Produced by The Philip Lief Group, Inc.

Berkley Books / New York

A Berkley Book
Published by The Berkley Publishing Group
A division of Penguin Putnam Inc.
375 Hudson Street
New York, New York 10014

PRINTING HISTORY
G. P. Putnam's Sons hardcover edition / January 1999
Berkley trade paperback edition / February 2001

Berkley trade paperback ISBN: 0-425-17650-9

The Penguin Putnam Inc. World Wide Web site address is
http://www.penguinputnam.com

The Library of Congress has catalogued
the G. P. Putnam's Sons hardcover edition as follows:

Going to the chapel : from traditional to African-inspired, and everything
in between—the ultimate wedding guide for today's Black couple
/ by the editors of Signature bride magazine ; produced by the
Philip Lief Group, Inc.
p.   cm.
ISBN 0-399-14463-3
1. Weddings—United States—Planning.   2. Wedding etiquette—
United States.   3. Afro-American—Marriage.   I. Philip Lief
Group.   II. Signature bride.
HQ745.G62   1999
395.2'2—dc21   98-27882 CIP

PRINTED IN THE UNITED STATES OF AMERICA

10 9 8 7 6 5 4 3 2 1

ACKNOWLEDGMENTS

This book has become a true labor of love for everyone involved, much like *Signature Bride* magazine. As publisher of *Signature Bride* magazine, I would like to personally say thank you to the following people for their vision, contributions, and dedication to this book and *Signature Bride* magazine. Without these people this book could never have been created.

Judy Linden, Fiona Hinton, and Diane Rhodes at The Philip Lief Group, and Adrienne Ingrum, Sarah Gearhart, and Amelia Montgomery, for seeing our vision and for putting their full support behind us and our book series. Thanks for everything. You have truly captured the essence of *Signature Bride* and have beautifully transformed the magazine into our newest creation, *Going to the Chapel: From Traditional to African-Inspired, and Everything in Between—The Ultimate Wedding Guide for Today's Black Couple*. Thank you for your talents and your patience.

To Denise Silvestro, Martha Bushko, Diane Lomonaco, and all the others at Penguin Putnam for believing in us and creating such a wonderful publication. I look forward to a long working relationship. To the staff at *Signature Bride* magazine—each and every one of you is truly appreciated more than you'll ever know.

And to the numerous others listed below whose help has been invaluable:

Michael Adams
Audra Alexxi and Lewis van Arnam of LVA Represents, Inc.
Sharon Ayers of Turning Heads Beauty and Barber Salon
Boyega and Jonathon Adewumi of Nigerian Fabrics and Fashions
Thony Anyiam of Anyiam's Creations International
Association of Bridal Consultants
Byron Barnes
Waheedah Bilal
Lee Bradley of The Gold Connection

Andrea Buckley of FTD Flowers
Harriette Cole
Patty Collette of Patty Cakes
Jim Collier, videographer
Vince Cowan of Vince Cowan Photographer
Nikki Davis-Webb
Andrea Fisher of the Greater Ft. Lauderdale Convention and Visitors Bureau
Lateefah Fleming-Williams
Peter Furla of Furla Photography
Herbert Garrett of Garrett's Photography and Video
Mary Gearhart, photographer and gallery owner, for her technical and moral support
Beverly Gianna of the New Orleans Metropolitan Convention and Visitors Bureau
Leona Gonsalves, artist and entrepreneur, for her inspired research
Larry Grasso, impresario of Mott Street, for his wit and sartorial wisdom
Mildred Greene
Eleanor Henderson
The customer service staff of Heritage Weddings™ mail-order catalog
Charles Hodges
Jacquie Hughett of the Greater Miami Convention and Visitors Bureau
Iman
Lois Ingrum, photographer
Charmaine Jones of Isn't That Special—Outrageous Cakes
Stacy Jones of Pioneer Balloon Company
Felischa Marye of Mary Kay Cosmetics
Sam Mattingly of 1-800-FLOWERS
Rev. Ella Pearson Mitchell and Rev. Henry Mitchell
Gerard and Eileen Monaghan of the Association of Bridal Consultants
Michael Morris of 52 Shades Photography and Video
Willie Myers of Myers Photography and Video
Kali Ndoye
Ruth Oliver
Reggie Payton
Lois A. Pearce of Beautiful Occasions

Barbara Pflaumer of Alfred Angelo
Beverly Reese of From the Earth to You
Yvette Rosado of Sasaki
Tony Rose of Tony Rose Studios
Polly Schoonmaker of Polly's Cakes
Frank Sciolino of Concept Creations
Jacqui Scott of Elegant Brides
Dorothy Shi
Margaret Spicer, Professor of Drama and Adjunct Curator, the Hood Museum, Dartmouth College, for her knowledge of fabrics and conservation
Jane Smith
Matthew Jordan Smith
James Spada
Brittanica Stewart
Ingrid Sturgis
June Terry
Monique Todd of the South African Tourism Board
Christine Valdes of the Tourism Marketing Alliance
Debbie Vyskocil of DLV Productions
Cookie Washington of Phenomenal Women Design
Carlos Webb
Winston Williams
Vietta Wright

And to my family and friends, thank you for being you. You've all been so involved with *Signature Bride* magazine and the development of the book. You've shared in both our joyous and not so joyous times. I truly appreciate your always being there.

And lastly, my deepest gratitude to our readers. Without your support, we wouldn't be doing what we do best. A lot of you have invited us into your wedding plans and your Big Day through your letters, e-mails, and phone calls. I personally feel I've attended each and every wedding! I wish you the best of everything now and forever more.

With sincerest thanks,
Debra Kronowitz
Publisher, *Signature Bride* magazine

THE PROJECT TEAM

Publisher
Debra Kronowitz, *Signature Bride* magazine

Editorial Director
Judy Linden

Project Manager
Adrienne Ingrum

Writer
Sarah Gearhart

Wedding Consultants
Amelia Montgomery
Linnyette Richardson-Hall

Illustrator
Kelvin Oden

Assistant Editors/Photo Researchers
Fiona Hinton
Diane Rhodes

SIGNATURE BRIDE MAGAZINE EDITORIAL ADVISORY BOARD

Iman
President, Iman Cosmetics
New York, New York

Linnyette Richardson-Hall
Past President, Association of Minority Wedding
Professionals; President, Premiere Event
Management, Ltd.
Baltimore, Maryland

Dr. Linda Owens
Psychologist, The Owens Group
Atlanta, Georgia

Lois Pearce
Director of Ethnic Diversity,
Association of Bridal Consultants
New Milford, Connecticut

Dr. Marlene Watson
Family Therapist, Allegheny University
Philadelphia, Pennsylvania

Deryl Wallace
President, Flowers to Remember
Vallejo, California

C O N T R I B U T O R S

We'd like to gratefully acknowledge and thank all the writers whose articles, which first appeared in *Signature Bride* magazine, are now used in this book:

Jen Beeh, "With This Ring," Winter/Spring 1996.

Harriette Cole, columns from Fall/Winter 1996, Spring/Summer 1996, Summer 1997.

Andrea Diaz, "Wedding Consultants, Good, Bad and Ugly," January/February 1997.

Crystal Downs, "A Look at the Bridal Consultant," Spring/Summer 1995; "Something Old, Something New," Winter/Spring 1996.

Melanie Gray, "Balloon Artistry," Summer 1997.

Gloria Green, "Not for Weddings Only," Spring/Summer 1996; "Hands Up!" Spring/Summer 1996; "You Deserve a Break for a Day," Fall/Winter 1996; "The Mane Event," January/February 1997.

Rolanda Hatcher-Gallop, "One Bride, Two Jobs," Fall 1997.

Kathleen Hayes, "Picture Perfect," Spring/Summer 1995; "Getting that Bridal Glow," Spring/Summer 1995; "Beyond Flowers," Fall/Winter 1995; "Planning the Ultimate Party," Fall/Winter 1995; "All Decked Out," Winter/Spring 1996.

Jewelle Hicks, "What You Need to Know About Flowers," Spring/Summer 1995.

Wilburt Jones, "Soul Food Buffet," Fall/Winter 1996; "The Morning-After Brunch," Summer 1997.

LaKellee Van Keuren, "Keeping the Faith," Winter/Spring 1996.

Gia LaDonna, "When it Comes to Hair . . . " Fall/Winter 1995; "When it Comes to Skin . . . ," Winter/Spring 1996.

Linda Lawson, "Fitness Countdown," January/February 1997.

Jacqueline Y. Metcalf, "Losing Unwanted Pounds," Summer 1997.

Catherine Poindexter, "You've Got the Power," Spring/Summer 1996.

Simona E. Rabsatt, "Surfing for Wedding Help," Fall 1997.

Mary Jo Rasmussen, "Choosing a Honeymoon Getaway You'll Both Love," Spring/Summer 1995; "Savor the Caribbean," Fall/Winter 1996; "Tropical Paradise," January/February 1997.

Ata Rivers, "Paradise . . . the Sights, Tastes, and Sounds of the Caribbean," Fall 1997; "Barging Offers Luxury and Romance," Fall 1997.

Sari Rubin, "Innovative Shower Ideas to Pass Along to Family and Friends," Winter/Spring 1996.

Ingrid Sturgis, "Rituals," Summer 1997.

Carla Underwood, "In-Laws and Out-Laws," Spring/Summer 1995; "Bridal Bubbly," Fall/Winter 1995; "Balancing Work and Marriage," Fall/Winter 1995; "Yours + Mine = Ours," Winter/Spring 1996; "Oh, Sweet Music," Winter/Spring 1996; "Editor's Note," January/February 1997.

Christine Valdes, "Reach for the Stars, Reach for Each Other . . . and Not Have to Reach for Your Wallet!" Fall 1997.

Theresa Volpe, "The Essential Finishing Touch," Spring/Summer 1995.

CONTENTS

Signature Bride weddings are all about Black love.

*I*F EVER THERE was a time for self-expressing, being true to yourself, and going for what you know, it's on your wedding day. Yet we editors at *Signature Bride* have noticed that the same Sisters who can transform an outfit from Sunday-go-to-meetin' into Friday-night-special often find themselves lost in the clone zone when the time comes to strut their stuff down the aisle—"Just forgettin' themselves!" as our grandmothers might say. Maybe it's because for so long we've been overly influenced by "rules" laid down by God knows who or urged to go with the flow and follow other folks' patterns. But there is help available, and you're holding it in your hands.

Going to the Chapel provides you with all the information you need to get married in your own individual style. As a woman of color, you may want to examine your perceptions of "bridal" and the kinds of statements you can make on that Day of All Days. We'll help you re-evaluate all the old rules, choose the ones that have meaning for you, creatively bend the ones that you find too confining, and break any that just aren't "you" at all.

We say explore *all* the options. If a long white gown and all the trimmings is what you've dreamed of since childhood and anything different would seem unfulfilling and flat-out strange, don't let anybody turn you around, saying it's not "Black enough." We'll help you embrace the traditional wedding with your own special touches and meaning. If wearing kente cloth and pouring a ritual libation for the ancestors best expresses your sense of heritage as well as your sense of style, we'll show you how to plan an Afrocentric ceremony that's as authentic or as eclectic as you desire. And if you're a "wild child" with your own all-tradition-be-darned taste, we'll give you dynamite information with which to explode those old bridal do's and don'ts and plan your day your way.

Maybe you're a little of each of these, wanting to observe some established traditions, create a few of your own, as well as put your personal *signature* on one of the most important events of your life. *Going to the Chapel* covers the whole gamut, all the ways to celebrate love and marriage across the spectrum of color and culture. We give you the guidelines and practices that were established in Europe centuries ago and have been handed down for generations in America. These we call "Traditional," in quotes, to acknowledge that there are *other* traditions—those of Africa and the whole African Diaspora—that may speak just as powerfully, or more so, to you. Whatever rituals and customs you want to plan your ceremony around, we'll help you do that. The only "rule" we lay down is that your wedding day is *your* day (even though your mother may lead you to believe otherwise): We want you to go for it, Sister. Let it express *you, your* love, *your* commitment!

This is our philosophy here at *Signature Bride* magazine, the only bridal lifestyle magazine for today's Black woman. We launched the magazine in 1995 and we're now proud to kick down the doors of bookstores with another first: *Going to the Chapel* is the first *complete* sourcebook for Black brides. You'll find it full of faces, styles, and references that are *you* and information and advice that will inspire and guide you and your bridegroom as you create your perfect ceremony.

So kick off your shoes and curl up with your man on your favorite couch. Let us show you all the exciting possibilities for self-expression available to you at every stage of planning. We'll help the two of you define your wedding fantasies and then bring them into the realm of reality. We'll take you step by step through all the intricacies of setting a reasonable budget, hiring the right vendors, choosing the perfect location for your special day. You'll find everything you'll need right here, gathered together in one book, to make your dreams come true.

Linnyette Richardson-Hall

—Linnyette Richardson-Hall
    Special contributing editor, *Signature Bride*
        magazine
    Past president, Association of Minority
        Wedding Professionals
    President, Premiere Event Management

It's _your_ day! The only "must" is _joy!_

YOUR DAY, YOUR STYLE, YOUR WAY

OU'RE SO DIZZY with happiness that you can barely think straight. You're getting married. Congratulations! Your head tells you there's lots to do, but right now your heart has taken over. Every fantasy you've had since childhood about your Day of All Days is dancing before your eyes.

This is exactly the time to listen to your heart and focus on those fantasies.

Wedding Trends for the '90s

Say good-bye to "the rules" and say hello to individuality when it comes to planning your wedding. The old "Traditional" guidelines may work for some couples, but for others flexibility and personal style win. We have compiled a list of current trends Sister-brides want to share with you:

1. *All for One and One for All.* **It's becoming the norm for couples to pay a portion of, or perhaps the entire, wedding tab.**

2. *Bringing Heritage to the Party.* **Choosing Afrocentric readings, invitations, and fashions, and jumping the broom are just a few things done to honor our culture.**

3. *Long-Distance Planning.* **Today it's not unusual for couples to live in one city, away from either family, or in two cities, away from each other. Couples in these situations are some times planning "honeymoon" or "destination" weddings that take place in exotic settings.**

4. *The More the Merrier.* **When your wedding takes place in a city other than where the majority of your family and friends reside, post-honeymoon receptions in your hometown give everyone a chance to celebrate with you.**

5. *Save-the-Date Announcements.* **The computer age offers couples a creative way to share their good news and ask their guests to mark their calendars well before formal invitations are mailed. You can e-mail or design and print your own announcement.**

6. *Music to Move the Soul.* **Consider jazz, R&B, reggae, or calypso. Look into using string instruments (piano, harp, and guitar) and a keyboard for your wedding ceremony and reception.**

7. *Hire a Bridal Consultant.* **With the majority of Sister-brides-to-be in the workforce, the services of a bridal consultant can help keep you stress-free and on budget.**

If you and your man take the time now to develop a vision of your ideal wedding, in as much detail as possible, you will be more likely to hold on to the elements that are most important as you move through the actual stages of planning and preparation.

If you envision all 200 of your nearest and dearest toasting you, you'll find a way to do it. If your dream is to exchange the vows that express your commitment in your own words on the shore of a Caribbean island at sunset, you can make your dream come true. Keep that grand toast and sunset in the picture.

Pay attention to your own inner voice and let your man do the same (before everybody else starts talking), as you imagine *your* perfect ceremony and celebration. For the moment forget the inevitable constraints of money, time, and social obligations.

Yeou have countless choices in planning your wedding festivities—from Afrocentric to African-American to European, from "Traditional" to just plain personal, from formal to semiformal to informal. Here are a few sample scenarios to get you started in your own process of selection:

Afrocentric

Picture this: You are wearing a beautiful wedding gown of *aso alaro,* an elaborately patterned Yoruba cloth, and your hair, makeup, and nails are looking better than they ever have in your life. You're poised to walk down the aisle to join your beloved. The air suddenly fills with the sound of dramatic drum cadences and your flower girl begins an African dance. When you reach the front of the roomful of your assembled guests, you and your man invoke the spirits of your ancestors by pouring a ritual libation. After you've exchanged vows, the officiant symbolizes your union by joining your wrist to your husband's with a string of cowrie shells. At the end of the ceremony, your guests and your groom's guests walk forward to embrace each other in the center of the room and then switch sides, to signify their full acceptance and support of each spouse.

Nikki and Carlos Webb decided on an Afrocentric wedding to share their pride in our African heritage with their friends and family.

Jumping the Broom

The broom has had symbolic significance in many African cultures—as the means of "sweeping away" the past and the influence of evil spirits, as a sign of the willingness to take on the responsibilities of a new family and home, and as an instrument of peace and harmony.

In the time of slavery in this country, African-American couples who were not allowed to marry in the eyes of the law adopted the ritual of jumping the broom to seal their vows and mark the beginning of their homemaking.

African-American

You're wearing your mother's wedding gown. The congregation has just sung your favorite gospel hymn in the church you were baptized in, and the minister who performed the ceremony is the same one who did the baptizing. Nearly everyone here is someone you grew up with—your grade school friends, your next-door neighbors, even the first boy you had a crush on. This is your "hood," and they've all gathered to see you on your Big Day (half of them are crying). You're husband and wife now, and you're about to jump the broom to symbolize your new life together before you head off to the parish hall for some of your grandmother's fried chicken and biscuits.

"Traditional"

You're standing with your father at the entrance to a beautiful cathedral filled with guests in formal evening attire. The tones of the *Trumpet Voluntary* echo joyously throughout the grand space. You glance over your shoulder one last time and then take the first of the steps that will lead you down the aisle to the altar and culminate in those familiar yet suddenly new and personal words: "I take thee to be my wedded husband, to have and to hold from this day forward . . ."

Jumping into the future together!

Lateefah and Winston Williams made
"Traditional" very *special* in their wedding choice.

Honeymoon Wedding

Or maybe you're standing on the shore of that Caribbean island. Twenty of your closest family members and friends have flown in for your "honeymoon wedding." You're all staying in private cottages near the sea, with a main house where you and your guests gather for meals and evening entertainment. *This* evening you'll be celebrating your marriage, toasting each other with rum punch, and dancing to reggae music on the terrace under the stars.

Michelle and Frank Reid brought their entire wedding party, including Michelle's parents, Thomas and Audrey Porter, to Guadalajara, Mexico, where they married in a beautifully landscaped villa with the ocean and mountains at their back.

Progressive Wedding

Or maybe you want a creative combination of several of these scenarios that takes place over several days: You get married in a small civil ceremony in San Francisco, where you and your groom live, then fly to his hometown in Mississippi for a reception (even a second, religious ceremony) with his family and friends, and then on to *your* family in Maryland for a post-wedding brunch before boarding the plane for your honeymoon in the islands.

These are just a few of your options (see chapter 11, "Your Ceremony, Your Way"). There are as many scenarios as there are brides and grooms. You may want to include traditional African rituals in your ceremony as individual touches rather than as a general theme. You may want a big family wedding, but not one that's quite so down-home. You may want a formal ceremony, but more contemporary than "Traditional"—with vows you've written yourselves, for instance. You may want the romance of a honeymoon wedding in a faraway place, but in Ghana instead of the Caribbean. Or perhaps your choice would be a progressive wedding that begins with a ceremony in Africa and with a reception at your homecoming in New York. Whatever your dream scenario, you will find a wealth of ideas and cultural offerings throughout this book—for every detail from invitations to keepsakes—as well as a complete list of resources that will help you make your dream a reality.

THE DETAILS OF YOUR DREAM

Set aside a quiet evening to begin to share your wedding fantasies with your fiancé. Our men are taking a much larger and more active role in the planning these days, and you may find that yours already has a clear vision. Carlos Webb knew he wanted to marry his bride-to-be, Nikki Davis, in an Afrocentric ceremony—and his vision matched hers: "I didn't feel any cultural ties to Western wedding traditions. We wanted to portray how proud we are of being of African descent. We wanted to consciously identify our marital union with our African roots and build a bridge for others to identify more with theirs. One of our goals was to educate our family and friends about wedding customs from the different regions of Africa."

Some men have a tougher time visualizing and verbalizing their romantic wishes. Give yours the kind of encouragement he needs. Maybe a candlelight dinner in your favorite restaurant would provide the right atmosphere and inspiration. Ask him about weddings he's attended that were especially meaningful to him. Let him read the scenarios given above.

Once you're both visualizing your dreams, use the following questions to help you develop a joint vision:

Where are the two of you? At your family's weekend house? In the church you grew up attending? In a beautifully decorated community hall? In an exotic setting—on a beach or a boat? In a formal ballroom? On the college campus where you first met each other?

What's the time of day and the time of year? Sunset on a summer evening? A winter's night with snow outside and a fire blazing in the fireplace? A soft spring morning? A crisp fall afternoon?

What kind of ceremony is it? A religious one in the church where you and your fiancé met? An interfaith ceremony with an officiant of each of your religions? A secular one presided over by a judge or justice of the peace? An African one drawing on ancient rituals?

What are each of you wearing? Are you, the bride, in an heirloom gown? A dress designed by a friend? Traditional African wrapped cloth or a gown with African-inspired details? Something *flyy* and sexy? What's *he* wearing? A grand *bubah* of rich brocade? A tuxedo with a kente cloth cummerbund? An elegant suit? Something vintage and wild?

Who's with you? All the important people in your life from childhood on? Those closest to you—your parents, your siblings, and your best friends? Just the two of you and a special witness?

Give each other time to express your answers fully and honestly. Really *listen* and be careful not to criticize if your visions at first seem very different. Jot down each of your ideas and work together at including the best and most dearly held aspects of both your dreams in your joint vision.

Some of your answers will help you define the degree of formality you want in your wedding. If you see yourself wearing a floor-length gown with a long train and a veil and several attendants, standing in a church filled with 100 or more guests in black tie and evening gowns, you're imagining a "Traditional" (Eurocentric) *formal* evening wedding. Strictly speaking, these are held in a house of worship, a hotel, club, or elegant home; the invitations are either engraved or printed; the ceremony is followed by a reception with drinks and a full dinner. The formal dress code is different if your ceremony is held before 6 P.M.

If you imagine something a little smaller that can take place at any time of day with fewer attendants and more latitude in dress, you're probably thinking of a *semiformal* ceremony. As the "semi" suggests, there are still formal elements involved, but they're more loosely interpreted. Your man and his attendants could wear dark suits and ties (daytime) or dinner jackets with dress shirts, bow ties, and vests or cummerbunds.

An *informal* ceremony can take place anytime (although daytime is most common) and just about anywhere. These are also usually the smallest ceremonies—you may choose to have only one attendant and a handful of guests. You could wear a suit or a dress of any length and your groom and his best man could wear coats and ties. (See chapter 4, "Your Signature Fashion," for more detail on formal, semiformal, and informal attire.)

Again, these are merely "Traditional" guidelines. Your ceremony need not conform exactly to any one of the definitions. You are free to have a hundred guests or more at your informal wedding if you wish, and formal doesn't mean that your eccentric Uncle Buddy can't relax enough to tell all those embarrassing stories about your old boyfriends. All the "Traditional" degrees of formality can also be interpreted and adapted to suit your cultural preferences. At a formal Afrocentric wedding, for instance, you and your groom could wear garments of African cloth and ask all your guests to come in African attire.

In general, formal weddings are the most expensive because they're larger and more elaborate, but even here there are ways to keep costs down. Wear your mother's gown instead of buying a high-priced designer dress. Have a buffet-style reception instead of a seated dinner. Get your Uncle Buddy's jazz band into tuxes to provide the music; if he's busy blowin' sax he won't be able to talk so much. Categories like "formal" and "informal" are just tools for you to use in establishing *your own* guidelines. As Nikki and Carlos decided when they were visualizing their ideal wedding, "Our main goal was to have a wedding that characterized our relationship, that was more personal, more spiritually meaningful. We customized our wedding by writing our own vows, designing our wedding garb, making an effort to incorporate into our ceremony African traditions and symbolism that were relevant to us and our feelings for each other."

When you and your fiancé have determined your joint vision, write it down in all its detail. It will be the basis for much of your decision-making and planning from now on.

DEFINING YOUR COMFORT ZONE

Now that you have your joint vision, review its main elements. Which ones are so central that you couldn't sacrifice them without losing the real meaning of your dream? Which ones would you be willing to modify or do without if time or money forced you to choose? If having 200 of your nearest and dearest toasting you at your reception is the most important part of your dream, perhaps you'll end up being toasted with sparkling wine at a brunch rather than champagne at a seated dinner. Maybe you'll be standing with your guests on the shore near a friend's beach house during that romantic sunset rather than on a Caribbean island.

Amelia Montgomery of Weddings by Amelia, a professional bridal consulting service based in Harlem, New York, suggests that couples address two potentially sticky issues in particular at this stage: how many people to invite and whether or not to include children. She's seen enough last-minute disagreements over these questions to recommend setting some limits early on.

If you and your fiancé take the time now to identify the elements that you consider absolutely essential—to establish the boundaries of your comfort zone with regard to possible compromise—you'll be able to preserve them as you turn your vision into an actual plan.

TURNING YOUR VISION INTO A PLAN

Every wedding plan has five basic elements:

- Financing
- Timing
- Location
- Type of ceremony
- Size

Let's look at your joint vision in relation to these elements.

Working out an adequate and acceptable plan for *financing* can be one of the most delicate pre-wedding tasks. According to "Tradition," the bride's family pays most of the wedding expenses. In the cultures of the African Diaspora, it is also the custom for the bride's family to host the festivities, although the groom's family makes a substantial contribution to the bride's family in other ways.

In the African-American community today, the most common alternatives for sources of financing are:

- You and your fiancé
- Your family or his
- A cooperative plan that includes all of these

Discuss these alternatives between yourselves before you approach your families. If you and your fiancé are independent enough and can afford it, you may decide you want to pay for everything, which can also mean that you have more freedom to do it your way. If you're just starting out and will need help covering the costs, perhaps the "Traditional" alternative is the one for you. The main thing at this stage is to *survey all the choices* (see chapter 3, "Plan Your Plan").

There may be circumstances in your lives that will influence your choice of *timing* for your ceremony. If you are in your final year of college, for instance, and one or both of you will be enrolling in graduate school, and you want to do so as a married couple, you'll probably set a date in the summertime. If either or both of you is in the military and you want to marry before you're stationed overseas or in order to qualify for married housing, that too will determine your choice of date. If you both have relatively flexible schedules, you can choose your favorite time of year and allow a generous period for planning.

The average engagement today lasts from eight to fourteen months, although it's always possible to marry either more quickly or more slowly. You may decide that you want extra time to save enough to be able to really go all-out or to be sure to be able to reserve your favorite site if you live in a large city, where you usually need to book a year ahead. Or perhaps, like Lateefah Fleming and Winston Williams, you also need the *emotional* time. "We were engaged for a year and a half," says Lateefah. "I couldn't concentrate on working and getting married. I was still in a very selfish stage." Winston adds, "I knew we could really make a run at this, but I wasn't financially or mentally ready to be married when I asked her. First you have to see God, then you have to be true to yourself."

Location is another crucial element, and one that may, in turn, affect timing. If it's always been your dream to be married at your family's beach house, you'll probably want to hold the ceremony in warmer weather. If you want to be married by the minister who baptized you, you'll need to find out when he's available. If you want all your friends and relatives to come, you should probably avoid a date that coincides with other family holidays (unless you want to combine your wedding with, say, a celebration of your parents' anniversary).

The *type of ceremony* you imagined in your joint vision may be one of the elements you consider beyond compromise. Religious and cultural matters are perhaps the most sensitive to consider in planning a wedding. If you share the same faith and manner of worship, your union can be a special spiritual celebration and even a joyous opportunity for religious observance. Talk with others of your faith about traditions old and new and get ideas from those who have been recently married.

If you and your fiancé come from different faiths, and you want to incorporate both in your wedding, begin now to explore all the alternatives for creating a ceremony that can accommodate both of your beliefs. (This may also be an opportunity for you to talk about your own spiritual values, something couples sometimes overlook during the excitement of dating.) Most religions now accept and perform interfaith marriages, though some officiants are more receptive to them than others. Ask friends who have had interfaith ceremonies or call the higher officials of your church for recommendations if your own clergy seem reluctant. Investigate all the options on your own, especially if you think that your families may feel uncomfortable with a faith other than their own. Family conferences about such important subjects, when you two are still undecided, can often only exaggerate the discomfort. Make a plan with your fiancé first. You may find that anticipated objections melt away in the face of your efforts to be inclusive.

Perhaps cultural traditions are important to you. If you two share the same cultural heritage and want to pay tribute to it in your ceremony, you need only discuss which of the rituals you want to highlight in your celebrations. If not, apply the same principles as you would in the case of different faiths. Consider choosing readings and symbols from both traditions for the ceremony, serving special dishes, and including special music and dances from both at the reception. There are many ways to embrace and celebrate differences in an event that symbolizes union (see chapter 11, "Your Ceremony, Your Way").

As Amelia Montgomery has already pointed out, the *size* of your wedding can be as important as any of the other elements. It's perhaps most closely connected to financing, since the more people you invite, the more it's likely to cost. Maybe you've envisioned a small, intimate ceremony—out of personal preference or because it will enable you to realize other aspects of your dream. If, on the other hand, a big gathering is one of your "won't compromise" elements, start to think about the ways you can achieve it. You'll need a location that can accommodate everyone—though that doesn't necessarily mean expensive—and a plan for celebrating *large,* which can also be done on a small budget.

Financing, timing, location, kind of ceremony, and size are all interrelated considerations in planning your wedding. All of them will be discussed in greater detail in chapter 3, "Plan Your Plan." For the moment, concentrate on achieving a mutual understanding of your options in regard to these elements. There's a piece of conventional wisdom that applies to the planning of a wedding: The way you and your man work together on this event is a good indicator of the way you will conduct your life together as a married couple. Of course you will also want to consider the feelings of your family and other loved ones on this most meaningful and emotional occasion. One of the best ways to do that is for you to spare them any disagreements you may have between yourselves and for the two of you to make some basic decisions now, in consultation with each other, so that you can then support each other completely in the days and months (and years) ahead. If the two of you are confident and comfortable with your own desires when you joyfully announce your engagement to the world, all those who care about you are more likely to feel comfortable, too.

HOW TO USE THIS BOOK

With your dream envisioned, your comfort zone established, and your options outlined, you're ready to get started on the actual plans, which will then be followed by more detailed stages of preparation. This book is designed to give you easy access to all the information you'll need.

Keep Talking

by Harriette Cole

Even in the best circumstances, friction flares from time to time as wedding plans develop. (This is your first fight, right?) After you and your fiancé have defined your comfort zone, find a healthy way of continuing to communicate through the subsequent stages of preparations. Establish one hour a week when you sit down to review plans—whether it's at dinner, on the way to work, on the telephone, or even on the Internet. Here are some guidelines to consider for your planning meetings:

1. Keep a list during the week of your questions and concerns, and recommend that your man do the same.

2. Unless there's timely information that can't wait, save your questions and concerns until the appointed hour.

3. Approach your meetings with love and tenderness.

4. When you don't agree on something, just agree to disagree for the time being. Next week each of you can come back to the issue with an idea that allows you both to "win."

5. End your meetings by determining what tasks need to be accomplished in the coming week and which of you will be responsible for them.

6. Have faith that you both will do the work at hand.

If you follow these guidelines, or a version of your own, both of you will be fully informed when your wedding day arrives. You will also have established a wonderful practice for regular communication throughout your marriage.

You may want to turn first to the *Bride's Calendar* at the back of the book (page 289). It will help you set priorities, establish and watch your budget, and keep track of things done and still to do—from the day of your engagement through the ceremony, reception, and honeymoon. It schedules and coordinates all the preparations, whatever your style of wedding, and is fully cross-referenced to the chapters of the book that deal in detail with each of its elements.

Throughout the text there are sidebars that offer useful tips on everything from African cultural accents to points of etiquette to recipes and sample menus from the Diaspora. Be sure not to skip the chapter on ways to keep your cool as the Big Day approaches. Check out the numerous line drawings and black-and-white photographs throughout that illustrate details and accessories. Use them in talking with the people who will provide you with services for your wedding and reception. A picture is worth a thousand words—and, trust us, you won't have time for a thousand words! Browse through the sixteen-page full-color album, picturing a wide range of wedding apparel—from Afrocentric to European, from traditonal to avant-garde—and a portfolio of registry gifts, floral arrangements, and balloon artistry, to give you ideas and inspiration. At the end of the book is a nationwide list of resources to help you locate and purchase the perfect bridal services and products, and a detailed index of all the information presented.

You've got each other and you've got the book—let's start planning your *signature* wedding.

The "Yes!" moment

WE'RE MAKING IT PERMANENT: ANNOUNCING YOUR ENGAGEMENT

So I turned from the realms of fancy
As remote as the stars above,
And into the land of the living
I carried the jewel of love.

—ANNIE L. BURTON

Carlos Webb: I was very nervous, even though I knew there wasn't a chance that Nikki would say no. We had been together five years and we were living together. But it was the biggest step I had taken in my life. I had the ring for about three days and was planning to propose at Nikki's favorite restaurant, but having the ring in my possession was making me very anxious, so in the middle of the night, I woke her up and said, "Let's go for a walk. Let's go to our favorite spot." Our spot is the steps in front of the Museum of the City of New York. She said, "No."

Nikki Davis: It was midnight. It was raining!

Carlos: So I had to figure out something else. The next day I made a cassette tape of our favorite love songs. I rented a car and told her I was going to pick her up from a class. I was so nervous, I ended up driving down a one-way street the wrong way! It was raining. I took her to dinner at Jezebel.

Nikki: It's my favorite restaurant. I was wondering why Carlos was acting so strange. I was enjoying my meal when I noticed that Carlos was barely eating. This was unusual because he loves to eat! And then as I was looking at the dessert menu, he was fumbling in his pocket and mumbling something about renter's insurance!

Carlos: I finally got the ring unstuck from my pocket. I designed it myself and had it handmade at the Studio of Ptah. [The ring has a sizeable central diamond buffeted by two smaller ones on each side that are cradled by gold ankhs on either side.] I just handed it to her. I was so nervous, I don't really remember what I said.

Nikki: I was so surprised and enamored with the ring that I barely heard what he was saying, and I began to cry. All I knew was that he was asking me to marry him. The waitress came over at just that moment and when she saw what was going on she said, "Oops. Did I interrupt something?" Then we went to our favorite spot on the steps in front of the museum.

Like Nikki and Carlos, the two of you will always remember the special moment when you became engaged. Right now, you surely feel like shouting the news from the rooftops and singing it out to strangers in the street. Soon you can do just that. Contain your joy long enough to make sure that all the people the two of you are closest to have heard it from you first, personally and privately. You wouldn't want anyone you care about to feel like the last to know. Think now of those who will be most affected by the news of your engagement.

TELLING YOUR PARENTS

If you are getting married for the first time, your parents will probably be among the first you'll want to tell, although if your fiancé is as truly "Traditional" as Winston Williams, whom you met in the previous chapter, they may already know. "We have to draw on what has gone before us," says Winston. "Parents, grands, aunts, uncles. Experience is the best teacher—their experience." So he spoke to Lateefah's mother and father about his intentions months before he proposed to her. "I was interning at her father's law office," he recalls, "and on the morning of my last day, I told her parents that I needed to talk to them. My heart was in my mouth. I

African and Caribbean Engagement Rituals

In many African and Caribbean cultures, marriage represents the union of two families, not just two individuals. Before a couple can even become engaged, they must ask the permission of their elders. Courtship often involves an elaborate series of negotiations—over several weeks or months—between the families of the young man and the young woman to make sure he can provide for her financial security.

Among the Koro People in Africa, the aspiring groom pays three ritual visits to the family of the girl he wishes to marry. On the first visit he gives them three shillings; on the second, four shillings; on the third, five shillings. He is then asked to bring three or four pounds and ten bundles of corn. If he cannot complete these payments in one year, he continues to make annual installments until he has given the full amount.

In the Virgin Islands, it is customary for the man to apply in writing for permission to court his beloved. Her parents then respond in writing. Before they marry, he must build a home for his bride. Some churches still practice the reading of the "wedding banns"—in which the minister announces a couple's intention to marry on three consecutive Sundays before the ceremony. This is a "Traditional" way to obtain the "license" to be wed, giving anyone who knows "just cause that these two should not be joined together" an opportunity to come forward.

Among the Thonga in South Africa, a young man puts on his finest ornaments and skins to make his betrothal visit. Afterward, his newly won intended accompanies him on his way back to his own village. At the place where they part, they tie knots in the tall grass as a sign of their love.

said, 'I'm dating your daughter, and she is the most beautiful, caring person I've ever met. I'm standing here in this office to ask if I can spend the rest of my life with her.' Her mother started crying. Her father said, 'No!'—and then, 'I'm just playing, we wouldn't have it any other way.' "

Your fiancé may have secured *your* "yes" first and now wants to make the "Traditional" gesture. There is no right or wrong way to proceed in these matters of the heart. If your parents know him and like him, it's perfectly appropriate for him to go to them for their blessing—alone, if he wishes, or with his happy bride-to-be at his side. If you're uncertain about how they'll react to the news, it may be best for you to prepare them in advance. If they've been hinting or nagging, forgive them and tell them in a way that will let them savor their knowledge of your decision.

If your parents only know *about* your fiancé (and vice versa) from your enthusiastic reports, you'll want to plan an introduction as soon as possible. In this case, postpone your announcement until they've had a chance to meet each other. You can avoid potential awkwardness by telling them of your engagement *after* they've met. Share the news with them by yourself, so they can express their reaction openly. If they have any reservations, you will be able to handle them more easily if your fiancé isn't present.

If your father or mother is no longer living, your fiancé may speak to the surviving parent. If he or she has remarried, advise your fiancé on what you feel is the best approach: If your stepparent raised you and has been an important part of your life, you'll naturally want that person to be present for the first announcement. If your parents are divorced, be guided by your own feelings and your sense of theirs. If they're still friendly, you may want to arrange for them to be together when you share your news. If not, your fiancé—or the two of you—may pay separate visits to each, first to the one you've been closest to. Again, there is no strict protocol except to be sensitive to everyone who's involved.

If necessary, gently remind your fiancé to tell his parents, too (alone, if they aren't well-acquainted with you); once he's talked to yours, he might assume all the talking's done.

When you and he have told both your parents, you may want to arrange for them all to meet each other by having them over for a meal or for coffee and dessert one evening. According to "Tradition," his folks should call on yours, by phone or letter if they aren't near enough to do so in person, and invite them to lunch or dinner, if possible, so they have a chance to become better acquainted. If they don't take the first step, it's appropriate for your parents to extend the invitation. "Tradition" aside, we recommend that the two of you take the initiative to get everybody together the first time. If your family regularly gathers for church on Sundays or for a weekly meal, these may be ideal opportunities to introduce your "new" family. Once they've met, encourage both sets of parents to get together without the two of you.

How you tell both sets of parents and bring them together at the beginning of your engagement can help set the tone for all future communication in the years ahead, and especially for the actual wedding planning and the division of responsibilities and expenses.

What to Do If Your Folks Aren't Thrilled

1. Be sure you have told your parents your reasons for choosing your fiancé.

2. Get them to state their objections as clearly as they can and listen carefully to their conerns. Make sure you understand what they are saying by repeating it in your own words.

3. Think about their concerns for at least a day, that is, "sleep on them," before responding to them or sharing them with your fiancé.

4. Speak to your parents on your own. Don't put your fiancé in the position of having to defend himself.

5. If they are worried about a difference in background or religion, about your financial security, or—if your fiancé has children—about your suddenly becoming a parent, reassure them that you've discussed these issues between yourselves and tell them your plan for handling them in your life together.

6. If you can't alleviate their concerns by yourself, seek the help of your minister or spiritual advisor, or some other close relative or friend whom your parents admire and who supports your engagement.

TELLING YOUR "OTHER" MOTHERS AND EXTENDED FAMILIES

One of the beauties of Black family life is its extended-ness. Grandmothers and grandfathers, "other" mothers and fathers—whether blood relatives or friends—can be just as important to you as your own parents. You may even want to tell *them* your happy news before you tell your parents. Make the occasion a special one—bring out their wedding album or engagement photographs; reminisce together about loved ones who may no longer be with you but would be excited for you.

TELLING YOUR CHILDREN

With more than 60 percent of our households headed by single parents, the number of African-American brides and grooms bringing children into marriages is substantial. If either you or your fiancé, or both, has children, you have probably already addressed the presence of an important new person in your life with them and their other parents. Children can be extraordinarily perceptive about these things no matter how much you try to protect them, and their father (or, in the case of your fiancé's children, their mother) will probably also have a sense of your relationship. Regardless of how well you and your fiancé have adapted to each other's family, marriage represents an official change in everyone's relationship to each other. Building bridges that can enable all of you to make the transition well is important work that begins with the way you announce your engagement.

The children should be told first, unless their other parents need to be prepared to help handle the children's responses. (The other parents should *not* be the ones to tell them, however.) Always tell your children this news by yourself, without your fiancé, to allow their true feelings to surface honestly. (This applies even to grown children, who can have even stronger feelings than younger ones.) If the children show signs of discomfort—or worse—when you make your announcement, this doesn't mean they won't eventually welcome the marriage. Remember that they need time to adjust. Give them regular, private opportunities to ask questions about their new stepparent and stepsiblings and to voice their concerns.

"Listen to your children, and when you finally think that you know what they're trying to express, listen some more," advises Dr. Liz Treiton, a family therapist practicing in New Orleans. With the increased activity and excitement leading up to the wedding, it can be easy to assume that your children are more comfortable with the new arrangement than they truly are. Sometimes they'll express their concerns *nonverbally*—acting out in school, becoming resistant to authority, or withdrawing from activities they normally enjoy. Dr. Treiton suggests setting aside time each day, once you've told them of your engagement, to ask questions like, "How are you feeling right now?" "Do you think I gave you enough attention today?" "Was there anything you wanted me to know that you thought I just didn't get?" Such efforts will help to create "safe zones" where your children will be able to open up, rather than act out.

As well as giving your children important "alone time" with you, continue to plan activities with them that include your fiancé. You may find that the two of you have some adjustments to make, too. "I had to learn to let Walter have equal control of my children," says Darlene Hunter, who had raised her two sons and one daughter alone for eight years. "Here I was, used to always having the final say about everything. I slowly began to let loose the reins as I began to trust Walter's decisions more." With time spent together with your children, your partnership as parents will grow more comfortable and trusting. Just be sure to spend the time. "No matter how busy we get," Walter says, "we try to do something as a family every week. Even if it's just going for a walk."

If your children and his are also going to be spending time together, help them begin to get to know each other now, to become familiar with each other's personalities and likes and dislikes— and be prepared for conflicts along the way. "If your children are suddenly faced with sharing everything that is dear to them—their personal belongings, their private space, and even their parent—don't expect this to be easy for them. Understand that these conflicts are necessary toward growth as a family," says Dr. Treiton. "Counsel them about what to do when disagreements with their new stepsiblings arise. Encourage them to be fair and to see the situation from each other's perspective."

Including your children in your wedding will help them feel a part of your bond and understand experientially that a new family unit has been formed.

Laying the groundwork for a successful stepfamily is a process involving respect—respect for your children's feelings and their right to express them, respect for the special bond they share with both natural parents, and respect for your spouse-to-be's position as co-captain of this new team. You may need plenty of patience and understanding during this process, but your rewards will be tenfold when your home is warm with love and acceptance in the years to come.

TELLING YOUR EX-SPOUSE(S)

If you've been married before and have no children, you should still think about whether to inform your ex-husband. It can be kinder and wiser to tell him directly rather than have him hear it through the grapevine, especially if you still live in the same town or share some of the same friends. If you aren't on good terms, or don't want to re-establish contact, a simple note will do. If your fiancé has been married before, encourage him to tell his ex, too.

Sample Wordings for Engagement Announcements

T raditional" wording, announced by the parents of the bride:

> Mr. and Mrs. Henry Palmer announce the engagement of their daughter, Nichole, to Gregory Driver, the son of Mr. and Mrs. George Driver of Hartford, Connecticut. Ms. Palmer, a summa cum laude graduate of Howard University, is a photojournalist in New York City for the *Amsterdam News*. Mr. Driver, who graduated cum laude from Vassar College and received his M.B.A. from New York University, is a systems analyst for AT&T, also in New York. An early autumn wedding is planned.

(Note: If the parents of the bride don't live in the city where the announcement is being made, you'd also include their place of residence: e.g., if this announcement is published in a New York paper, you'd specify "Mr. and Mrs. Henry Palmer of Atlanta.")

If your parents are divorced, and neither has remarried:

> Mrs. Olivia Palmer (or she may use her maiden name with her married name, "Mrs. Patterson Palmer") announces the engagement of her daughter, Nichole, to Gregory Driver . . . Miss Palmer is also the daughter of Mr. Henry Palmer of Atlanta.

(Note: If your parents are still friendly, they may want to make the announcement jointly: "Mrs. Olivia Palmer of Chicago and Mr. Henry Palmer of Atlanta announce the engagement of their daughter, Nichole . . ." Otherwise, the one who's raised you—usually your mother—does the honors.)

If your mother has remarried:

> Mr. and Mrs. Charles Greene (her new married name) announce the engagement of Mrs. Greene's daughter, Nichole Palmer . . . Miss Palmer is also the daughter of Mr. Henry Palmer of Atlanta.

GOING PUBLIC

N ow that your closest loved ones know, you can sing and shout—or at least publish your news as widely as you'd like. Announce it in newspapers and on the Internet, tell friends, fellow church members, sorority sisters, co-workers, and e-mail correspondents.

(Note: Here the mother has chosen to announce the engagement with her new husband, with whom the bride may be especially close. It is also acceptable for both natural parents, even if remarried, to announce jointly: "Mrs. Charles Greene of Chicago and Mr. Henry Palmer of Atlanta announce the engagement of their daughter Nichole Palmer . . .")

If one of your parents is no longer living:

Mr. Henry Palmer announces the engagement of his daughter, Nichole, to Gregory Palmer . . . Miss Palmer's late mother was the former Olivia Patterson . . .

(Note: This wording allows you to pay a special tribute to the deceased parent, perhaps mentioning his or her profession or special achievements.)

If both parents are no longer living:

↬ You may ask a close relative or friend to make the announcement:

"Mr. James Palmer announces the engagement of his niece, Nichole Palmer, to Gregory Driver . . . Miss Palmer is the daughter of the late Mr. and Mrs. Henry Palmer.

↬ Or, if both your and your fiancé's parents are deceased, you may announce the engagement yourselves:

Nichole Palmer, a photojournalist, is to be married to Gregory Driver, a systems analyst for AT&T, in early autumn. Miss Palmer is the daughter of the late Mr. and Mrs. Henry Palmer of Atlanta. Mr. Driver is son of the late Mr. and Mrs. George Driver of Hartford, Connecticut.

If you're remarrying:

Mr. and Mrs. Henry Palmer announce the engagement of their daughter, Nichole Palmer Parks (if you kept the name of your previous husband) to Gregory Driver . . .

Your fiancé can adapt these guidelines to the circumstances of his parents.

Formal Announcements

The "Traditional" place for you and your fiancé to make a formal announcement is in the newspapers where you live now—both the African-American weekly and the general dailies—as well as in those of your hometowns. If you're recently widowed or divorced, however, it is considered more respectful to spread the news of your engagement by word-of-mouth and only publish a wedding announcement. Black Muslims and orthodox Muslims also wait to make an announcement until after the marriage has taken place, and then do so in a publication such as the *Muslim Journal* or the *Final Call,* where the wording often takes the form of a simple "congratulations."

If you want to publish an engagement announcement, contact the society or lifestyle editors of the papers where you'd like it to appear and find out their requirements. Most now have a recorded list of the information you will need to submit. Sometimes they will send you a form to fill out instead. In either case, you will usually be asked to supply details of your and your fiancé's education and occupations as well as the names, residences, and occupations of both your parents (even if they are divorced or no longer living) and the date of your wedding. In naming the date, just give the month, for reasons relating to home security, even if you have already chosen the day. If either you or your fiancé had a previous marriage, the publication may also require that you note that. You may also note whether you are planning to change your name.

Some African-American weeklies may allow you to compose your own announcement, in which case you could include other details that might be important to you, or personalize it for an audience who may know you well. In most cases, though, you will have to conform to the style the paper uses in its lifestyle pages, so review them before you make your submission. In the traditional wording, your parents make the announcement, but there are guidelines to follow for different circumstances.

You may also want to publish a photograph along with the announcement. It is now common for the two of you to be pictured together, although you may choose the more "Traditional" option of a picture of you alone. Either way, this can be an opportunity for you to begin your search for the right photographer for your wedding (see chapter 5, "Picture Perfect" for more details). Again, review the lifestyle pages. If a photograph you see there appeals to you, check the credit or contact the newspaper to find out the source. Today, couples sometimes arrange for what is called a "lifestyle shoot," a session that takes place outside a studio, in a natural setting, such as a park, a garden, or even at home. Photographs taken during such a session can be used for announcements, for an easel display at the reception (to be signed on matting by guests), framed as thank-you gifts for your attendants and families, and ultimately included in your wedding album. Be sure whatever photograph you submit conforms to the newspaper's specifications (usually 8" x 10" or 5" x 7").

Depending on the size of the area the paper serves and its frequency of publication, you should submit your announcement 10 days to 6 weeks before you'd like it to appear. Large metropolitan papers often cannot publish all the announcements they receive, and some no longer publish engagement announcements. Others run announcements more than once a week and might have more space on a weekday than on Sunday. If your announcement is selected to run, an editor will usually call to confirm the copy a week or two in advance.

Informal Announcements

If you belong to a church or other spiritual community, you will also want to share your news with the other members. Religious and spiritual support can be a strong foundation for a marriage and a source of comfort and renewal in the life ahead of you. Ask your minister to make the announcement at the end of a service or during the coffee hour. Be sure to write down the details for him, especially if you and your fiancé belong to the same church. (You don't want any confusion about who's marrying who if there are old boyfriends or girlfriends who are also members.) You may want to invite the whole congregation to the ceremony but also need the minister to make it politely clear that they're not all invited to the reception. When you see Mrs. So-and-So and all her relatives in line at the buffet table, it'll be too late. If you don't have an announcement period on days of worship, see if you can insert a few words in the church bulletin.

Sororities, fraternities, college alumni associations, social clubs, and civic groups are an important part of Black life and places where you'll also want to announce your news. If you meet frequently and have no publications for members, ask your chairperson to schedule an announcement on the next agenda. Or call your organization's secretary in time to get a line or two into the next alumni newsletter or magazine: "AKA Soror Nichole Palmer ('92) will be tying the knot in September with Gregory Driver (Vassar '90), a member of Alpha Phi Alpha."

The news will probably circulate naturally around your workplace once you mention it over coffee to one or two co-workers. But you might want to make a special point of telling key individuals if you think there will be concerns about time off or the future of your employment. It's always a good idea to tell your boss personally. Send an interoffice announcement if you want to make sure that everyone knows or if you want to issue a group invitation to the ceremony. Again, be clear about what part of the festivities you're asking people to attend: "To Everybody: I'm settling down, but I'm not putting down my camera. I'm going to marry Gregory Driver, whom some of you have met when he's been waiting for me on deadline days. You're all invited to a big wedding/picnic in September. Exact date tk." In some corporate cultures, it's the kind of news that's reported in in-house newsletters: "Gregory Driver, who's been with us for eight years as a systems analyst, is getting married this fall to Nichole Palmer, a photojournalist. Our best wishes to the happy couple."

You'll also need to notify the personnel department if you are planning to change your name, add your spouse to any insurance plans, or designate him as a life insurance beneficiary.

E-mail distant friends and relatives, asking them to mark their calendars if you've set the date: "Gregory Driver, whose name you've probably noticed cropping up a lot lately in my messages, has popped the question! He's a great guy with a good job (systems analyst for AT&T). We're hoping to get married this fall. More details to follow . . ." You can even go online with your news. Some of the wedding sites on the Internet offer you the opportunity to share your announcement with other users.

CELEBRATING THE NEWS

Another way to announce your news is to have an engagement party. These can be as formal or informal as you choose and are usually held soon after the engagement has been announced. By "Tradition," your parents— or, if they're no longer alive, a close relative or friend—host the party in the setting of their choice, at home or in a club or restaurant. They ask the guests—including your fiancé's parents—by written invitation to join them "in honor of Nichole and Gregory." Handwriting is fine, but most stationery stores carry preprinted engagement party invitations that have blanks to fill in for the name of the couple, the date, time, place, and the name of the hosts. If you're planning a very formal party and have enough time to get invitations printed, you can order customized ones that might also include a photograph of you and your fiancé and/or a romantic verse in addition to the particulars of time and place:

You are cordially invited to attend an

Engagement Party

given in honor of

Susan Miller and David Kennedy

on Saturday, June fifth

at two o'clock in the afternoon

Park View Club

404 Broadway

Madison, Wisconsin

Mr. and Mrs. Michael Miller

Since some guests will probably want to give engagement gifts, it can be helpful for you to register before the party (see chapter 8, "Giving and Receiving with Grace"), unless you specify on the invitation "no gifts, please."

Some couples choose to have a receiving line with both sets of parents to greet guests as they arrive at the party. Then at some point after everyone is assembled, your father or "like a father" can bring out a bottle of champagne to toast your future happiness, followed by your fiancé toasting you and your parents, and his parents toasting yours—and so on, until *everybody* feels pretty happy.

Your fiancé's parents may also want to host a gathering, especially if they live in another city and want an opportunity to introduce you to *their* friends and family. The only "Traditional" rule is that *your* parents have the chance to throw the first celebration.

Most folks we know opt out on the engagement party "Tradition" since they're already looking ahead to the wedding and thinking about expense. We think it's a good excuse to get everybody together early on, even if the two of you just call them all up and invite them over for a backyard barbecue, get out the beer and the boom box, and swap dating stories with happy endings. It's perfectly acceptable to have an inexpensive, casual gathering.

If there's another family occasion coming up—a birthday or an anniversary, for instance—you might add a cake that announces your engagement as part of *that* celebration. Winston Williams, whom you last saw getting the blessing of his future in-laws, decided to turn Lateefah's graduation day into an engagement party: "I thought her graduation was the single most important event in her life up to that time, and I asked myself, 'How can I enhance that? Propose to her!'"

He picked up the ring that morning, went to the ceremony, and sat in the audience with her family. "I took out the ring and they passed it down the row from her father to her mother to her sisters to her grandmother and grandfather from Indiana to her other grandmother and grandfather to her aunts. They were all nodding that they liked the ring while the graduation speakers were talking." After Lateefah had gotten her degree, she came over and started hugging everyone, still not knowing what Winston was up to. She laughs, "I hugged my mother and she said 'Hug Winston.' I hugged my grandmother and she said 'Hug Winston.' I just didn't get it. I was so excited. It had taken me so many years to finish college. I was one of those who dropped out and then went back. So finally, after I had hugged everybody else, I hugged Winston." And that was the moment Winston chose to get down on his knee and ask her to marry him. Graduation attendees around them went wild. Her girlfriends started shouting, "Go Teefah, go Teefah!" But Winston says, "I didn't hear anything except Lateefah. My hand was shaking bad, but I slid the ring on her finger." The barbecue her parents had planned as a graduation celebration became an engagement celebration, too.

You may still choose to forego a party altogether at this stage and save up for an even bigger bash after the wedding. It's up to you, but we say celebrate that announcement!

RINGS AND THINGS

The first rings were given in Africa. Ancient Egyptians used gold bands to represent marriage—the circular shape for eternity, the precious metal for beauty and durability. They wore them on the left hand on what we still regard as "the ring finger" because they believed a vein ran from there directly to the heart.

If your fiancé hasn't already presented you with an engagement ring, and you desire one as a symbol you'll wear everyday to commemorate your vows to each other, you'll need to broach the subject gently. Treat it as your first joint purchase, without any recriminations. You might start by saying that a ring not only represents your commitment to each other, it reflects your personality and style, and the values and traditions you hold dear. Some couples do without an engagement ring for a variety of reasons. Not wearing a ring does not make you any *less* engaged.

If you do decide to shop for a ring and don't already have your ideal one in mind, exposing yourselves to all the existing options will help you develop your own ideas. Look at as many choices as possible—visit jewelers, consider family heirlooms and antiques. You may even ultimately decide that you want to design your own.

Today there are a number of possible variations on the "Traditional" arrangement of the man giving the woman an engagement ring and wedding band, and, for a double-ring ceremony, the woman giving the man a wedding band. You may choose to give *each other* engagement gifts and only give rings at the wedding. You may select a jeweled wedding band rather than an engagement ring *and* a wedding band. He may want to give you his grandmother's engagement ring, perhaps reset in a more contemporary style. You may both want something even more personal—rings that incorporate reminders of your courtship, your occupations, or hobbies, or elements of your heritage.

Money truly isn't everything. You can find or design rings that will be lasting expressions of your love for each other whatever your budget. You may discover that what you thought of as restrictions turn out to be opportunities for creativity.

Selecting a ring that you will wear for the rest of your life is a process that takes time and care. If you've always dreamed of the traditional diamond solitaire in a gold or platinum setting, you will need to know some of the basic ways of evaluating and talking about diamonds before you begin shopping. There are four main qualities to consider in choosing a diamond:

- Color (its whiteness)
- Clarity (its flawlessness)
- Cut (its shape and facets)
- Carat (its weight)

These are known in the trade as the "4 Cs." Decide which are most important to you. You don't have to have a "big rock" of several carats to have a beautiful ring. Cut and setting can be just as important. Page through catalogs, browse through stores, note the features and prices of the rings you like best. When you've identified the look you like within your price range, find several reputable jewelers with wide selections and

All that Sparkles—Tips on Choosing the Perfect Diamond

The Four Cs

Color: **The rating of how white, or "colorless," the diamond appears—from D to Z, with D being the clearest and each letter thereafter indicating increasing amounts of yellow or brown tint to the body color. (These are not the same tints found in the very costly and desirable "colored diamonds" that are yellow, cognac, pink, purple, or blue.)**

Clarity: **A measure of flawlessness. Although most diamonds sold as jewelry today will apear flawless to the naked eye, there are no "perfect" diamonds. Using 10-power magnification, diamonds are graded based on the number and magnitude of internal and external flaws, with F (flawless) as the highest grade, and I (imperfect) being the lowest.**

Cut: **The basic shape, faceting, and finish of a stone that plays a large role in its ability to reflect light.**

Carat: **The measure of a diamond's weight. One carat is approximately 200mg.**

Basic jewel shapes

| Round | Oval | Marquise | Emerald | Pear | Heart |

begin to try on rings and narrow your choices. Beware of so-called "good deals." Find out how long the jeweler has been in business, whether they have a certified gemologist on staff or an appraisal lab on the premises. Do they handle sizing, cleaning, and stone tightening?

Once you find the ring you want to buy, it's wise to get an objective appraisal. Some stores will offer you a "contingent purchase" that will enable you to return a ring if you find that its value has been misrepresented. When you make the purchase,

From simple to elaborate to Afrocentric, your choice of settings is endless. Rings can be purchased with a stone or you can add a stone of your own.

you should also receive a detailed receipt that describes your ring and the stone's weight, shape, color, and setting as well as a diamond certificate for stones of 1 carat or more. Insure your ring on your renter's or homeowner's policy (which is what Carlos Webb was mumbling about at the beginning of this chapter).

If you don't feel you can buy a new diamond, perhaps there's an heirloom diamond in the family—in a brooch or a necklace, if not a ring. Regardless of its setting, you should first have the jewel appraised by a certified gemologist to determine its condition and value. If it's already in a setting you like, you may find that all it needs is a good cleaning and tightening. If you'd like to have it reset, the appraiser can probably offer some referrals or you can gather recommendations from family and friends.

Estate sales and antique shops are other sources for rings. Years ago, when there were fewer jewelry stores, pieces were individually designed and hand finished, and more valuable stones were often used. Again, you should first get an appraisal of any piece you like. All these options can be considerably less costly than buying a new ring.

You may decide on another stone besides a diamond. Sapphires and rubies are the next most durable. Using your birthstone or just a stone of your favorite color can add personal meaning to your ring. You can always use smaller diamonds as accents if you feature a different stone. Adding engraved inscriptions on the outside or inside of the ring is another way to personalize it. Consider using a romantic line of poetry, a traditional African saying, or words of your own or a favorite song that tell of your love.

The composition and style of the setting complements and enhances whatever stone you choose. Again, your own eyes and your own taste should be your main guides. Gold is the traditional metal for an engagement ring and wedding band, but white gold (that uses a nickel alloy) is also popular, and platinum, which is stronger than gold and was more commonly used before World War II, is experiencing a revival. Some rings combine metals—platinum and gold, for instance. Karats are a measurement of the purity of the gold: 24 karat means 100 percent gold; 18 karat is 75 percent gold; and 14 karat 58.5 percent. The higher the karats the softer the gold, so it is actually advisable to use 18 or 14 karat in a ring that will be worn regularly. Platinum is either 90 percent pure (marked IRIDPLAT or PLAT 900) or 95 percent (PLAT or PLAT 950). The styles of settings you can choose from, again, are numerous, and range from the fancy filigree of the early 20th century to the prong setting made popular by Tiffany's to the more recent "tension setting" in which the stone is almost entirely visible and actually held in place by pressure from the ring itself. Maybe you'll decide on a simple setting that will leave room for future additions, such as stones to mark special occasions like anniversaries and the birth of children. Ring finishes can be polished or matte, plain, textured, or etched.

If you want a ring that's *completely* different, you might want to contact a designer who can help you create your own. Some retail jewelers have in-house designers. Check Resources at the back of this book as well as your local Yellow Pages and newspapers, and the ring fingers of people you know.

Gold bands with Egyptian ankh motif.

"Find a designer who has a wide range of design capabilities, not just one style. Make sure they're designing to your tastes not just their own. It's not the designer's symbol of marriage. It's yours," says Tammy Kohl, owner of Takohl Design Studio in Chicago. Be sure to see a preliminary sketch or model, and allow plenty of time for possible changes.

Some jewelers are now designing rings in ethnic or cultural patterns and styles. "We're creating a full line because it's becoming so popular," says Darren Collins, president of HLC Jewelry Master, Co., in Princeton, New Jersey. According to Lee Bradley of the Gold Connection in St. Louis, Missouri, popular styles chosen by Black couples include *ankh* and *Adinkra* designs, as well as African fertility and commitment symbols. For couples who want to combine "Traditional" and Afrocentric designs, Bradley has created an engagement ring with a "Traditional" central diamond surrounded by a band containing Afrocentric symbols. Both Collins and Bradley say their companies also take a lot of custom orders. Most designers are will-

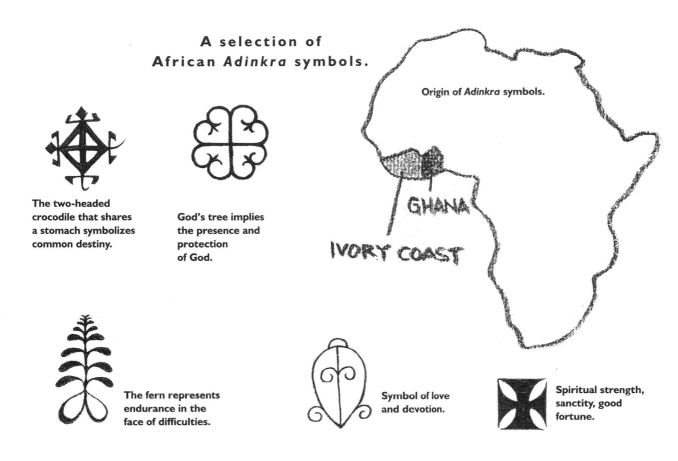

A selection of African *Adinkra* symbols.

Origin of *Adinkra* symbols.

GHANA

IVORY COAST

The two-headed crocodile that shares a stomach symbolizes common destiny.

God's tree implies the presence and protection of God.

The fern represents endurance in the face of difficulties.

Symbol of love and devotion.

Spiritual strength, sanctity, good fortune.

ing to research a particular motif or custom to find a style that represents a specific culture. Many even have reference material and art books on hand. You can do your own preliminary research in local libraries and museums. (The latter sometimes have gift shops that sell reproductions from their collections.)

Whatever ring you choose—old or new, "Traditional" or totally personal—remember that its true value lies not in its cost but in the meaning that it has for the two of you.

TAKING CARE OF BUSINESS

Along with the romance and celebrations, there are some practical matters that need to be addressed at this stage. Getting married requires a license, may involve a change of name and address, and, if you wish, a prenuptial agreement.

Call your local marriage license bureau to find out when and where to apply and what documents, blood tests, and fees are necessary. Each state has its own requirements and "waiting periods" so you don't want to leave this until the last minute only to find out that your license won't be valid for the date of your ceremony! You can expect to be asked for your birth certificate, passport (or other proof of citizenship), and the relevant legal documents if you are divorced or widowed.

If you're taking your fiancé's name (or he's adding yours to his) and/or changing your residence, you must remember to squeeze in some time to notify everyone who needs to know—the Social Security Administration, passport office, magazine and newspaper subscription departments, bank(s), credit card and utility companies, the library, and any organizations you may belong to. Send a letter to each that explains that you're getting married and need to have your records changed. Include all the pertinent information—your account number(s), the date you want the change to take effect, the correct spelling of your married name, your new address and telephone number. Sign the letter with your maiden name, keep a copy for yourself and follow up with a phone call ten to twelve days after mailing. Unfortunately, you must take care of your driver's license in person. To avoid standing in line forever, make it a point to be at the facility at least 20 or 30 minutes before the doors open.

Prenuptial agreements may seem too "businesslike" when you're in love, but they can not only protect your assets and the interests of any children you may be bringing to the marriage, they can also be useful tools for evaluating your attitudes toward money and your expectations for your relationship. Almost anything that pertains to your life together can be written into such an agreement—down to the division of housekeeping duties—although it can't be guaranteed that every clause will hold up in court. The safeguarding of heirlooms or property that you want to be sure remain in your family should the marriage not last is perhaps the most powerful reason for drawing up a legal document. You should each hire your own lawyer with whom to determine and discuss the details individually and allow plenty of time to review all the provisions carefully before you sign.

You're officially engaged. You've made your announcements; you've got a ring. Everybody's full of congratulations. You're the happiest you've ever been. Gather all that positive energy to begin the process of planning a ceremony that brings together family and friends, old traditions and new, the heritage of your past and all your hopes for the future.

Changing Your Name and Address

To use this checklist, fill in the names, addresses, and phone numbers of the companies and organizations you will need to notify. Check them off when you make your first contact and again when you follow up.

	ADDRESS	TELEPHONE

Legal Documents: _____

    Social Security _____

    Passport _____

    Voter Registration _____

    Driver's License _____

    Car Registration _____

    Insurance _____

Banks: _____

_____

Credit Cards: _____

_____

_____

Doctors: _____

_____

_____

Utility Companies: _____

    Telephone _____

    Gas _____

    Electric _____

Magazine and Newspaper Subscriptions: _____

_____

Organizations and Clubs: _____

_____

_____

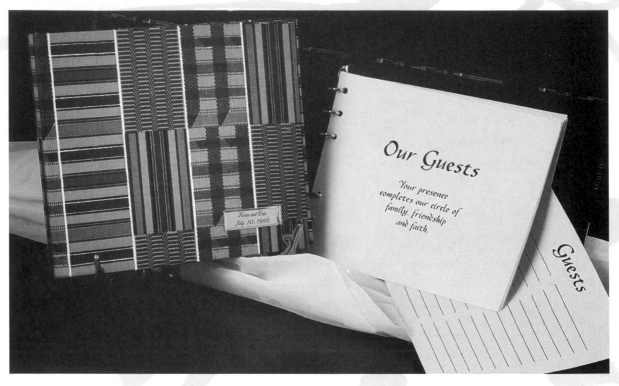

This guest book is just one of the Afrocentric resources available for planning and recording your wedding.

Guest book courtesy of Heritage Weddings™ mail-order catalog.

THREE

PLAN YOUR PLAN:

GETTING ORGANIZED

LANNING OUR WEDDING didn't feel like work," says Nikki Davis, whom you met in chapter 1, of her preparations for her Afrocentric ceremony. "Carlos created questionnaires for us to use when we interviewed all the vendors. Many appreciated and respected how organized we were. We had obviously done our research."

Whether you plan to walk down the aisle wearing satin or *aso alaro,* to African drums or the "Wedding March," your wedding is the creative opportunity of your lifetime. It's a chance to express your love for each other, to acknowledge your family and friends, and to recognize the elements of your heritage and style you feel are most important. Integrating all these elements into the perfect ceremony and celebration, and including all the people you want to be there to witness or participate, is a process of loving, careful planning.

Let's review the dream scenario you created in chapter 1. Perhaps you had a vision of your extended family and your man's 40 frat brothers with their wives or girlfriends, all boogying in a rooftop restaurant overlooking the Atlanta skyline in June, on the anniversary of your first date. We told you not to worry at that point about cost or other practicalities. So you tried to forget that you've just started paying off those college loans and your folks and future in-laws are straining to get the younger siblings through school. You didn't limit your vision even knowing those family members and frat brothers are scattered from Maryland to California. You wrote down every detail of your dream scenario although you couldn't believe there was any way to make it come true.

We're glad you trusted us enough to let yourself fantasize, and now we'll show you how to preserve the heartstring elements of your joint fantasy—the aspects that mean the most to you—even if you're working with a shoestring budget. If you're one of those blessed Sisters who has it going on in the finance area and can afford your fantasy, we'll show you, too, the secrets of good decision-making, creativity, and organization—that are the most important factors in producing the wedding of your dreams.

EIGHT KEY DECISIONS

The key points of your fantasy will be the key points of your planning. Look back at the questions in chapter 1 (p. 9).

- ✤ Where are the two of you?

- ✤ What's the time of day and the time of year?

- ✤ What kind of ceremony is it?

- ✤ What are each of you wearing?

- ✤ Who's with you?

Write down your answers if you haven't already. They are the foundation of the main decisions you will now make in the first stage of your preparations.

Turn next to the Bride's Calendar at the end of this book. You'll see that it's based on a 12-month engagement, which is the optimum lead time for booking popular sites and vendors. The priority of tasks remains the same regardless of the length of your particular schedule. Don't despair if you have only six months; it's possible to produce an elegant, meaningful wedding in even less time, although you may need to recruit or hire additional help (see Key Decision #5).

In this chapter we'll address the top eight decisions you'll need to make, on which many of your subsequent plans will depend. We'll show you how to:

1. Set up a planning system

2. Establish a realistic budget

3. Find the ceremony and reception location(s) that will suit your budget

4. Set a date

5. Divide the work

6. Make the first calls to sites

7. Choose your wedding party

8. Make your guest list

Key Decision #1: Set Up a Planning System

Many wedding guides take an almost military approach to the planning process. Do this, do that, left, right—marshalling all the details into tidy, separate lists, single file, and then marching down the lists with perfect discipline until the last item is crossed off. Well, you have to be organized, but we at *Signature Bride* advocate a more "organic" style. We believe the most meaningful aspects of *your* total vision should be your ultimate guide, rather than minute points of etiquette.

In chapter I, after you and your fiancé developed your dream scenario, you defined your "comfort zone" in regard to financing, location, time, kind of ceremony, and size, identifying the elements that were most important to you and the ones you felt you could compromise without sacrificing the heart of your vision. Review the boundaries of your comfort zone once more before you proceed. Remind yourselves of the elements you consider non-negotiable and commit yourselves to preserving those. Otherwise, adopt an attitude of flexibility. Don't allow details that are less significant to you obscure the overall picture. Although we present the key decisions in this chapter in a certain sequence, the order in which you make them will be determined by *your own* sense of priority. If that rooftop celebration means the most to you, you'll adjust the date and time and number of guests accordingly. If the extended family and frat brothers are more important, you might need to sacrifice the rooftop restaurant for a site that fits your budget.

Having said that, we do advocate setting up a system of organization that will help you keep a record of all the information you'll be gathering and all the decisions you'll be making from these first ones on, until the Big Day.

Buy one of the commercially available wedding planners, or a date book or calendar that will enable you to keep track of your planning schedule. Then use the structure of this book as the basis for the rest of your system, whether you apply it to index cards, pages in a loose-leaf notebook, or files on your computer. Once you know the total amount you have to spend (see Key Decision #2), set up a master budget sheet with categories that correspond to each chapter of this wedding guide, from 4 to 15. Then designate a card or a page or a file for each of those categories. As you collect the names and numbers of vendors, record them in the appropriate places and leave room to note the dates and times of your contacts as well as comments about your conversations. When you start making expenditures, put them in the corresponding slots on the budget sheet.

You should also set up a clippings file for each category so that you can store newspaper and magazine ads, articles, and business cards for easy access and reference. As you begin to book your reception site, caterer, photographer, florist, etc., you'll need to file receipts and contracts for each. Start a "samples sack" to hold swatches of material, stationery patterns and papers, cosmetics, and perfumes.

Always keep a written version of your vision handy in your planning system.

Key Decision # 2: Establish a Realistic Budget

Is it a surprise to you that a wedding in just about any culture at any point in history is a major undertaking, financially and otherwise? You're making a very important rite of passage, one of life's most precious and pleasurable ones! As editors of a bridal magazine, we've learned a lot about weddings and offer you this sage advice: Let it be an occasion for joy, not for putting anyone into debt.

After you and your fiancé have written down your joint vision and your "comfort zone" of compromise and created a planning system, it's time to consider the costs. We recommend that you establish an *affordable* budget at the outset, even if that means letting go of some of your more elaborate ideas. Remember that the budget must cover not only the cost of the ceremony and reception, but rings, wedding attire, flowers, photography, invitations, transportation, and the honeymoon. Of these, the reception and all it entails—food, music, decorations—is usually the largest single expenditure, averaging about a third of the total cost, with the engagement ring and honeymoon as close seconds, followed by photography, music, and flowers.

There's no hard and fast rule for determining an "absolute cost." Amelia Montgomery, of Weddings by Amelia, has planned weddings that have ranged from $7,000 to $30,000 and acknowledges that it's possible to pay much more, or much less, depending on size, location, vendors, and all the other trimmings. The only real rule of thumb to go by is what you or your contributors can truly afford.

WEDDING COST BY CATEGORY

CATEGORY	PERCENTAGE OF WEDDING TOTAL
RECEPTION	28.3
CONSULTANT	15.0
WEDDING RINGS	11.5
PHOTOGRAPHY	6.6
BRIDE S GOWN	6.1
MUSIC	5.2
FLOWERS	4.6
BRIDAL ATTENDANTS APPAREL	4.5
REHEARSAL DINNER	4.2
MEN S FORMALWEAR	3.2
INVITATIONS, ANNOUNCEMENTS, ETC.	2.8
ATTENDANT S GIFTS	2.1
MOTHER OF THE BRIDE APPAREL	1.7
BRIDE S VEIL	1.6
CLERGY/CHURCH FEES	1.2
LIMOUSINE	0.9
BRIDEGROOM S ATTIRE	0.8

Wedding cost by category, from the Association of Bridal Consultants.

Sample Budget Sheet

Here is an example of a personally designed budget developed for a couple who married in New York City. The Budget Master column is compiled by a software program used by the couple's bridal consultant and is based on the couple's stated budget of $18,000. The Budget column shows the adjustments the couple made to the standardized budget allocations. As they used the budget sheet, they filled in the Actual Cost and Balance Due columns to keep track of expenses. The sheet indicates the reality of most weddings—couples spend more than they plan to!

CATEGORY	BUDGET MASTER	BUDGET	ACTUAL COST	BALANCE DUE	AMOUNT OVER/UNDER
Accessories	$90.00	$106.17	$151.63	$0.00	$45.46
Bridal Consultant	$2,700.00	$1,500.00	$2,632.13	$0.00	$1,132.13
Bride's Attire	$900.00	$983.45	$1,176.97	$0.00	$193.52
Cakes	$450.00	$350.00	$400.00	$0.00	$50.00
Ceremony	$216.00	$935.00	$1,190.00	$0.00	$255.00
Drummers	$0.00	$250.00	$275.00	$0.00	$25.00
Entertainment	$720.00	$1,300.00	$1,600.00	$0.00	$300.00
Flowers	$720.00	$433.00	$521.00	$0.00	$88.00
Gifts	$90.00	$100.00	$216.50	$0.00	$116.50
Groom's Attire	$0.00	$123.99	$123.99	$0.00	$0.00
Honeymoon	$2,034.00	$2,100.00	$2,500.00	$0.00	$400.00
Invitations	$360.00	$546.66	$665.95	$0.00	$119.29
Photography	$450.00	$250.00	$400.00	$0.00	$150.00
Reception	$5,760.00	$5,150.00	$7,829.85	$0.00	$2,679.85
Rehearsal Dinner	$1,080.00	$295.00	$295.00	$0.00	$0.00
Rings	$1,800.00	$2,273.25	$2,381.50	$0.00	$108.25
Transportation	$180.00	$350.00	$550.00	$0.00	$200.00
Videography	$450.00	$350.00	$600.00	$0.00	$250.00
Wedding Programs	$0.00	$150.00	$185.00	$0.00	$35.00
Grand Totals:	$18,000.00	$17,546.52	$23,694.52	$0.00	$6,148.00

Wedding Costs Worksheet

Reception _____

Consultant _____

Wedding Rings _____

Photography _____

Bride's gown _____

Music _____

Flowers _____

Bridal attendants' apparel _____

Rehearsal dinner _____

Men's formalwear _____

Invitations, announcements, etc. _____

Attendants' gifts _____

Mother-of-the-bride apparel _____

Bride's veil _____

Clergy/church fees _____

Limousine _____

Bridegroom's attire _____

Unless you and your fiancé decided in chapter 1 that you were going to cover all your wedding expenses yourselves, your very first order of budget business—now that you're getting down to business—is to discuss your financing plans with your families.

In many African cultures, the bride is married in her own village and her family prepares and hosts the wedding feast. The groom's contribution to the occasion is the *lobolo* or "bride price," which through the centuries has taken a number of forms, from mats and baskets to iron rings probably obtained from foreign sailors to beads from European traders to cows and oxen and, by the nineteenth century, to money. We "modern" African-Americans may shrink from the idea of a "price" for a bride, but the cultural meaning of the *lobola* custom is very much rooted in the importance of family in Africa. One family "loses" one of its members to marriage and the other restores the balance by making a material gesture of its ability to care for the new bride. We now have many more options for financing a wedding and for showing respect and appreciation for our new relatives, but you may want to keep our ancestors' basic principles of family balance in mind as you address money matters.

No one ever feels totally comfortable discussing money, so take some time to consider the circumstances that will enable everyone involved to speak as freely and honestly as possible. Sometimes uneasiness about the issue—or just the desire to please—can cause people to overextend themselves. Make sure you create a situation where wishful thinking combines with good judgment.

Talking with Your Family/Talking with His Family. If you and your fiancé are young and still establishing yourselves financially, and your family is willing and able, you may have decided in chapter 1 that the "Traditional" arrangement of having the bride's parents pay most of the costs was your plan of preference. Many parents consider this one of their great privileges, along with giving you your moral training and helping with your academic education—and they may feel there's no discussion necessary. Such was the case with Joseph and Temple Jean Fleming. "We didn't ask Lateefah's parents to pay," says Winston Williams, "they just did it. When I got their blessing a few months before I asked her to marry me, they made it clear they wanted to handle it. I bought the ring and hadn't really thought about all the other stuff to pay for! But they took care of 98 percent of it—or more!" Lateefah confirms, "I paid for some little things. Winston paid for the honeymoon. Everything else my parents took care of. I think they were happy to do it because after I spent years dating a bunch of bums, I was finally marrying someone they deemed worthy."

Even if there's no question that your parents will pay, do still present your vision of the wedding to them in all its details (by yourself, if you anticipate any awkwardness), using the sidebar as a guide to the "Traditional" division of expenses and responsibilities. Parents do not have the right to dictate everything just because they're going to be financing the event; on the other hand, if you're going to accept their generosity, you must be able to accept some of the limits and expectations that may come with it. Make your and your fiancé's needs and desires known as clearly and completely as you can. Then give your parents time to respond honestly; they may need to discuss their feelings and make an assessment of their resources privately.

If they respond with a vision that's very different from yours, listen to it carefully and don't react too quickly. Be willing to compromise on those less significant details. Discuss all your differences thoroughly and come to a general agreement before you start making any other preparations.

If your parents want to pay but simply can't afford the kind of wedding you envisioned, and you have no other source of financing, here's where those heartstring elements come into play. Face the fact that if you want that rooftop reception it will be for only 30 of your closest family and friends. Or if it was the big throng of loved ones that really tugged your heartstrings, maybe you'll see the skyline of Atlanta from Woodruff Park, rather than a rooftop, during an outdoor wedding with a barbecue reception for all 200 guests. In short, consider your options: having a big homespun event, or a small ceremony now and a big bash later on, when you've had some time to save up for it. Or you can think about extending your engagement. If you were planning to get married in six months, maybe an additional six would give you a better financial base. (But be aware that we, and most wedding professionals, advise against engagements longer than 18 months; the emotional strain can outweigh any financial benefits.)

If your parents are unable to pay, *his* parents may offer to cover a substantial part—or all—of the expenses. ("Traditionally," the main contribution of the groom's family has been to host a dinner for the members of the wedding party and their guests on the night of the rehearsal for the ceremony.) In this case, you should convey their offer to *your* parents on your own, giving them the opportunity to react freely, uninhibited by your fiancé's or his parents' presence. Be very mindful of your parents' feelings. They might be embarrassed by consenting to allow your future in-laws to shoulder the costs, and it's their right to refuse. If your parents accept, be sure to let them contribute in any way they can. It's still a good idea to get both families together and present your joint wedding vision so that everyone is included at this stage, regardless of the size of their contributions.

To avoid awkwardness, make sure all bills are sent directly to the people responsible for payment. Put both sets of parents' names on the invitation and give both the traditional places of honor at the ceremony and reception.

A Cooperative Plan. Perhaps you and your fiancé decided that the most comfortable alternative for everyone—both financially *and* emotionally— was for the two of you, your family, and his to share the expenses of the wedding equally. This idea has cultural support in the fourth principle of the Kwanzaa Nguzo Saba—Ujamaa, the concept of cooperative economics—and shared responsibility is fast becoming the most common form of wedding financing in the Black community.

As Nikki and Carlos found out when they invited their mothers over to talk about the budget and plans for their Afrocentric wedding, achieving "cooperation"— financial and otherwise—requires mutual respect and understanding. "My mother knows our roots are in Africa and she's proud of it, but she doesn't have the same connection we do to being of African descent," says Carlos. "She wanted the wedding to be in her church," Nikki chimes in, "but in the end she was great—she said, 'I

Who "Traditionally" Pays for What

The Bride

- Groom's wedding ring
- Groom's wedding gift
- The services of a bridal consultant (may be shared with other contributors)
- Gifts for her attendants and other key participants
- Personal stationery
- Blood test/physical examination
- May host a pre-wedding bridesmaids' party if the bridesmaids don't
- Hair stylist and makeup artist
- Wedding gift log
- May provide housing for out-of-town guests
- Wedding guest book

The Bride's Family

- Engagement party
- Wedding gift for the bride and groom
- Bride's gown, veil, accessories, and trousseau
- Invitations, announcements, calligraphy, and postage
- Ceremony, including rental of sanctuary if necessary, fees for organist, choir, other musicians, and sexton, aisle carpets, and other decorations
- Reception, including food, beverages, music, and decorations
- Flowers, including bouquets for the bride, bridesmaids, and flower girls, boutonniere for the father of the bride, and arrangements at the ceremony and reception site
- Engagement and wedding photography/videography
- Gratuities
- Transportation for the bridal party to the ceremony and from the ceremony to the reception
- Security arrangements for the gifts

The Bridesmaids

- Bridesmaids' attire
- Travel expenses
- Lodging

- Group wedding gift for the couple
- May host a shower for the bride
- May host a pre-wedding bridesmaids' party

The Bridegroom

- Bride's engagement and wedding rings
- Bride's wedding gift
- Groom's attire
- Gifts for the groomsmen
- Personal stationery
- May host bachelor party if his attendants don't
- Blood test/physical examination

- Marriage license
- Clergy fee
- Corsages for the mothers, grandmothers, and other honored female guests
- Boutonnieres for his attendants and himself
- May provide housing for out-of-town attendants

The Bridegroom's Family

- Their wedding attire, travel, and accommodations
- Wedding gift for the bride and groom

- May host a bachelor dinner
- Rehearsal dinner

The Best Man and Ushers

- Attire for the ceremony
- Travel expenses
- Lodging

- Group wedding gift
- May host the bachelor party
- Decorations for the getaway car

Out-of-Town Guests

- Travel expenses

- Lodging

Nguzo Saba: The Seven Life Principles of Kwanzaa

1. *Umoja*—**Unity**
2. *Kujichagulia*—**Self-determination**
3. *Ujima*—**Collective work and responsibility**
4. *Ujamaa*—**Cooperative economics**
5. *Nia*—**Purpose**
6. *Kuumba*—**Creativity**
7. *Imani*—**Faith**

want you to have whatever makes you happy. You will have my support.'" "She didn't let her feelings get in the way," agrees Carlos. "She gave us the financial and emotional support we needed. And everyone was like that. It was so wonderful. Our immediate family contributed in any way they could—money or services—so that we could have the wedding *we* wanted." "We paid maybe a third of the cost ourselves," says Nikki. "We were so fortunate to have so much financial support that everything was paid for by the day of the ceremony."

In Nikki and Carlos's case, the budget discussions with their mothers were an opportunity for airing differences that opened the way for a wonderful feeling of acceptance and unity. Approach your own budget talks with the same combination of confidence about your vision and openness to the feelings of others. Remember to be appreciative of whatever contributions others make and to be flexible, too, about the total budget you agree on. If you decide to split costs equally, make sure that each contributor can afford his or her share. If one contributor can spend much less than another and feels awkward about it, adjust all the contributions down to match.

You and Your Fiancé. Even if the two of you are in a position to pay for everything yourselves, that doesn't mean you can—or should—ignore the wishes of your loved ones. Financial freedom isn't freedom from concern and sensitivity. As the customs of our ancestors show us, weddings are family affairs in the best and fullest sense. The ties that have supported you in your lives so far—and the new ties that you'll be forming with your marriage—need to be recognized and nurtured. Still plan to meet with both your families early on to share your vision. If they want to make some kind of contribution, accept it gratefully and graciously.

You'll breathe a sigh of relief once you've set a budget. Record the total amount on your master budget sheet and break out what each contributor has agreed to pay. If he or she will be covering a specific cost—say flowers—note that, too, and write the amount and name of the contributor in the corresponding section of your planning system as well.

Key Decision #3: Find the Ceremony and Reception Location(s) That Will Suit Your Budget

Return once more to your dream scenario and review the elements of geographic location, kind of ceremony, and actual setting, reminding yourself of their relative importance in terms of your comfort zone. Find your notebook pages or index cards for Ceremony and Reception. We're going to show you how to decide on the geographic location(s) and help you develop a list of possible ceremony and reception sites that fit your vision so that you can then assess them in relation to your budget.

Geographic Location. If you want to be married in the town where your parents live, as a symbolic send-off from the home of your childhood to the new home you will make as an adult, with your husband, skip this section and go directly to Ceremony Sites below. That's one less decision for *you*, Girl!

Today most people live in several places in the course of a lifetime, and "home" to you may mean something different from where your parents live now or where you were raised or even where you've spent most of your grown-up years. It is much more common now for a couple to hold their ceremony where *they* live, especially if neither has strong ties to their parents' current places of residence and if they're paying their own expenses. If the majority of those you want to attend live where you live, having a local wedding can also mean that more of them will be able to come.

What if you envisioned yourself on that rooftop in Atlanta, but most of your fiancé's frat brothers live on the West Coast? Consider the *progressive wedding* we mentioned in chapter 1, for which you have the ceremony in one location, say Atlanta, and the reception in another, say Los Angeles (and even a day-after brunch in yet another location). Or perhaps there's a college reunion coming up in a few months that those frat brothers will all be attending and that can double as a celebration of your nuptials. The progressive wedding means more travel expenses for you and some long-distance planning for which you'll need help (see Key Decision #5), but it can also mean that you can share your happiness with both your nearest *and* farthest loved ones. If you're considering a progressive wedding, make a list of possible destinations and call your travel agent to check the costs of transportation (maybe you can make several stops on the way to your honeymoon). Record the fares and schedules on your Ceremony or Reception sheet, whichever applies.

If you saw yourself standing with your guests on the shore of a Caribbean island or in a village on the west coast of Africa, you were thinking of a *honeymoon wedding* (also known as a "location" or "destination" wedding) in which your guests join you for a few days before you and your groom go off into your own private sunset. More and more resorts and cruise lines offer wedding facilities and services, consultants (who will even find you a dress), and special packages. It could be that the main preparations you'll have to make are reservations. Peruse the travel section of your Sunday paper to get an idea of the range of options and prices. In this case, list your choices in the Honeymoon section of your planning system. Consult your travel agent, or call the U.S. Black Travel and Tourism Associates (Resources) for a referral. If your destination is outside the United States, or if you want to be married on shipboard, make a note to ask your agent about the necessary documents and other requirements.

Are you considering holding your ceremony in a historic setting of African-American significance? There are hundreds of choices across the country—churches, hotels, whole districts of buildings and businesses that have been recognized and preserved, many of them still active. You can begin your list of possibilities by consulting the book *African-American Historic Places,* a joint publication of the National Register of Historic Places and the National Park Service. Turn to Resources at the back of this book for other guides, talk to friends who've had weddings in culturally significant places, and add new places to your list as you gather them.

Ceremony Sites. Once you know the locale in which you want to be married, the *kind* of ceremony you envisioned in chapter 1 will influence your choice of the actual site. If you'd like to be married in a *house of worship* by an officiant of your faith, gather and write down the names and numbers of several possibilities to call about availability, fees, and other requirements (see Resources under Clergy). In many religious and spiritual traditions, premarital counseling is an essential part of the preparations for a wedding and something you'll need to plan for.

If you and your fiancé are of different faiths and decide you want a representative of each to participate in your ceremony, make a note to ask whether this will be

Choosing African-American Historic Sites

The United States has thousands of sites that hold historical significance for African Americans. Michael Adams, an architectural historian and author of two books, *Some Style and Elegance: African-Americans at Home* and *Harlem Lost and Found: An Architectural History,* offers these guidelines on finding romantic, historically important sites for your wedding:

↪ For exterior sites, notice if it is well maintained. "Grant's Tomb and Riverside Park are terrific sites for garden weddings," Adams offers as examples.

↪ "And the Great Hall at City College is newly restored," he adds, citing the second guideline: look for spectacular sites, great rooms, grand entryways, elegant stairwells, outstanding architectural features that have been restored to their former glory.

↪ And finally, he adds, know your history—or ask those who do. "St. Phillips Episcopal is the third oldest African-American congregation in the U.S. Abyssinian is probably the most powerful and influential church in the country. Mother AME Zion is the oldest African-American congregation in New York state. It was pastored by Paul Robeson's brother. The *spirit* of these sites is as important as their edifices."

possible at the location you're considering. Couples who plan an interfaith ceremony sometimes have an officiant from each but choose a location that is associated with neither—a country inn or summer home, for example, rather than a house of worship.

Planning a *civil ceremony* instead of a religious one? Your choices of locations range from city hall to your own living room and include just about everywhere in between. Civil ceremonies—whether they're held in city hall or the mahogany-paneled library of your friends' weekend home—can be just as romantic, and just as meaningful, as any religious ones. If you decide on city hall, you can still have a gathering of friends and family in another location afterward.

An *Afrocentric ceremony* can be held in either a church or a civil setting. Some couples choose to have a co-officiant administer African rituals at their religious ceremony (see Resources under Clergy). Other couples simply want to incorporate African details—customs, clothing, music, or decorations—into their ceremony, whether it's civil or religious. As with an interfaith ceremony, you'll need to ask if this is possible at sites you're considering.

Write down the possible sites that are right for the ceremony you envision in the Ceremony section of your planner.

Although most couples choose to have their ceremony and reception in separate locations, you might have decided you want to have both in the same place. Many houses of worship have facilities that can accommodate receptions and many officiants are willing to perform a wedding at the location of your choice. Just be sure to confirm that it's an option when you make your first calls, which we'll prepare you for as this chapter continues.

Reception Sites. If you know you want to have a separate reception, develop another list of possible sites. Even if your heart's still set on that rooftop restaurant, and you'll trim your guest list to get there, brainstorm for a few other acceptable options just in case it's already booked and so that you'll have other prices for comparison. If your ideal site is an outdoor setting, for instance, consider the public botanical garden or the grounds of the country club. Be sure to keep convenience to your ceremony site(s) in mind as you consider possibilities.

Shop around, ask your friends, look at the ads in the style sections of your local papers, consult our Resources. Also be open to just plain inspiration. Nikki and Carlos found their ideal site when they weren't even looking. "We had planned to go to Africa to be married and have a reception here at home at a site we would decorate with an African theme. But when we attended an open house for Kwanzaa at the Akwaaba Mansion [in Brooklyn, New York] we said, 'This place is perfect!' We walked in and felt enveloped by all the culture and historical significance. The African and African-American decorations were just what we wanted. We felt that no major decorating would be necessary to create the setting we wanted. It allowed us to experience everything we desired." Their other decisions flowed from their decision to have the wedding and reception at Akwaaba Mansion. They wanted to use both the outdoor and indoor facilities, so a warm-weather date was a must, and the size of Akwaaba Mansion dictated the maximum number of guests they could invite.

You'll be surprised at the number of locations that double as reception sites. Here are some ideas to help you begin your search:

Museums. Imagine your guests sipping champagne amidst priceless works of art. The elegant "decor" of a museum provides a regal atmosphere and eliminates the need for anything more than table decorations. Be sure to ask whether catering services are available, what facilities are available for musicians (you may have to be "unplugged"), whether insurance is required, and what restrictions apply (you may not have access to galleries themselves).

Historical Sites. If you've always envisioned your reception in a place with the intimacy of home and an added sense of history and romance, consider renting space in a landmark building. Most communities have at least one, and it may have period architectural details and furnishings, a formal garden, even special significance for your particular heritage. Contact the local historical society for information or consult one of the published guides to historic places, including those for African-American sites we mentioned earlier (see Resources). Again, you may find that certain restrictions apply. Some sites rent the entire building; others only make one or two rooms, or just the grounds, available. Some offer catering, others only kitchen facilities. Rental schedules may also be limited.

Boats. A sunset on the water, the city skyline in the background—what can equal the beauty and tranquility of a shipboard reception? If the city in which you're being married has a harbor, check the Yellow Pages under Boats—Charter to find lines that offer entertainment facilities. Many offer wedding packages that include everything from dinner to decorations and music. You can indeed sail into the sunset after your ceremony.

Country Clubs. With their lush lawns, comfortable lounges, and dining rooms, country clubs can be luxurious settings for wedding receptions. While some are "members only" clubs, others are open to nonmembers. Their staffs are usually very experienced with these events and many offer all-inclusive packages. You might also find that you have less competition than you would at a banquet facility that may have several receptions going on at once and the prices are usually comparable.

Hotels. A hotel can be a practical as well as an elegant choice for a reception. If you're going to have a lot of out-of-town guests, it might make sense to hold your celebration in a place where many of them can also find overnight accommodations. Older hotels often have ornate ballrooms and grand staircases that lend a majestic atmosphere to your festivities.

Restaurants. Maybe you want to return to the scene of your first dinner date to celebrate your wedding. Many restaurants offer reception services—from food and drink to music and dancing—either in a private room or during off hours.

If you're planning a *long-distance or progressive wedding* with a reception in a town or city where you don't live but where other family members or friends do, see if they'd be willing to act as "location scouts" for you. Let them know your vision and your budget and ask them to start gathering information about (even taking photographs of) sites they think would be suitable. If you're planning your reception in a place where you don't know anybody, get the number of the local Chamber of Commerce from directory assistance and make a note to call for recommendations, or consider hiring a wedding consultant who can help you with long-distance planning (see Key Decision #5).

If you've decided on a *honeymoon wedding* in an all-inclusive resort or on a cruise ship, write down questions to ask your travel agent or the site's concierge or manager about the reception facilities available and their cost. If you want to find a special out-of-the-way place to celebrate at your destination, consult tourist guide books for the area and ask friends and family who may have visited there for recommendations as well. Again, a long-distance wedding consultant can be of tremendous assistance.

Jot down your list of possibilities and the relevant phone numbers on your Reception sheet.

Key Decision #4: Set a Date

When the two of you envisioned your dream wedding in chapter 1, you had a time of year in mind. It may have been determined by your personal schedules—the beginning of graduate school, for instance, or the prospect of a job or military transfer. You may have preferred a season that has always seemed the most romantic to you—fall, when you had your first date, or spring, when he caught you humming that sexy love song to yourself and finally said, "I love you, baby." You may have focused on a certain time of year when more of the people you'd like to invite will be available or when you'll all have more time to celebrate—say, during the summer if you're both teachers with a lot of friends in the same profession. If you both have busy working lives and want to include as many of your family members as possible, you might have imagined a holiday wedding, a time when family will naturally be gathering. Or perhaps you thought you'd like to honor your heritage by holding your ceremony at a time in Black history of special significance to you. Whatever your choice, time of year can affect expense. Keep in mind that although June is still the most popular month to be wed, the majority of ceremonies are held from May to October. If that's where your ideal time falls, you may need a bigger budget and a longer schedule for planning. On the other hand, if location is more important to you than time of year, you might find a bargain at your chosen site in the off-season months,

MARRIAGES BY MONTH

DEC.	5.8%
NOV.	6.4%
OCT.	9.7%
SEP.	12.8%
AUG.	11.3%
JUL.	9.5%
JUN.	13.2%
MAY	10.3%
APR.	7.5%
MAR.	5.3%
FEB.	4.5%
JAN.	3.7%

Marriages by month, from the Association of Bridal Consultants.

especially January and February, when there's much less competition for the most desirable sites and services.

Now move from your dream season to a calendar and decide on a specific date, with a couple of backups in case the site you choose is already booked. The most popular days for weddings are Saturday and Sunday. Thus they are usually the most expensive choices as well as the ones requiring the longest lead time for reservations. Weekdays are less in demand and can offer advantages in cost and last-minute scheduling.

The time of day can be as important as time of year and location in determining the other details and costs of the occasion. A church wedding at eleven o'clock with a reception immediately following means your guests will probably be expecting lunch. If your budget won't allow you to serve a full meal, you might consider a slightly earlier ceremony, where you could offer coffee and cake, or a later one—early afternoon, for instance—where you could have a menu of finger foods, along with cake and champagne. Dinnertime receptions are generally the most expensive.

Think, too, of your guests and how far they may have to travel. An evening wedding can create the need for overnight accommodations and the expectation of day-after festivities. Maybe that's exactly what you want, an extended celebration—

just be sure that each decision you make fits your total vision and budget (see chapter 12, "Celebrating Your Union in Style: The Reception").

Record your top two or three choices of date and time on your Ceremony and Reception master lists.

Key Decision #5: Divide the Work

As you've now begun to realize, there's no denying that planning a wedding—just like most things in life worth having—takes work. The amount of time required will obviously depend on the size and elaborateness of your ceremony. The shorter the length of your engagement, the more concentrated your effort will have to be.

Turn again to the Bride's Calendar at the back of the book and assess your own schedule realistically against it. You have three options for accomplishing the tasks outlined:

- Hire a consultant

- Get help from your family and friends

- Do it yourselves

All three have their advantages and their drawbacks—again, just as most things in life. The option you choose will be the one that best fits your personal style, circumstances, and schedule.

If you and your fiancé work full time, decide whether you want to spend all your free time on wedding plans. Working together on this important event can enrich your relationship, but if you both feel constantly pressured to get everything done, it can also be an unnecessary source of stress. Your mother and friends may be eager to pitch in, but it can get complicated when there are too many cooks stirring the pot. Those closest to you may want to help but have busy schedules like yours. A bridal consultant might be just the godsend you need. Of course, some consultants also have dictatorial streaks and hiring a "professional" can make it a challenge to retain your *personal* touch. Consider all the alternatives carefully now. Discuss your vision and your concerns with your fiancé, friends, and family. Contact people you know who've used consultants and ask about their experience. If you have any doubts about being able to pull it all off without professional help, make some appointments to talk to consultants yourself.

Consultants. African-American brides have only recently begun to seek the services of a professional in planning and executing their weddings. We used to take on all the responsibility ourselves—either because we thought we *should* or because we were afraid we couldn't afford help. We at *Signature Bride* have heard lots of stories about our Sisters who, by the time the Big Day arrived, were so tired that they were snapping at everybody in sight and couldn't enjoy their own celebrations.

A good bridal consultant can save you time and money as well as wear and tear on your nerves. Her job is to know about all the resources available to produce the kind of wedding you want, *within your budget.* She can play the "bad guy" with vendors, negotiating the best prices (she often has pre-arranged discounts because of the volume of work she refers), reminding them of important details, and insisting on perfection. She can advise you on questions of etiquette, supervise the rehearsal and ceremony, and work behind the scenes to insure that everything runs smoothly.

She might even save the day. Amelia Montgomery tells us how an overwhelmed bride, who had tried for months to do it all herself, finally threw in the towel and answered the Weddings by Amelia ad in the Big Black Book. She'd had no one to help her so far, except an equally overburdened matron of honor. Her caterer had gone bankrupt; she hadn't yet ordered her gown, her attendants' dresses, or her invitations. Her fiancé thought she was doing "just fine" and that hiring an "outsider" would be a waste of money. She promised him that she'd pay and asked Amelia to come to the rescue. In the two months remaining before the ceremony, Amelia got everything back on schedule—she found another caterer at the same price, ordered the invitations and flowers, arranged for music. In the end, the bride was able to breathe a sigh of relief and the bridegroom had to admit he'd been wrong. He gave Amelia the biggest bear hug he could muster. So if you have any doubts about being able to pull it all off in the time you've got, consider talking to a few consultants now.

A consultant can do as much or as little as you like. If you just want to kick back until the Big Day, show up, get married, and get down—all in perfect style, of course—you can tell your consultant exactly what you want and let her do the rest. If you have a florist you use regularly and a caterer you want to deal with personally, that's possible, too; a consultant can handle other arrangements, or simply advise and guide you in making your own. If you're planning a cultural wedding—Afrocentric or

Afro-Caribbean or African-American—an ethnic or cultural heritage consultant can be expert at weaving the details throughout the whole event. If you're planning a progressive or honeymoon wedding, there are also consultants who specialize in long-distance planning.

"A wedding is a major financial investment—you may be spending $20,000—you want to be sure you're getting good advice," cautions Lois A. Pearce, director of Ethnic Diversity and the Connecticut State Coordinator of the Association of Bridal Consultants and one of only 12 in the world who have achieved the professional level of Master Bridal Consultant. "You should have the same expectations of your consultant—regarding training, experience, and expertise—as you would for any of your other wedding vendors." How do you find the consultant that's right for you? Word of mouth is one good way. You may have attended a wedding recently where everything seemed to go off without a hitch. Everything looked great and the bride received numerous compliments. When all the hoopla has died down, ask her who was behind the scenes. Find out if their working relationship went as smoothly as the wedding itself. If you belong to a large religious congregation that has a marriage and wedding ministry, your place of worship can be a source for consultants. Ask your clergy: In many cases you can receive the services of a professional who would cost hundreds of dollars outside of the church at only a minimal cost—even for free if you're a regular member. Bridal consultants attend bridal shows to advertise their services and be interviewed by prospective clients; at these you have a chance to compare several at once. We recommend you contact the Association of Bridal Consultants (ABC), an international organization of over 1,000 members that trains consultants and enforces a professional code of ethics, which will give you referrals in your area (see Resources).

Once you've set your budget and made your key decisions on options for location and date, begin interviewing. It's best if you and your fiancé, or a close friend or relative who can give you a second opinion, meet in person with a consultant you're considering. Bring as much information to your meeting as you can at this stage, along with a list of tasks you'd like to be handled, knowing that some of your thinking may change should you decide to hire a consultant. Bring your written vision, too, so the consultant can get the broadest and most detailed idea of your taste and style and needs.

Pearce suggests asking the following questions to assess the consultant's level of expertise:

Categories of Consultants and What They Cost

Full-Service Consultants coordinate every possible aspect of the wedding—from the early stages all the way through to the end of the reception, including limousine service, tuxedo rentals, and hotel reservations. Often they receive discounts or commissions from vendors that can cut costs considerably.

Partial-Service Consultants assist the bride midway through the planning stages, after she has already hired most of the vendors.

Wedding Day Coordinators supervise the rehearsal, wedding ceremony, and reception only.

Ethnic or Cultural Heritage Consultants specialize in incorporating the couple's ethnic heritage into the wedding theme, as well as offering the other standard services.

Most full-service wedding consultants charge a percentage (10 to 20 percent) based on the total cost of the wedding and reception, often with an additional flat fee for supervising on the day itself. Partial-service consultants and wedding day coordinators usually charge either an hourly fee or a flat rate for specific services, which can include follow-up with vendors, organizing deliveries, and developing "duty sheets" for the members of the wedding party. These fees vary considerably across the country. You can ask the Association of Bridal Consultants (see Resources) for price ranges in your area.

Make sure the quoted price includes everything you've asked for and get all the terms in a written, signed, and countersigned contract. You can expect to pay a deposit, with the balance due on the day of the rehearsal, although, again, the terms will vary according to the services you've contracted for and the area where you live.

- How many years have you been consulting?
- How many weddings have you worked on?
- What is your professional training and affiliation?
- How do you keep up with the current trends?
- Have you handled any wedding like the one we envision?

As you ask these questions and share your vision, see how the consultant responds. Does she "get" what you want, seem interested and knowledgeable, listen to your ideas before she tells you her own? Is she organized? (What's the state of her office?) How you interact with a consultant is a major factor in deciding whom to hire. "This is the person you're trusting for guidance and to watch over your money," emphasizes Pearce, "so she should be someone you like and have confidence in." Also ask for a list of references for both clients and vendors (call them!) and to see samples of her work, that is, photographs of weddings she's coordinated.

Help from Family and Friends. Sharon Cofer, a 25-year-old public accountant in Richmond, California, planned her May wedding in Philadelphia while working a 50-hour week. She enlisted her mother, Thelma Carson, to help her put together a traditional Afrocentric ceremony. "I didn't need a wedding planner when I had someone asking to help out," Cofer explains. "I think that brides who do their own weddings should take the opportunity when someone offers. But they need to be specific and clear as to what they want that person to do." Her mother agrees and adds that time and organization are the other main ingredients: "We'd each work eight or more hours a day, then come home and put in three or four hours working on the wedding." They had 18 months from the time of Sharon's engagement to the day of the ceremony and used every minute of it to do their homework and make arrangements.

Lateefah and Winston were on such fast career tracks that they were relieved and happy to let her mother do most of their planning. "She could think a lot clearer than I could," says Lateefah. "Our lives are stressful enough. I was just graduating and I got a job at HBO. Maybe this was selfish, but my main focus was killing them in the work world. We would have had a small, quick barbecue or just sent out announcements if we'd planned it ourselves—except we really wanted everyone to come. With my mother's help, it worked out right!" They ended up with a church wedding and 215 guests. "It was an absolutely perfect day for us," Winston agrees.

Maybe you'd rather recruit your older sister (who's been through it more recently) or a girlfriend or two, especially if they're going to be acting as attendants (see Key Decision #7). Again, your needs and who you think you'd work with best will determine your choice.

Doing It Yourselves. If you're marrying a man like Carlos, whose enthusiasm for planning his wedding was as strong as his fiancée's and who shared the responsibilities equally, you will find wedding planning a labor of love. "Thank God we wanted the same thing," Carlos remembers. "I felt fortunate to have someone who had the same deep connection to our African heritage that I do." "It was truly a fifty-fifty effort," says Nikki. "I think it's really important to have a groom who is *involved.*"

Amelia Montgomery notes that an involved groom is becoming the norm among Black intendeds. Still, Carlos met with some puzzled reactions: "People told me, 'Just sit back and relax. It's the bride's day.' I said, 'I'm there, too, and I have just as much interest in this as she does.'" Doing your wedding planning together can be great preparation for true teamwork in your marriage.

Whomever you choose to help you, remember that planning a wedding is a process of collaboration—not only with your man, but with your families and friends, consultants and vendors, everyone from the person who prints the invitations to the one who sets the tables for the feast. Our ancestors understood that it took more than two people in love to make a marriage, and by the same token it takes more than two to make a wedding. Just be sure to establish the boundaries you feel comfortable with right at the beginning. (Consider giving everybody a written copy of your vision.) If your family has offered to do the cooking, for instance, sit down with them well in advance to determine what will be on the menu. Listen to their suggestions, but let them know that the final decisions are yours. It's a delicate business staying in charge when you can't do everything all by yourself. Looking back at her mother's participation, Lateefah muses, "The only drawback was that I'm extremely nosey. I need to know everything. Mommy took control and that sometimes annoyed me." "But that doesn't compare with the benefits," Winston reminds her, and Lateefah nods in agreement.

With tact and organization it's possible to involve your loved ones in the preparations. Let them lighten your load. You will love them even more on the Big Day.

Key Decision # 6: Make the First Calls to Sites

Now that you've got a budget, geographic location(s), several options for dates, times, and specific sites, and a plan for the division of labor, you can start making calls to get information about the places where you're considering holding your ceremony and reception. (If you've decided to hire a full-service wedding consultant, she'll be making these calls and reporting to you, so you can go ahead to Key Decision #7.) Get out your Ceremony and Reception sheets again and review your choices. Decide whether your ceremony site or your reception site is the most important to you and plan to call the places on that list first, since their availability might influence your choice of date for the other site.

Right now you are focusing on three things:

- ✦ Cost
- ✦ Capacity
- ✦ Availability

Churches and other houses of worship, if they charge for the use of the space at all, usually charge a flat rate, with separate fees for clergy, organist, choir, and other staff members who may participate. Prepare a list of questions to ask at each ceremony site:

- ✦ What does the cost you're quoted cover?
- ✦ What additional services do they offer and at what price?
- ✦ How many people will the site seat?
- ✦ Is the site and your chosen officiant available on your preferred dates? Is it permissible to bring in an officiant from another faith or spiritual tradition?

(If you're planning your reception at the same site, read on for additional questions.)

Most *reception sites* charge by the head, so these initial estimates will help you determine how many people you'll be able to invite, given your budget. Again, prepare a list of questions, which will need to be a little more detailed at this stage than for your ceremony site(s), since receptions usually involve food and drink as well as music and decorations:

- ✦ How many people can the site accommodate? Are there parking facilities?
- ✦ Does the site provide catering? May we use our own instead? May we have access to kitchen facilities?
- ✦ Is it permissible to serve alcohol? Will the site provide it?
- ✦ Does the site charge by head, flat fee, or both? What is the average cost for a reception at the time of day we're planning ours? What does it include?
- ✦ Does the site provide music and decorations? May we supply our own instead?

- Are our chosen dates available?

- How soon should we book? (The most popular reception sites often need to be booked at least a year in advance.)

- Do you anticipate a change in costs before the booking deadline?

The answers you get (record them in the appropriate sections of your planning system) should enable you to narrow down your choices and even make your final decision about a site. See chapter 11, "Your Ceremony, Your Way" and chapter 12, "Celebrating Your Union in Style" for follow-up questions and the next stages in the booking process.

Don't panic if the first quotes you get seem outrageous or if the dates don't jive. That's why you have backup choices. With persistence and ingenuity, you'll find the place that's within your budget *and* your vision. Remember the meaningful part of your dream. If it's 200 guests—all the extended family and frat brothers—do not let the cost of the cloth napkins at the most expensive restaurant in town scare you.

When you know the seating capacity of your top choices for ceremony site and per head estimates for the reception, you have the numbers you need to make the guest list and choose your wedding party. All the key decisions you've made so far now culminate in the last two: asking the key people who were with you in your original vision to join you for the Big Day.

Key Decision #7: Choose Your Wedding Party

Childhood friends, sorors, frat brothers, "partners in crime," your closest, dearest, blood-sweat-tears relationships. Savor them now as you imagine your Big Day, because one of the most meaningful and pleasurable parts of your wedding preparations is to ask those who mean the most to you to stand up with you as you make the commitment of your lifetime.

"Traditionally," the formula for determining the number of attendants you *need* for the ceremony is based on the ratio of one usher per 50 guests. For the sake of balance in the wedding party, couples then choose to have the same number of bridesmaids as they have ushers. (Ushers don't necessarily have to double as groomsmen, who also march in the processional.) Amelia Montgomery and other professional bridal consultants who serve the African-American community have found

The groom and his ushers in full Afrocentric garb.

that one usher per 20 to 25 guests is more effective at Black weddings, where guests have a habit of showing up fashionably late on "CP time" and all at once. A higher usher-to-guest ratio means that you're less likely to have gridlock at the entrance to the church. But even if you decide to up the number of ushers, you don't need to have a bridesmaid to go with each one.

Your bridesmaids may be able to provide the help we mentioned in Key Decision #5—assisting with tasks before the wedding and coordinating details on the day itself—especially if you've decided not to hire a consultant. We've heard so many touching stories of Sister-friends, those special maids or matrons of honor—whose title in the wedding distinguished not just their emotional role but their special support in choosing bridesmaids' attire, scheduling fittings, addressing envelopes, keeping track of gifts, even helping the bride interview and select vendors. If you have such a friend, do honor her! Should your groom have friends whose social and organizational skills are as strong as their emotional ties to him, by all means encourage him to choose them and allow them to share their talents in planning your Big Day.

Nikki and Carlos, who did all the planning themselves, decided to have only one attendant each and tried not to burden them with wedding preparations, partly because they didn't want their friends to feel like they'd been asked to do a job rather than to celebrate. But Nikki now admits, "One thing I would do differently, I would delegate more toward the end. The last forty-eight hours before the wedding were overwhelming. I was up sewing African fabric for our altar cloth the night before and finishing up other minor details the morning of . . ."

Consider the budgets of those you want to ask as well as their availability. "Traditionally," bridesmaids and groomsmen pay for their own travel and accommodations and the cost of their wedding attire, although you and your fiancé (or your families) can offer to help if you're in a position to do so.

It can be a gesture of embracing your new families for each of you to include a member of the other's among your attendants, but it isn't a "rule." If your best friend is a Brother, it's now increasingly common to ask him to be your "person of honor." Ditto if your man's best friend is a Sister. Ask all your attendants at the same time to avoid hurting anybody's feelings by making him or her seem like a second choice or afterthought.

If there are children—your own or friends' or other family members'—that you'd like to participate in the ceremony, there are plenty of possible roles for them. Consider their ages, temperaments, and attention spans carefully. Generally speaking, the right age range for junior bridesmaids and junior groomsmen or ushers is 10 to 14 (junior ushers should be at the upper end of that range). Flower girls, pages, ring- and trainbearers should be 5 to 7 years old. If your wedding is going to include "jumping the broom," you could have a young person join the processional just before the bride to sweep away the evil spirits as she walks down the aisle. The parents of the children you include in your wedding party should be present at both the rehearsal and the ceremony. It is "Traditionally" their responsibility to pay for the child's wedding attire, but be sensitive to their needs. You may want to help out.

Your wedding party, those you choose to stand up with you on this most important day, is key to making the engagement period and the celebration meaningful. Choose with love and labor in mind.

The Wedding Party:
A Description of Each Role

Your Queen Diva (Maid or Matron of Honor)

- Helps coordinate bridesmaids' activities before and during the ceremony

- Attends all pre-wedding parties

- May arrange the bridal shower

- May help record shower and wedding gifts

- May act as an official witness for the marriage license

- Unofficially calms the bride's nerves

- Helps the bride dress for the ceremony and for departure from the reception

- Greets the officiant(s) if the wedding is at home

- Arranges the wedding gown train before the processional and rearranges for the recessional (if there are no pages)

- Holds the bride's bouquet and gloves and the groom's wedding ring during the ceremony

- Bustles the bride's train and removes her headpiece before the reception

- Keeps track of the bride's personal items at the ceremony and reception

- Stands next to the couple in the receiving line

- Helps with introductions of guests and with directing the photographer at reception

- Sits on the bridegroom's left at the bridal table

Your Princess Divas (Bridesmaids)

- Help with pre-wedding activities and errands

- Attend all pre-wedding parties

- May co-host a bridesmaids' lunch or bachelorette party

- May help to prepare wedding favors and place cards

- Stand with the couple in the receiving line

- Circulate at the reception, acting as deputy hostesses

Little Divas (Junior Bridesmaids)

↬ **Usually 10 to 14 years old**

↬ **Walk with the bridal party**

↬ **May be dressed in smaller versions of the bridesmaids' dresses or in dresses more appropriate for their ages**

↬ **May stand in the receiving line**

Your Man's Main Man (Best Man)

↬ **Attends all pre-wedding parties the bridegroom attends**

↬ **May act as second official witness for the marriage license**

↬ **Makes sure the groom arrives on time—properly dressed and prepared!**

↬ **Does not walk in the processional**

↬ **Oversees the ushers; designates those who will escort the immediate family**

↬ **Keeps rings, license, and any honeymoon tickets safely tucked away**

↬ **Holds the bride's wedding ring during the ceremony**

↬ **Delivers the officiant's fee**

↬ **Stands in the receiving line**

↬ **Keeps track of the bridegroom's personal items at the reception**

↬ **Delivers the first toast at the reception**

↬ **Helps the bridegroom change for the honeymoon getaway**

↬ **Makes sure all the luggage for the bride and groom is put into the getaway car**

Buffalo Soldiers (Groomsmen/Ushers)

↬ **Assist the groom with any pre-wedding, wedding, and post-wedding duties**

↬ **Attend the pre-wedding parties the groom attends**

↬ **Seat guests at ceremony**

↬ **Unroll the aisle runner after the bride's mother is seated**

↬ **Decorate the getaway car**

Little Buffalo Soldiers (Junior Ushers)

- Usually 10 to 14 years old
- Don't usher guests, but may put the pew ribbons in place
- Walk in the processional and recessional

Pint-sized Petal Pusher (Flower Girl)

- Usually 5 to 7 years old
- Immediately precedes the bride in the processional, tossing petals along the runner
- May carry the guestbook around at the reception to collect signatures

Rubber Band Mini-Man (Ring Bearer)

- Carries clever substitutes for the wedding bands to the altar tied with ribbons to a satin pillow
- Walks right before the flower girl in the processional; beside her in the recessional

Pages

- Walk with the bridal party in the processional and recessional

Trainbearers

- Walk in a pair right behind the bride and carry her train up and down the aisle

Key Decision #8: Make Your Guest List

Having roughly determined the size of your wedding, based on your budget and estimates of cost per person at the various sites you're considering, you can now begin to put names to all the numbers by starting the first draft of your guest list. This can be a tough task. The only argument Nikki and Carlos had during their planning was over who to invite: "I wanted everyone I've known since birth to be there. My childhood friends. My high school friends. College friends. Work friends. I kept delaying the process of actually making a list because I knew I couldn't ask everybody. I still feel bad that I didn't invite the couple who jump-started our wedding talks. They were friends of friends and not close to us, really. So I didn't remember them when I finally did my list," Carlos confesses. Nikki eyes Carlos affectionately and adds, "Because we didn't do our lists early, we couldn't invite others to fill the spaces of those who couldn't attend. But, as it turned out, we had only a handful of guests who couldn't make it." Their experience points to at least one of the ways—early selection—to avoid some of the disappointments that can plague the process of compiling your guest list.

If you're planning to have your ceremony and your reception in separate locations, consider inviting everybody and their cousin to the ceremony and keep the numbers (and expense) down at the latter. If you've decided to have the whole celebration in one place and have to observe limits because of the capacity of the facility (or because of preference), you can have your attendants politely spread the word in advance that it will be a small, very private occasion. Then send announcements right after the ceremony to those you weren't able to invite (see chapter 7, "Your Invitation"). Or, as we suggested earlier, if you found your budget fell short of your vision, do your own version of the progressive wedding, over time rather than distance: Have an intimate ceremony now and schedule a large reception in a few months.

Even if you don't have many restrictions on size, you'll have to draw the line somewhere. You're not obliged to invite the steady boyfriends or girlfriends of all your guests or to give your single friends the option to invite an escort. Although many of the bridal books say to expect a 25 percent rate of regrets from those you do invite, the percentage is often much lower in the African-American community. Consultant Amelia Montgomery finds that in her experience it is closer to 10 percent for Black weddings. If you send your invitations out early—two months ahead of the date, instead of the standard four weeks—you'll give out-of-towners plenty of time to respond, and you may be able to add some guests as others decline.

The best approach to compiling a master guest list is to start with four individual lists:

- ❧ The bride's
- ❧ The groom's
- ❧ Her parents'
- ❧ His parents'

Compile each of your lists separately, without consulting each other. That way you'll have a more accurate sense of the true common ground between them when it comes time to start compiling one master list. Don't forget to include on your list your bridal party, your grandparents, other family members, and the ceremony officiant(s), even though you may have already invited them informally. Give each other as much free reign as you can at this stage—these are your "wish" lists. Later you'll have to set some limits according to your budget and the kind of financial plan you've decided on. If you and your fiancé are paying most of the expenses, you might want to form your own lists first and give your families a ballpark figure to work with for their own. If *they're* paying or you've made a cooperative agreement, discuss a general apportioning of numbers before you begin.

You can start your lists on sheets of paper since you won't be needing addresses until the later stages. Put your final "master" list on index cards or on your computer in the Invitations file rather than on sheets of paper for easy updating and correcting and as a log for responses once you've actually mailed the invitations.

Once you have your first round of lists, you can begin the "weeding out" process. If the grand total far exceeds your budget or the size you've all agreed on, ask everybody to focus on their absolute musts. If your parents insist that their next door neighbor, whom you've never met, is a "must," remind them that you're all having to be selective. If there are too many in the next-door-neighbor category, and you and your fiancé are paying or sharing the costs, you may have to say "no" gently or suggest a larger financial contribution. If your parents are paying, they may be the ones to put their foot down. "We started out with a collective list of four hundred nineteen. My mother said, 'We can't afford a wedding for four hundred!' So we all cut our lists down until we reached three hundred. In the end, two hundred fifteen came," recalls Lateefah.

Once you have a master list that's acceptable to everybody, and a secondary list of those you'd like to invite if others can't come, gather the addresses, double-check the spelling of each name, and enter the list on your computer or in your card file.

Now that you've made the eight key decisions, go back to your original vision and see how those "heartstring" elements are coming to life. Take a well-deserved moment to congratulate yourself on laying a firm foundation for the rest of your planning.

Continue collecting ideas and adding new touches. Remember that nothing is "hard and fast" at this stage. There is always room for enhancement or for a better way to implement a concept you already had. Half the fun is refining all the details of your vision.

Page through magazines, catalogs, and the food and style sections of your local papers on the look-out for hairstyles, recipes, makeup techniques, honeymoon locations, helpful hints, and unusual nuggets of information. (And file them all in your planning system!)

Another great source of information in our high-tech age is the Internet. There are now numerous bridal sites, many of them offering multicultural tips and ideas. The MelaNet (melanet.com), for instance, is geared specifically toward the Black surfer. Covering everything from Kwanzaa to what's happening in the African Diaspora, their "Online African Wedding Guide" offers suggestions for incorporating your heritage on your special day. Whether you're looking for the perfect gown, researching the history of African weddings, or selecting your invitations, Melanet's guide can help answer your questions.

The Knot, one of the largest online wedding resources and the only one that can be found on both America Online (keyword: Knot or Weddings) and the World Wide Web (www.theknot.com), has an Afrocentric Weddings Area that features everything from advice from Harriette Cole (special contributing Editor to *Signature Bride* magazine and author of *Jumping the Broom*) to an African-American designers showcase to Cafe Beulah recipes. Internet bridal sites are usually national in scope so they can be especially helpful if you're planning your wedding from a distance or progressively, in several different locations. On some of them you can even post your engagement and wedding announcements. (See Resources for other sites.)

Browse and interview, surf and shop, consult as many sources as you can, evaluate and compare all the products and services available. Enrich your ideas and expand your choices. You're about to start turning your dream into a reality.

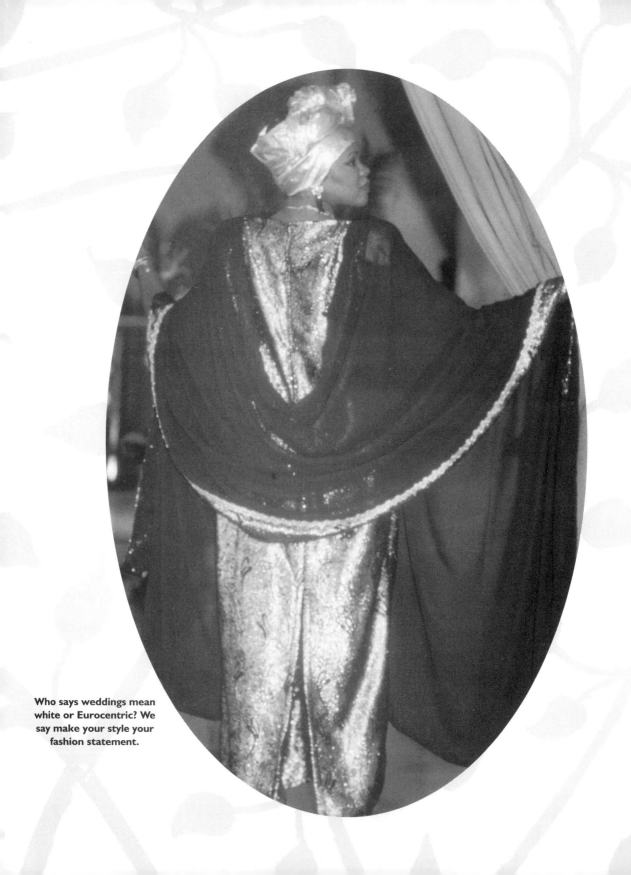

Who says weddings mean
white or Eurocentric? We
say make your style your
fashion statement.

YOUR SIGNATURE FASHION

ORUBA QUEEN, SISTER-DIVA, African-American princess, Slammin' Sexy Spandex—pure old-fashioned bride or one like no one's ever seen—you need the dress to match your dream. Re-envision yourself in that perfect wedding scenario you imagined in chapter 1. Regal but not uptight, romantic *and* sophisticated, elegant yet daring, vintage chic: Whatever your style, whatever your size, and the size of your pocketbook, you'll be wearing that dress on your Big Day.

The winning move—choosing your *signature* gown.

The white Victorian gown, updated to reveal some saucy shoulders.

Evening gown or bridal gown? Only the color tells.

A pattern of glory—like the pattern of your new life together.

Simply white, simply gorgeous. A white wedding gown need not be synonymous with "froufrou."

Bridal Gown Portfolio: If It's White, It's All Right

Very fitted, perfect for the very fit bride.

Marrying in a conservative church? This white beaded gown provides full coverage, yet the fit provides full femininity.

An alluring, shoulder-baring gown underneath.

79

Only the color says "bridal" in this easy, elegant gown.

Extravagance!

Notice the slimming effect the judicious use of lace provides to this beautiful, full-figured bride.

Ball gown or bridal gown? You guessed it.

Forget price for a while. Concentrate first on defining the dress of your
dreams. Look back at your answer to "What are you wearing?" from
chapter 1 and write a description down in the Wedding Attire section of your planner, making sure to include your ideas about style, color, and fabric. Perhaps you've
already clipped some photographs from magazines of dresses you like. If not, you
may want to make a simple sketch (for your eyes only) of the basic lines and length
you have in mind to keep before you as we discuss your basic options—"Traditional"
or Afrocentric—and explain the "technical terms" that go along with them.

"Traditional"

Throughout human history, the color
white has symbolized innocence, purity, and
joy. The tradition of the white wedding gown
was established fairly recently, during the
Victorian age in 19-century England, to represent wealth and status in addition to the
ancient associations of the color. Today, no-
tions of "Traditional" bridal attire have
evolved to include the whole range of
"whites"—from ivory to ecru—as well as
other colors and a variety of styles, from classic to contemporary. The accompanying fashion portfolio is meant to let you "browse"
through the styles available to you.

"Traditional" wedding gowns have a
language all their own, and it's best to acquaint
yourself with the vocabulary before you begin
your serious shopping. The types of fabrics
and the variety of styles available can be con-
fusing. Tulle, toile, and taffeta, charmeuse,
chiffon, and shantung—how's a Sister to
know? And what about those necklines? Well,

**The white updated Elizabethan gown maintains
its romantic aura.**

The "Traditional" Wedding Gown:
A Verbal and Visual Guide

Silhouettes

Ballgown: **fitted waist and bodice with a full skirt**

Basque: **similar to the ballgown, but waist drops to a point in the front**

Empire: **high-waisted (below the bust) with a narrower skirt**

Mermaid: **hugs the body to the knees, where the skirt flares out**

Princess: **closely fitted from shoulder to waist (which has no seam) with a skirt that then tapers out to the floor**

Sheath: **follows the contour of the body from the shoulder down**

Necklines

Bertha: **high neck with a cape-like collar that covers the shoulders**

Fichu: **low-cut, with an attached scarf-like garment piece that drapes around the neckline**

Jewel: **just around the base of the throat**

Queen Anne: **rises to the base of the neck in the back, frames the shoulders and scoops low in the front**

Sabrina: **from the tip of one shoulder to the other, in front and back**

Sweetheart: **shaped like the top of a heart**

Sleeves

Balloon: **full, gathered, elbow-length**

Cap: **just "caps" the shoulder**

Dolman: **sleeve cut in one piece with the bodice, wide at the shoulder (with no shoulder seam) and often narrowing to the wrist**

Fitted Point: **long, slim sleeve that ends in a point just below the wrist**

Gauntlet: **removable sleeve that extends from just above the elbow to the wrist**

Leg of Mutton: **full from the shoulder to the elbow, then fitted to the wrist**

Pagoda: **fitted from the shoulder to the elbow, then flares out in tiered layers to the mid-arm in front and the wrist in back**

Trains

Sweep: **extends 8 to 12 inches on the floor**

Chapel: **extends 3½ to 4½ feet from the waist**

Cathedral: **extends 6½ to 7½ feet from the waist**

Extended Cathedral: **extends 12 feet or more from the waist**

Fabrics

Charmeuse: **a liquid, slinky fabric, usually silk**

Chiffon: **soft, sheer, lightweight fabric of cotton, silk, nylon, or rayon**

Crepe: **soft crinkled fabric**

Devore: **a patterned velvet in which some of the pile has been removed to expose the underlying weave; gives the appearance of a kind of velvet lace**

Organza: **sheer and lightweight, as chiffon, but with a stiff finish**

Panne: **a shiny, slinky velvet**

Satin: **a kind of weave that adds sheen to the surface of a fabric, usually cotton or silk**

Shantung: **a heavier silk with a nubby texture**

Taffeta: **a lightweight, crisp, shiny silk**

Tulle: **a fine net, usually of silk or nylon, often used for veils or overskirts**

"Traditional" Guidelines for Formal, Semiformal, and Informal Wedding Attire

Formal Daytime (before 6 P.M.)

Bride: **Floor-length gown with train and coordinating veil, gloves, shoes, and hosiery.**

Bridesmaids: **Long or short dresses with coordinating gloves, shoes, and hosiery.**

Bridegroom and Groomsmen (and Fathers): **Gray morning (cutaway) coats, gray striped trousers, gray vests and ascots or four-in-hand ties, optional top hats, spats, and gray gloves.**

Mothers: **Long or short dresses, coordinating hats (optional), gloves, shoes, and hosiery.**

Formal Evening (after 6 P.M.)

Bride: **Floor-length gown with train and coordinating veil, gloves, shoes, and hosiery.**

Bridesmaids: **Long dresses with coordinating gloves, shoes, and hosiery.**

Bridegroom and Groomsmen (and Fathers): **White tie—full dress, with black tails, white formal shirt with wing collar, white pique vest, and white bow tie, optional top hats and gloves.**

Mothers: **Long or short evening dresses with coordinating hats (optional), gloves, shoes, and hosiery.**

Semiformal Daytime (before 6 P.M.)

Bride: **Long or short gown with coordinating veil or hat, gloves, shoes, and hosiery.**

Bridesmaids: **Dresses no longer than the bride's with coordinating gloves (optional), shoes, and hosiery.**

V-neck's pretty obvious, but Bertha or Sabrina? Who *are* these people who have necklines named after them? The way it looks is more important than the word for it, but knowing the words can help you feel more confident about what you want and assist you in communicating with designers and salespeople. Read the descriptions as you page through magazines and use the glossary in this chapter to learn some of the most often used terminology.

Bridegroom and Groomsmen (and Fathers): **Gray strollers with striped trousers, pearl-gray vests, white formal shirts, four-in-hand ties, and homburg and gray gloves (optional).**

Mothers: **Long or short dresses with coordinating gloves (optional), shoes, and hosiery.**

Semiformal Evening (after 6 P.M.)

Bride: **Long or short gown with coordinating veil, gloves, shoes, and hosiery.**

Bridesmaids: **Dresses no longer than the bride's with coordinating gloves (optional), shoes, and hosiery.**

Bridegroom and Groomsmen (and Fathers): **Black tuxedos (or white dinner jackets with tuxedo pant for summer or warm climates), white formal shirt, vest or cummerbund, bow tie.**

Mothers: **Long or short dresses with coordinating gloves (optional), shoes, and hosiery.**

Informal Daytime and Evening

Bride: **Long or short dress or suit with hat or veil (optional), gloves (optional), shoes, and hosiery.**

Bridesmaids: **Dresses or suits no longer than the bride's, gloves (optional), shoes, and hosiery.**

Bridegroom and Groomsmen (and Fathers): **Business suits or blazers with trousers of a color and weight appropriate for the season and time of day.**

Mothers: **Long or short dresses or suits with gloves (optional), shoes, and hosiery.**

When you're considering all the possible styles, consider too the features that will be most flattering to you. If you have the shoulders of life, you might want an off-the-shoulder gown that will play them up. If you have great legs, maybe you'll choose a short skirt with a long dramatic train. If you're one of those Sisters blessed with a tiny waist, show it off with a form-fitting bustier. If you have a back, baby, emphasize that behind with a body-hugging mermaid gown. If you're full-figured, flaunt it. Think about the features of your anatomy that your man most appreciates and be sure your wedding gown highlights them. You may feel that your breasts are too big or your butt sits too high, while your man may be driven wild by what you consider figure flaws. Your aim is to drive him wild down the aisle (tastefully). So choose a style that flatters what you and *he* believe are your best assets.

Different designs can also *de*emphasize your so-so points. A long sheath can add height. A princess (or A-line) silhouette can streamline your midsection. Long sleeves can slim down your arms. A low neckline can be more flattering to a hefty bust than a trying-to-hide-it high one. A ballgown silhouette can be just the right style for your wonderful heavy hips.

Women of the African Diaspora come in every conceivable hue, from fantastically fair to exquisitely ebony. Consider choosing a color other than egg-shell white that complements your complexion best, or maybe even a color that makes a statement all by itself. Besides the many varieties of off-white and almost-white, wedding gowns today can be found in red—a symbol of fiery power—and even black, for its dramatic effect.

Review the "Traditional" guidelines for formal and semiformal wedding attire at this stage, too, so that you can begin to think about how you will coordinate the clothing of your groom, your attendants, and your immediate family with your own. Formal weddings are very popular right now and some of you will want to *get dressed* for this special occasion as you've never gotten dressed before, all the way to a cathedral-length train and white tie and tails. Others will want to relax the "Traditional" code. Again, as we emphasized in chapter 1, these guidelines are just that—general definitions to assist you in planning the overall look of your wedding.

Afrocentric

Whether you want to wear full African dress or incorporate African elements into your "Traditional" gown, you can do so. Today there are more and more Black designers who specialize in Afrocentric clothing and whose work is available to you, both custom-made and retail (see Resources under Fashions).

June Terry of Ferandun (Ghanaian for "love and sweet") Fashions in New York, has been designing African-style wedding attire since 1965. Inspired to wear African garments herself by a co-worker from Liberia, June was eventually asked by a woman who became her first client if she could make a wedding dress in the same

A wide variety of Afrocentric wedding clothing is available today. Unlike Eurocentric attire, African wedding fashions are often coordinated outfits for the bride and groom. Headgear is an integral part of African ceremonial clothing, and designers usually include this as part of their design.

African Wedding Attire

Jonathan Adewumi, president of Nigerian Fabrics & Fashions in Brooklyn, New York, reminds us that Africa is a vast continent containing many different populations and cultures. In Nigeria alone, there are three ethnic groups—Yoruba, Igbo, and Hausa—and within those a number of different wedding customs and practices.

The Yoruba People of Southern Nigeria

Aso Oke is a handwoven fabric of cotton and silk with metallic (silver and/or gold threads) customarily worn by the Yoruba people at weddings. The bride would have to request this fabric in her choice of color three to six months before her ceremony.

Traditional Yoruba attire for the bride is a four-piece wrap set, including a *boubah* (blouse), *iro* (wrap skirt), *iborun* (shawl) and a *gele* (head wrap).

The bridegroom would wear a four-piece garment consisting of an *agabada* (a long ceremonial robe) worn over a *dashiki* (a tunic top and long pants) with a *fila* (hat).

The Christian Nigerian

Christian Nigerians celebrate weddings for three days. On the first day, a Friday, the couple must get permission from their families and the blessings of their elders to marry. On Saturday, the ceremony takes place, with the bride wearing either a wrap of *asoke* or a European-style wedding gown. Sunday is then the "Day of Thanksgiving," when the new bride wears a dress of white or off-white lace or a combination of *asoke* and lace.

Muslim

Fatou Ndeye Sall, a Manhattan-based designer of African-style garments, tells us that in Muslim parts of Africa, the bride wears three different outfits in one day of celebration. She walks to a nearby "beauty place" (parlor) for each change of clothing and also refreshens her makeup.

From 10 A.M. to 1 P.M. she wears a *taille basse*, a European-style formfitting dress. From 1 to 5 P.M., she wears a *mamboye*, an African loose-fitting outfit with a wrapped skirt and head wrap. From 5 to 9 P.M., she dons a Western-style white bridal dress.

style. "I didn't know at first what she wanted. Then she described the type of outfits she saw me wear—wrapped skirts with loose, flowing tops (*boubahs*) and head wraps. 'Sure,' I said. 'What color would you like?' That was the beginning."

Ever since, June's line has had an Afrocentric emphasis. She uses African fabrics—both solids and prints—and African colors—the tones of the earth and the sky, rich browns, yellows, blues and gold. Weddings in Africa have always been more colorful occasions than the "Traditional" European-style and much less "uniform" in dress. The flexibility of African style can also be shaped to any figure.

June draws on many sources for her designs: "I have researched the fabrics and customary garments. I have seen many outfits at the United Nations from both East and West Africa and asked about their construction. I've talked to people of various African religions about how their ceremonies are performed and what garments they wear."

If you are considering wearing Afrocentric or African-inspired attire, you must first decide how African you want your clothing and ceremony to be. Do you just want to wear an African garment in a Christian ceremony or do you want all the accessories and rituals to be African, too? Will your family be involved and will they be able to accept this style of wedding? Like the garments she creates, June is flexible. She's designed everything from fully Afrocentric weddings to weddings where the bride has worn a "Traditional" white gown for the ceremony and an Afrocentric dress for the reception. Her main concern is that her client feel comfortable in the garment: "The beauty of the African style, which involves draping and wrapping fabric, is that it gives the bride such freedom of movement," says June.

Fashion designer Cookie Washington of Phenomenal Woman in Charleston, South Carolina, agrees. "You need to feel comfortable because it is different," she explains. "If a bride isn't quite sure that she wants her 'costume' to be so elaborate, she may opt for an African-inspired design—a blending of African and European materials and cut. A little kente cloth goes a long way. Her groom may be in a traditional tuxedo with a kente cloth lapel, and the groomsmen with kente cummerbunds. Anything is possible on your day!"

With any dress you choose you need to have a number of fittings—Afrocentric attire is no different. Cookie holds four sittings with her bride, June holds three. "The initial appointment is where the bride and designer need to be clear about the dress and design. A bride may be saying she wants African, but after talking and sketching what she is really saying, she actually may want European with a touch of African," says Cookie.

Both June and Cookie urge brides to "get clear" on the dress—the intimate details and the overall design. Photos or sketches work wonders when talking with designers.

At the second fitting every designer or bridal salon should insist that you bring the accessories you will be wearing on your wedding day: best fitting undergarments, pantyhose, shoes, and jewelry. "This is critical," says Cookie, "because it is here where the fine-tuning begins. If a bride shows up at this fitting without the right bra or with the wrong size shoe, it can throw off the entire look of the dress. She won't be happy, I won't be happy. It's a waste of time for both of us."

The third and fourth fittings are no different. Each time you go for a fitting you must take along the necessary props. After all, you want to look beautiful on your special day.

A FASHIONABLE FIT

Whether you see yourself in a "Traditional" gown (even if it's one with a contemporary twist) or in African attire, you have a number of possible options and sources:

- ↝ Buying from a bridal shop or department store

- ↝ Restoring and altering an heirloom gown

- ↝ Having a gown designed

- ↝ Buying from a consignment store or renting

Ideally, you should start your search for the perfect gown 9 to 12 months before your ceremony. Price re-enters the picture when you really begin to shop. Having estimated the cost of your ceremony and reception in chapter 3, you'll know approximately what remains in your budget for your other wedding expenditures. According to the Association of Bridal Consultants, most brides spend about 9 percent of their total budget on their attire (including dress, headpiece, and accessories), a little more than they spend on flowers, photography and music, individually. Set a preliminary figure that you know you can afford and that aligns with your priorities. If other parts of your wedding are more important to you than what you wear,

Headpieces, veils, jewelry—all mix in their charm with your dress for your *signature* look.

adjust your allotments accordingly. As you actually start to look at dresses or consult designers and compare prices, your preliminary estimate may also need to be modified.

Take an honest friend whose opinion you can trust along with you when you shop—maybe your maid of honor, who can also help you keep bridesmaid dresses in mind as you go. Wear a strapless bra that will allow you to try on every kind of neckline, and shoes and hose that will be in keeping with the general look you're going for.

If you know you want to wear a particular necklace on your wedding day, bring it along to make sure it's compatible with the dresses you're considering. And remember that your gown, though it may be the center of attention, isn't everything; your hairstyle and headpiece are an important part of the picture. Perhaps they will be determined by the dress you choose, but if you already know that you'll be wearing an heirloom veil, for instance, or that you want your hair braided high and held in place by pearl encrusted pins, these factors will influence your shopping. Take a Polaroid camera with you so you can have a record of various looks to ponder at home.

Buying from a Bridal Shop or Department Store

Perhaps the most common choice for brides is the shop (or department in a larger store) specializing in bridal attire. These carry many of the top designers' lines and the salespeople are trained to advise you on every aspect of your wedding ensemble. Ask brides whose dresses you've admired for recommendations, consult our Resources under Fashions and your local Yellow Pages under Bridal Shops.

Call ahead to schedule an appointment. Avoid weekends if you can, which are usually the busiest times, and allow longer than a lunch hour. Tell the staff:

- The time of year and time of day of your ceremony

- The degree of formality

- Your budget

Ask what fabrics are most suitable for the season of your wedding and your price range, as well as what styles they'd recommend for your particular figure.

Most of these shops stock only "samples" of each style in one or two sizes for customers to try on and then special order the dress accordingly. Your salesperson will pin the sample to give you a sense of how a dress will look in your size or have you try a similar dress in the right size.

Some bridal shops have a discontinued samples rack, or hold sample sales at reduced prices. Be sure to ask about these and other ways you might save. A style you like may be available in a less expensive fabric or with less elaborate detail. Lateefah got a bargain on her gown when her mother's friend, a wedding coordinator, sent her to a shop that was having a sale on returned dresses.

Smaller shops, whose selections may be limited by space, also sometimes host "trunk sales," where a designer or her representative comes to show the complete line. If there's a designer whose look you like, you might find exactly the right version of it at one of these, although you'll still pay full price.

When you've found a gown you like—one that makes you look like the bride of your dreams—spend some time walking around in it, even sitting down. Be sure to consider comfort and ease of movement. If you feel like the dress is wearing you, no matter how great you look in it, you might want to keep looking. Even if you're sure "this is the one," you may want to take a day to think about it and make certain you've covered enough possibilities to make a final decision. Gowns at bridal shops are usually custom-fitted and there are often penalties for cancellation once they've been ordered. Get your shopping friend to snap a picture and make a note of the manufacturer's name and the style number in your Fashion planner for any gown that you're considering.

Once you've made your final decision, get a full description of the dress—including manufacturer, style number, color, size, and any special details or agreed-upon alterations—in a written contract that also states the terms of purchase (including deposit and payment schedule and cost of alterations), dates of fittings and final delivery, and policy in case of cancellation or return.

Order your dress in the size that you are that day (even if you hope to be smaller on the day of your wedding). You can expect to have at least two fittings, possibly three or four. Make the appointment for the first fitting when you order your gown and be sure to record it on your calendar. Try to schedule your last fitting as close to the day of your ceremony as possible to be able to allow for the positive results of your pre-wedding fitness program!

Restoring and Altering an Heirloom Gown

Maybe you've already unpacked the gown your mother or aunt or "other mother" has had stowed under the bed for all these years, the one she wore and saved in the hope that you would someday wear it, too. It may be a little out of date—that pointed bodice and show-nothing neckline—but it's beautifully preserved (see the sidebar "Preserving the Memories") and its meaning is far beyond the trends of fashion. It almost fits—just a little tuck here . . . and, well, maybe a little letting out there. (They don't make "foundations" like they used to, you're probably thinking. But we'll show you even better ones available today!) An heirloom gown can provide the perfect combination of "Tradition" and personal expression. If you don't have one in the family, see Resources under Fashions and check your local Yellow Pages under Bridal Shops for those specializing in antique and vintage gowns.

If your heirloom gown needs restoring and/or altering, a good dressmaker

Preserving the Memories

I f you want to be able to pass your "Traditional" gown or Afrocentric wedding attire along, you'll want to plan now for storing it in a way that will preserve the fabric and color for years to come. You may want to use a professional service (your local dry cleaner or tailor can probably give you referrals), but it's possible to store your gown at home if you take proper care.

First, arrange to have your gown cleaned immediately after the wedding—stains not visible to the naked eye can do their damage over time. You can ask a member of the bridal party or your family to drop it off for you. When you return from your honeymoon, you can complete the process.

A gown should never be stored in a plastic dry-cleaning bag where moisture and dust can accumulate, and longer gowns of heavier fabrics should never be stored hanging, only flat. If you have a shorter lightweight gown you can hang it in a cloth garment bag on a padded hanger. Otherwise, you will need to purchase acid-free paper (long enough to avoid too much folding) and some acid-free tissue paper from a fabric store or textile conservation supplier. Carefully fold your gown, placing tissue paper in each fold and stuffing the sleeves and bodice to prevent creasing, and store it in the box away from moisture, extreme temperatures, food, or other impurities. If you want to keep your gown in your hope chest, be sure to line the chest with acid-free paper or a cotton sheet so that the fabric won't come in contact with the wood, which can discolor it.

Gently unpack your gown once a year or so to check on its condition and arrange for additional cleaning if necessary.

can advise you on your choices. Again, check our Resources and your Yellow Pages. Many bridal shops offer alteration and preservation services or referrals. When it's not possible to match the original fabric or lace, there may be ways to insert new material that's compatible or to adjust the hemline, neckline, or sleeves to compensate for the effects of aging. If the fabric has deteriorated but the lace survives, consider having an "heirloom headpiece" made from what's intact.

Having a Gown Designed

Maybe your idea of personal expression is a one-of-a-kind version of the "Traditional" wedding gown or African-style garment. There are many professional designers who will make a gown just for you, from the first sketch to the final fitting.

You can get exactly the look you want—from Fortuny (left) to Fable Character—by hiring your own designer.

Black Designers of Note

This is a list of notable Black fashion designers, some of whom design African-style wedding garments and others who focus on more "Traditional" gowns. A few of the designers specialize in areas other than bridal, including mother-of-the bride, wedding night, and honeymoon wear. Contact the designers to find out about their latest lines.

Anyiam's Creations International
Thony Anyian
Langley Park, Maryland
301-439-1110

Cassandra Bromfield Designs
Cassandra Bromfield
Brooklyn, New York
718-398-1050

Elegant Brides
Jacqui Scott
Hallandale, Florida
954-458-0229

Ferandun Fashions
June Terry
Manhattan, New York
212-698-6389

Franklin Rowe International
Franklin Rowe
Manhattan, New York
212-967-8763

Images of Royalty International, Inc.
Rev. Doris Tongo
The Bronx, New York
718-328-5484

Ites International
Millie David
Atlanta, Georgia
770-916-1142

JRH Millinery (headwear, more suited to bridesmaids and mothers-of-the-bride)
Johnnye Hansford
Plainfield, New Jersey
908-753-7214

Depending on fabric and style, this can be less expensive than buying a ready-to-wear or custom-fitted dress, so if you have the dream, at least investigate the reality. You may even have relatives—or secret-seamstress friends—who could stitch your dreams into cloth, especially if you can use an existing pattern as a basis. If you select and purchase your own fabric, you can also save, even with a professional designer (although you should always seek the designer's help and approval).

Laurie's Fashions
Laurie A. Sanders
Queens, New York
718-217-2899

Mario Uomo
Bruce Mario Gage
Chicago, Illinois
312-829-UOMO

Michael Joseph Designs
Terri Stevens
Chicago, Illinois
708-388-7435

Nigerian Fabrics and Fashions
Jonathan and Boyega Adewumi
Brooklyn, New York
1-800-ADEWUM6

Only VanEssa!
VanEssa Holley
Brooklyn, New York
1-888-MY TOUCH

Phenomenal Women Design
Cookie Washington
Charleston, South Carolina
803-769-4927

The Private Stock Collection
(wedding night and honeymoon wear)
Lottie Farahh
St. Louis, Missouri
314-426-7761

Shirley's Bridal and Pageants, Inc.
Shirley Jenkins
Elgin, Illinois
847-468-0337

Suädé
Abdur Rahman
Newark, New Jersey
973-639-1083

TMF Designs, Inc.
Therez Fleetwood
Manhattan, New York
212-714-8058

Consult our Resources under Fashions as well as the Yellow Pages under Bridal Shops and Fashion Designers for names. (Bridal shops sometimes have designers on staff.) You might also call fashion departments at local universities and art institutes, where you may find less expensive aspiring designers who can create a dress that might also help them create a career.

Visit more than one designer before making your final decision. Ask to see samples of their work and for references from previous clients. Along with the information about the time of your ceremony, its formality, and your budget, bring pictures—or sketches—of dresses to help illustrate your concept and any ideas you have for color or special detail.

Get an estimate of the cost and the schedule, including time for seeing a preliminary sketch and getting the necessary fittings (usually three). As always, put all the terms of your agreement in writing, and do *not* pay the full fee up front.

Buying from a Consignment Shop or Renting

If you don't mind wearing a gown that's been worn before, consignment shops can offer both vintage gowns and the latest styles for less. Renting is probably the least expensive way to go, although if you need alterations that will add to the cost. Of course, if you rent you won't have an heirloom to pass along, but you'll have all those fabulous photographs and the memories to go with them. Again, the Bridal Shops listing in the Yellow Pages will indicate which ones also handle consignments and rentals.

THE CROWNING MOMENT

You study your image in the mirror: The graceful scoop neckline edged with embroidered *Adrinka* symbols, the satin Princess-line that flows elegantly to the floor, a glimpse of your chapel-length train trailing romantically behind . . . Everything looks perfect, and yet something is missing. Then the seamstress places your tiara and veil on your head. The crowning moment. The image is complete.

What you wear on your head complements your wedding dress and adds the finishing touch to your overall appearance. Pearls, sequins, flowers, ribbons, the fabric of your gown—any of these materials can serve as a basis for a headpiece, in any number of styles, from tiaras and circlets to hats and wraps. And veils of any number of lengths may be attached—from a blusher that simply covers your face to a cathedral-length veil that flows three-and-a-half yards from your headpiece.

Most bridal shops sell (or rent, if you're renting) headpieces and veils in addition to gowns. And if you're having your dress custom-made, the designer will design and make them. There are also shops that specialize only in veils and headpieces.

"Traditional"

Even if you will be having yours designed, try on a variety of ready-made headpieces to get a sense of what looks best with your face and hair and gown. Experiment with different shapes as well as styles. Ask your salesperson or seamstress to advise you and keep these general principles in mind as you survey the possibilities:

- You might want to choose one feature of your dress to repeat in your headpiece—a rosette or a bow, for instance—but you probably shouldn't start introducing new elements.

- If you choose a fabric-covered headpiece—a headband, for instance—it should be the same fabric as your dress.

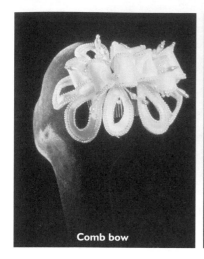

Comb bow

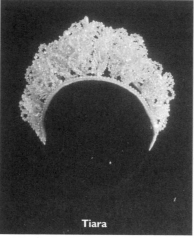

Tiara

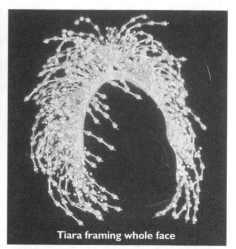

Tiara framing whole face

A sample of headpieces with and without veils that can complete a "Traditional" wedding gown.

Tiara with veil

Floral headpiece with veil

↬ Coordinate the shape and style of your headpiece with the shape and style of your dress—a broad-brimmed hat might be too much for a simple sheath but just right in combination with the fullness of a ball-gown silhouette.

↬ Consider comfort as well as "looks."

If you have long hair, try on headpieces with your hair up *and* down to determine which you like and which feels most comfortable. Remember that a headpiece is usually more decorative than functional; you'll have to rely on clips and combs and pins to keep your hair in place.

Veils, like headpieces, come in many shapes, sizes, and materials. Again, you want to complement, not contradict, the style and line of your dress. Compatibility and comfort are the key concerns. In general, the length of your dress can be a guide to the length of your veil. If you'll be wearing a chapel-length or cathedral-length train, for instance, it's "Traditional" to wear a chapel-length or cathedral-length veil. If there's lace in your dress, the veil should match.

Today, the trend is toward simple elegance, fewer layered veils and few "poufs." Some brides are choosing to do away with the veil altogether in favor of headpieces with decorative trim such as jewels or flowers.

Afrocentric

Most of the Afrocentric headgear June Terry creates is based on the *gele,* or head wrap, worn in many African cultures. Depending on the shape of the face and the desired height, she uses from 3 to 10 yards of fabric that matches the dress to make the wrap. She often attaches from 5 to 10 yards of tulle as an African adaptation of the "Traditional" veil. For the most height and the most regal effect, she sometimes stuffs tulle *inside* the *gele* as well.

The *gele* adds the final regal touch to this bride, stunningly adorned in finery from the Motherland.

Some of her brides prefer a constructed hat (such as a pillbox) instead of a wrap. In these cases, she also matches the fabric of the dress and adds decorative trim—gold braid or embroidery, for example—and may attach tulle as well, depending on the bride's preference. "Not every style of headgear suits everybody," she notes. The bride should look and feel good according to her own personal style and the style of the wedding.

SHOES, GLOVES, AND LEGWEAR

Your shoes, like your headgear, should be in keeping with the overall look of your wedding ensemble. Simplicity and comfort should also take precedence over hobbling down the aisle or across the dance floor, and elegance can still be comfortable. Unless you've had plenty of practice walking and dancing in elaborate footwear, stay away from high, narrow heels and complicated straps.

Brides—both "Traditional" and Afrocentric—often choose to wear shoes of the same fabric and color as their gowns and sometimes have them dyed to match. Look in the Yellow Pages for Shoe Dyers or ask for referrals at stores that carry fine footwear. Be sure to find out whether dyeing will shrink the shoe before you settle on size and place your order and give them a swatch of your gown.

You may want to find shoes that incorporate one or two decorative details of your dress—a pattern of seed pearls, for instance, or a scalloped edge. If your dress has a period flavor, you might want to reflect *that* with a high-cut pump for a Renaissance look, a brocade mule reminiscent of the 1930s. Whatever shoes you select, break them in a little before the Big Day; scuff the soles so you won't go sliding down the aisle.

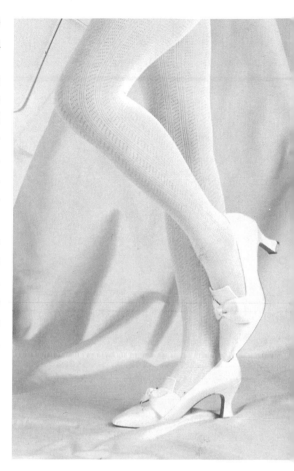

Whether yours is a "leg man" or one with a foot fetish, you want to be heart stopping when he gets that "glimpse of stocking" under your gown and a fatal attraction when he goes for the garter.

Gloves are optional. The simple rule to remember is the shorter the sleeve the longer the glove:

- ✎ Full-length sleeve = wrist-length or no glove

- ✎ Cap sleeve or short sleeve = elbow-length glove

- ✎ Sleeveless or strapless = over-the-elbow glove

Hosiery can also be a subtly romantic detail of your complete ensemble. If you plan to do the "Traditional" garter toss, you'll want to make doubly sure that the point of departure is beautifully clad.

You may decide on pantyhose for comfort and the streamlined effect, but if wearing stockings and a garter belt would give you an extra glow, we say go for it, girl! In either case, there are three rules for choosing hose:

- Match your skin color as closely as possible. In one short generation our choices have widened exponentially. Nearly every major hosiery manufacturer offers a good array of colors for Black women.

- Try the hose on with shoes or at least on your hand against the shoe. It might match in the package but look totally different meshed with your coloring.

- Try the hose against your skin and next to your dress to be sure everything's in harmony.

You may decide that you want to use your hose to add a dash of color or decorative detail to your look. Many fine stockings have sexy contrasting seams or lacy patterns, even interwoven pearls, that can pick up motifs from your gown. Think about adding an ankle bracelet, if you're comfortable wearing one, that will catch the eyes of onlookers as you dance your first dance. Be sure to buy an extra pair (or two!) of the hose you select, just in case.

A GREAT FOUNDATION

What you wear *under* your gown, whether it's "Traditional" or Afrocentric, may not be visible to your assembled guests, but it can contribute to your inward feeling of luxuriousness and confidence and to your outward appearance of total togetherness. Lifting, smoothing, and sculpting, ensuring that nothing interferes with the proper fit and flow of your gown—undergarments are truly the foundation of your wedding day look.

Your seamstress or salesperson can advise you on the appropriate slip for the gown you've chosen. If it has a long, full skirt you may need a crinoline or other stiff material to support it. If your gown has lacework or diaphanous (delicate, see-through) fabric, make sure that what shows through is skin, or a foundation of a compatible style and color. Never wear a black slip under white or light clothing!

The style of the sleeves, neckline, and back of your dress will determine your choice of bra. Again, your salesperson or seamstress can recommend the right style. (Some bridal salons also carry undergarments.) You may need a "convertible" model with straps that you can detach for a strapless dress or cross for a sleeveless one or fasten at the base of your neck for a halter-style. A dress with a low-cut back will require a long-line bra that fastens at the waist. (A long-line bra can help keep other things hidden, too.) We repeat, choose for comfort as well as effect. Look at what's available from the bra manufacturers you're used to wearing everyday before you venture into new lingerie territory. Whatever style you choose, have your bra properly fitted and secured (even sewn inside your gown) so that you won't be fooling with straps and constantly checking to make sure nothing's in view that shouldn't be.

If you want extra fullness, Bodylines, Inc., has developed a new version of its *Curves* breast enhancers for women of color. Like the original, the new version is made from a specially formulated medical-grade silicone gel. And now it contains a warm brown tint that actually blends with your own natural skin tone. The enhancers are waterproof and fit inside any underwire bra, swimsuit, or bustier. They have the same weight, density, and bounce as human breast tissue.

Today's "slimming" undergarments are—thank goodness—a far cry from the restrictive girdles of yesterday. No more complicated contraptions that could hold up the honeymoon! (Although you can still find some that will give you a bit of "Undress me, Husband" foreplay that will hold things up very nicely, if you get our meaning.) Made of Lycra or spandex rather than whale bones or binding elastic, "foundations" no longer have to hamper your movements to help "control" your figure. A one-piece body suit may be the simple solution to your undergarment dilemmas.

A few weeks before your ceremony, try wearing your wedding undergarments during the day to make sure you can move easily and aren't constantly "adjusting" yourself. Remember your Big Day is a time to be completely covered in the luxurious fabric of your choice *and* to feel good underneath it all. Comfort and sexiness *can* co-exist!

Lateefah took months to decide on the style and color of her brides-maids' dresses. Once they were selected, we chose our tuxes and were fitted in an hour," Winston chuckles.

Brothers tend to have "style." Maybe your man has a great sense of fashion and likes to shop. Maybe he's even been helping you pick out your gown and has been planning his own outfit to go with it. Or perhaps he definitely has style but his concept of clothing himself means replacing his favorite five T-shirts or dress shirts every couple of years. He may need your (tactful) help in dressing for this occasion.

"Traditional"

Fortunately, the "Traditional" choices in men's wedding wear and formal attire are less overwhelming than in women's. And again, "Tradition" is only a guideline. Today's grooms, like today's brides, are incorporating more of their own personal styles into their wedding clothes. "While black tuxes remain the most popular choices for weddings, they're more loosely interpreted (even more loosely fitted) and the accessories are bolder and more colorful," says Chuck Remley, vice-president of Modern Tuxedo in Chicago.

In tux deluxe. Simple tuxedo (left). And with vest, simply "untuxable"— that is until after your reception getaway.

Tuxedo Terms

Jackets

These may be single-breasted or double-breasted (the latter may look more flattering over a larger stomach)

Lapels

Shawl: a continuous, slightly curved line from the shoulder to the first button

Peak: narrow, upward cut just below the collar; the lower lapel protrudes beyond the upper

Fishmouth (Notch): a wider, triangular opening, with the upper and lower lapel the same width

Shirts

Collars: stand-up; wing (points fold outward to resemble wings); turn-down

Stays: stiffening material inserted in the points of the collars to hold them in place

French cuffs: turn-back cuffs that require cuff links

Studs: fastenings inserted to close the shirt front when there are no buttons, often in precious materials—gold, onyx, or diamonds

Shoes

Black patent leather slippers (opera slippers): sometimes trimmed with satin

Black formal shoes: very streamlined tie shoes

Accessories

Cummerbund: used to hide any other hardware at the waistline (suspender buttons or clips, for instance); always wear with pleats opening upward

Waistcoat/vest: can be a nice counterpoint to the jacket; alternative to a cummerbund

Tuxedos are the "Traditional" attire for men at *semiformal evening* weddings. All follow the same basic form, with the same basic elements—jacket, pants, shirt, bow tie, cummerbund or vest, and optional suspenders (braces).

But there are a variety of colors and details to choose from, as Remley points out, and this is where *your* creative input can certainly help. Winston's experience demonstrates the basic principle of selection: Whatever your groom and his attendants wear should coordinate with your dress and your bridesmaids' in style and degree of formality. It can be a nice touch for the color or pattern of the groom's accessories to reflect details of your gown. If you're wearing a rich brocade, perhaps he could wear a vest of the same fabric, for instance. Or if your dress is trimmed in kente cloth, maybe he'll wear a cummerbund to match. It's "Traditional" for his best man to wear accessories that distinguish him slightly from the other groomsmen—perhaps a different boutonniere or bow tie.

Remley reports on some current trends to keep in mind as your groom (and you) put his look together: High-cut vests in a variety of patterns, from geometric to paisley, are gaining popularity. Colorful patterns are also replacing black when it comes to bow ties. And, in a real departure from "Tradition," some grooms are even giving up bow ties altogether and wearing banded collars or collarless shirts.

If your man chooses to wear a white or ivory tuxedo-cut dinner jacket or full suit for a summer wedding, be sure it matches the white of your gown. Pastel shirts and jackets are not as popular as they once were, but if he and his ushers go pastel, coordinate their color with the bridesmaids' dresses. And diplomatically remind them to wear dark shoes and socks with a dark suit and light shoes and socks with a light suit.

For a *semiformal daytime* ceremony (before six o'clock), the groom and his groomsmen may wear gray "strollers" (tuxedo-cut jackets) with waistcoats, striped trousers, shirts, and striped ties.

Formal weddings in the Western tradition have a more complicated dress code. After six o'clock in the evening, "white tie" is the most formal option: the groom and his groomsmen wear black tailcoats and trousers with white accessories—shirts, waistcoats, and bow ties—and may even wear black top hats and white gloves. If you indicate on your invitation that you want your guests to wear formal attire, too, male guests wear either white tie or black tie (tails or tuxedos) and women wear evening dresses, long or short. For formal daytime weddings (from ten o'clock through the afternoon), the groom and his groomsmen wear gray morning coats (a cutaway with a single tail), gray striped trousers, gray waistcoats, shirts with wing collars, and ascots (a scarf-like tie) or striped ties.

Shopping

Most grooms rent their wedding wear, since there are few other occasions that call for tuxes, tails, or morning coats today. The total cost of the men's attire—for both the groom and his attendants—averages about half of what the bride spends on her outfit alone.

Look under Fashions in our Resources and under Tuxedo Rental & Sales (which includes all formal wear) in your Yellow Pages for shops near you. If you're being married in a different place than you live, or if you have out-of-town attendants, ask when you call to make your appointment whether the company has an outlet where your ceremony will be held and whether you can have a "long-distance" fitting and then pick up your tuxedo on site.

Remley has some tips on what to look for in the shop *and* the clothing:

A wearable (danceable!) fit is super-important for his wedding day tux.

Personal service. Choose a shop that specializes in formalwear. These shops are more likely to have quality merchandise and experienced and attentive staff.

Quality of fabric. Choose worsted wool and look for names you recognize, such as Christian Dior, Perry Ellis, Giorgio Armani, and Hugo Boss. Avoid poly-wool blends and styles from the shop's "own collection."

Fit. Pants should touch the top of the shoe. Sleeves should come to the wrist bone. Button the jacket to make sure there are no "gaps." Tuxedos today are being worn slightly oversized through the shoulders, with a looser fit in the trousers.

When renting the tuxes, be sure to get the accessories. Some grooms prefer to buy and keep them. In either case, be sure to ask the rental staff or salesperson to show you the best way to tie or adjust the accessories.

Most formalwear shops also rent and sell all the accessories—from shoes to cummerbunds to ascots. We strongly suggest that men consider renting formal shoes if they don't own a pair (see "Tuxedo Terms"). Many a handsomely-fitted tuxedo has been "undercut" by heavy or off-color footwear.

Afrocentric

In a reversal of the "Traditional" Western wedding colors, June Terry suggest dressing the *groom* in white, which is associated with African ceremonial occasions. The most common choice of ensemble is a dashiki suit—consisting of a loose tunic-like shirt and wide-legged pants—worn under an *agbada* (a large robe) with a hat, all made out of the same fabric and heavily embroidered. For contrast, his attendants usually wear a darker color—blue or black or dark stripes—that harmonizes with the bridesmaids' outfits, and two-piece suits (dashikis without the *agbada*).

Of course there are as many variations on men's Afrocentric formal dress as there are Black men and designers. Every color and just about any fabric pattern is acceptable. Eurocut tuxedos with African fabric accessories are also a fine choice. These can be enhanced with Afrocentric headgear.

The Afrocentric tux.

Underwear

Encourage your groom to pay some special attention to *his* underwear. (Maybe he'll let you shop with him.) There are some sensuous choices out there for him, too— silk boxers, for instance, or an old-fashioned but sexy style made of fine dress-shirt cotton and held on with tabs and buttons rather than elastic. If he's wearing "Traditional" formalwear, his undershirt should be of the sleeveless, "athletic" style, to avoid bunching and "extra seams" showing at the shoulders and neckline of his dress shirt. He may want to choose a silk rather than knit for the occasion.

As you gaze at each other in all your wedding finery, you'll have the secret pleasure of knowing what's *underneath*, too. . . .

One of the reasons you're marrying him.

Following the lead of the "Traditional" wedding gown, the bride's attendants have often been decked out with ruffles, bustles, and bows that no Sister would be caught dead in outside a wedding processional. Today, for reasons of fashion as well as expense, many brides are moving away from the "one-time-only" dresses they asked their attendants to wear in the past. Because bridesmaids usually buy their own gowns, brides are now trying to give them more versatile choices, selecting a look that can be equally suitable for other occasions or that can be easily adapted—a dress with a sleek underskirt, say, and a fancier detachable overskirt.

"Traditional"

"Traditionally," the bridesmaids' dresses complement the bride's in fabric, style, and formality. They also all "Traditionally" match each other, although the honor attendant usually wears something to distinguish her role (a different shade from the others or a slightly different, but compatible style, for instance) and the junior attendants wear versions appropriate to their ages.

Consider your Sisters' different sizes and shapes and choose a style that will work on everybody if you want all of them to be dressed alike. If you have your heart set on a particular color, try to make sure it's one that will harmonize with their skin tones and hair. It took some time for Lateefah to find the right common denominator for her attendants: "My older sister wears a size eighteen to twenty, my little sister is tiny, and the

Choosing a dress your bridesmaids can wear again and again will make your wedding even more joyful for these closest of friends.

for parties . . .

In selecting your bridesmaids' dresses, be sure to give your Sister-friends a chance to sparkle on *your* special day and wear their finery again and again . . .

or cultural events.

other bridesmaids ranged from size fourteen to size six. I took into account everybody's body type. And they all looked good in the dress." If you're willing to bend "Tradition," perhaps you'll decide on the dress and let each attendant decide on her own color. Another alternative is to choose the basic length (the only "rule" is that theirs are never longer than yours), style, and color and let each select her own dress.

Besides the dress, there are headpieces, shoes, and jewelry that make up the total package, and the total expense. All these elements should be compatible with their dresses and yours, as well as the general look of the whole wedding party. Keeping them all simple is elegant as well as less costly. A comb with a silk flower in the color of the dress can be a beautiful headpiece. If you want to give your attendants latitude in selecting their accessories, set some guidelines to ensure an overall harmony of appearance: Shoes should all be in the same color family with heels of approximately the same height. Gloves (which are optional except for "white tie" and very formal daytime weddings) should all be the same length, appropriate for the length of the sleeves. Jewelry should all be of the same type—a single chain or strand of pearls, for instance.

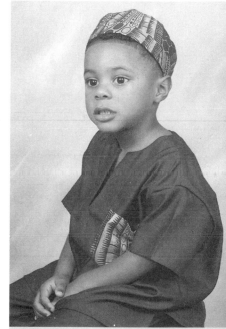

Child attendants—flower girls, ring bearers, and pages—can present some special wedding attire dilemmas. Comfort and ease of movement is especially important for children, though of course you'll want to choose clothes that are, again, suitable for the season and degree of formality and compatible in color and style with the rest of the wedding party. Consult the parents, even shop with them and the children, before you make a final decision.

It is "Traditional," especially at formal weddings, for the flower girl's dress to echo the bride's, though it

Comfort and ease are the keys to dressing children in the bridal party. Naturally show-stealers, only common sense is needed to make them adorable.

shouldn't be a miniature version. A young girl will have trouble walking in a floor-length dress and dealing with too many complicated fastenings and details.

"Traditional" formal attire for boy attendants is a child-style suit in a fine fabric, such as satin or velvet, depending on the season. Older boys may wear "adult" tuxedos or suits to coordinate with the men.

Involve the children in the process of selection and have them practice wearing and walking in their outfits before the ceremony.

Afrocentric

Although it's unusual for bridesmaids in a "Traditional" wedding to wear prints, they are used often in Afrocentric wedding attire. Bridesmaids are often advised to select a fabric that will complement the bride's dress. Although all bridesmaids' outfits are usually made out of the same print, they may want to experiment with color. "If there are six bridesmaids and the print comes in six colors, I'll use a different one for each outfit," says June Terry. "It's an elegant sight to see a row of women all dressed the same but all individual as well." Depending on the time of day and time of year of the ceremony, June may choose colors suggestive of the sunset, for example, or of autumn.

Afrocentric gowns or wraps need not be limited to prints and colors. Metallic colors, golds with "super wax" (metallicized fabric) royal blue, for example, are a beautiful choice for bridesmaids. "Traditional" gowns using Afrocentric fabrics or accessories (like capes or boas) are also popular.

The bridesmaids' outfits usually consist of two pieces—a *boubah* (loose blouse) and *lappa* (wrapped skirt)—with a *gele* (head wrap) in matching fabric (and always smaller than the bride's). Because young girls often have trouble with wraps, consider choosing a style with elastic in the waistlines of the skirts and a ruffle on the sleeves or hem to give a more youthful look.

For the ring bearer and pages, look for pants that match the groomsmen's and tops in the same color as the flower girl's and junior bridesmaids'.

Another option is to blend the "Traditional" with the Afrocentric by choosing European-style garments made of African fabrics in African color combinations, such as royal blue and gold or black and gold.

Shopping

The basic sources for your attendants' wedding attire are the same as for your own. Your honor attendant can be an enormous help in the shopping process—as your sounding board in narrowing down the choices, in coordinating and scheduling fittings, and in running general interference when conflicts arise.

Consider each Sister's budget and choose something you know everyone can afford. If you have your heart set on expensive matching dresses, you or your family can offer financial assistance—or ask at the department store or shop where they'll be buying their dresses about setting up a bridesmaids' registry to which you make contributions that help to cover the costs. Listen to your bridesmaids' concerns about such factors as price, comfort, and design. Keep lines of communication open to maximize pleasure and minimize pressure. And always maintain your sense of humor. Remember, your attendants are there to support you in making your dream a reality.

Deciding what you and your groom and all your attendants will wear for your wedding, planning every detail from head to toe, from the first through the final fitting, until the moment when you see in the mirror the stunning reflection of all your dreams—this whole process, perhaps more than any of your other preparations, brings you closer to the romance and ritual of your special day. When you look back at your wedding pictures, much of what you see will be your adornments. Take the time to know your style and make choices that will endure.

PICTURE PERFECT

THE NERVOUS MOMENTS before you walk down the aisle . . . the kiss that seals your vows . . . your first dance as husband and wife . . . the toss of the bouquet . . . these are some of the special wedding moments you will want to have preserved in photographs and perhaps on video.

Professional wedding photographer Lois Daniels Ingrum of St. Louis, Missouri, laughs out loud when asked the final question of our interview with her: whether there are differences in photographing weddings of Black couples.

"Yes!" comes with a guffaw from this veteran photographer of hundreds of weddings of couples of all kinds, as if to say, *Need you ask?* "White couples want the key moments of the weddings, those posed and positioned storybook images, and the photographer needs to be sure to get those shots from the proper angle, with the right light, and so forth. Our folks want all that, too, but they want that shot of Grandma dancing with the groom, and the one of Uncle Bubba with tears in his eyes! Weddings are more like family reunions for Black folks. It might have been years since Uncle Bubba got dressed up or since cousin so-and-so came up from Mississippi. It might be the first time in years the entire family was together in a photo. We tend to want a lot more family shots as opposed to just the bride and groom. And every family has their own little traditions that they want a picture of. So the photographer has got to get to know not only the bride and groom and the wedding party, but the family and friends who might fade into the background at another wedding. The photographer needs to be sensitive to Black folks and understand our culture. He or she should be able to fit in and ask questions to find out who is who, who's traveled a long way to get there, what's special about this child or very old person walking with a cane. I see myself as preserving Black family history and culture, not just taking pictures. Many Black couples tell me they cherish their special wedding shots of older or seldom seen family members most of all!"

FINDING THE RIGHT PHOTOGRAPHER

Finding such a photographer, one who will capture the magic of the people and moments of your wedding and produce the perfect wedding album, takes time. Experts advise you to start looking as soon as you've chosen your ceremony and reception sites and up to a year before your wedding date.

"I'm booked a year in advance," says Ingrum. "People can't believe it when they call me, say, six months before the date, thinking they are calling *early,* and I tell them I'm sorry. 'A *year!*' this one Brother said. 'Mm hm,' I told him. But after he looked at my portfolio, he and his fiancée changed their date so I could shoot their wedding. Couples know photographs are really important."

Get recommendations from family and friends who've hired photographers whose pictures you've liked. Check our Resources and your local Yellow Pages under Photographers. Look in local and regional bridal magazines for ads that display photographers' work, and in the style or society pages of your newspaper, especially the African-American weekly, for wedding pictures that appeal to you. Clip the photographs you like and contact the photographers for an appointment. Visit bridal shows where photographers specializing in weddings will have booths or displays.

During your initial research, you should decide whether you want to hire an independent photographer or a studio. Whereas studios often use multiple photographers (many of them working as freelancers), independent photographers can usually offer more individual attention and a shorter chain of command. Studios may provide more services—videography as well as still photography and in-house printing and album assembly, for instance. On the other hand, most independents will know videographers they've worked well with before whom they can recommend.

GETTING TECHNICAL

Interview at least three photographers before you make your final decision—even if the ones you're considering are friends or relatives. Look first of all for someone with lots of experience with weddings, who's good at working with people, who understands that this is your Big Day and that you want everything to be perfect. "Someone who doesn't shoot from thirty to fifty weddings a year is *not* a professional wedding photographer," says Lois. "I hear stories all the time from couples who hired the photographer at the newspaper or the portrait studio—professional photographers, sure!—who didn't do a good job on their wedding photos. Each area of photography is a specialty. Shooting weddings is as different from photojournalism as delivering a baby is to brain surgery, even though both are done by doctors."

Be sure to ask whether he or she has experience photographing people of color. Lighting and choice of film are extremely important: People of color absorb more light than white people, so the f-stop and shutter speed need to be adjusted accordingly, and certain brands and types of film capture skin tones more accurately.

"I feel it's best to get a Black photographer who is used to lighting and shooting Black people. For example, Kodak film gives more of a red tint to the skin. Fuji film gives a more natural look to Black skin. And I use a half-stop lighting dif-

This wedding party includes all the beauty of our diverse race.

ference between shooting a person of color and a white person. Because Black folks' skin can be as white as white folks' to deep black with bluish undertones, the photographer at a wedding really has to know how to make all skin tones look natural," Lois explains.

Discuss the style of photographs you want. The trend of "wedding photojournalism" or "lifestyle photography" is catching on as more couples want to capture spontaneous moments. (But be wary of using a *photojournalist* as your wedding photographer, as Lois Ingrum mentioned above. They're often used to taking vertical shots of single subjects, when weddings need horizontals that can accommodate all the bridal party and relatives.) And consider black-and-white photographs in addition to, or even instead of, color. Black-and-white has a timeless quality, whereas color can look dated or faded in years to come. Photographers can also add spot color to black-and-white photographs—a technique known in the trade as "hand coloring"—which can lend a period look. Or black-and-white can be processed with a sepia toner to give it an antique brownish tint.

View samples of the photographer's work and look for the qualities you're after:

- A variety of styles, both posed and candid

- Evidence of technical competence (all the shots are sharp, clear, and well-lit)

- A coherent overall effect (the pictures really give you a sense of the occasion)

Ask for client references, especially clients of color, and check them. Be sure to meet the photographer in person, especially if you're considering going through a large studio. (Some won't let you meet the photographer until the actual day of the wedding, a factor you should consider in making your choices.)

Also ask whether the photographer has shot at the site of your ceremony and reception before; it can be useful to have someone who is already familiar with the lighting requirements at a particular location. Most wedding photographers use a flash, either built into the camera or attached by a bracket to get a slightly better angle of light. Another option is strobe lighting, which is more powerful that the on-camera flash but requires a separate stationary setup and thus limits the photographer's mobility.

Finally, find someone you like, who listens to your ideas rather than dictates to you, who seems to understand your vision and is willing to capture it on film. The ability to work with all types of personalities under stress, to take direction while offering creative suggestions, and to see and record everything that's important while remaining unobtrusive are essential characteristics of a good wedding photographer. (And while you're at it, ask if they have any good tips on decorators, caterers, and musicians. As the quiet bystanders at receptions, photographers often get to see exactly how good the other vendors are at their jobs.)

Once you've narrowed your choices, cost is likely to be a deciding factor. An independent photographer is usually more expensive than a studio, but studios often retain ownership of the negatives, which can keep you from shopping around for the best reprint costs and therefore end up costing you just as much or more.

"Yes, I'm higher than the big studios," sighs Ingrum. "I don't compete on price, I compete on service, individual attention, and providing each couple with their own unique album of memories."

Ask the photographer how his or her rates are based; some charge a flat fee for a certain number of hours, then charge overtime. Get the specifics of what's included in the cost; find out whether he or she shoots more than the standard album quantity (standard usually means couple, wedding party, ceremony, and reception shots); ask if he or she shoots candid, spontaneous shots at no extra cost; find out what lighting methods are available.

Some photographers offer "wedding packages" that include finished albums, along with a certain number of loose prints. Be sure the package you choose has everything you want and find out about whether you can order extras later and at what cost. You can always opt for just buying loose prints and assembling your own album, a project that you and your groom might enjoy sharing as a ritual to begin your married life.

Before you make a deal, get all the terms in writing in a contract that both you and the photographer sign, even if you're hiring a friend or relative. "Contracts are a no-exception thing," comments Ingrum. "Even if it's your mother, sign a contract." This should include the name of the photographer and any assistants, his or her backup (whose work you should also see), the date, the time frame (with fees and provision for overtime), the location(s), the cost of equipment, the ownership of the negatives and proofs, the number of frames to be shot and whether the shots will be formal or candid or both, and the schedule for the delivery of proofs and prints. If you're buying a package, be sure that everything it includes is spelled out—the number and size of the albums, the number and dimensions of the prints in each, specific shots or locations that have been agreed upon, and the delivery date.

You'll be asked for a deposit of an amount that varies from photographer to

Creative Camera Work

- Let your photographer snap a few off-guard pre-wedding moments—when you're putting the finishing touches on your makeup, surrounded by your bridesmaids.

- Try a "fashion-style" shoot of you and your groom in your wedding day finery.

- Leave disposable cameras on the tables at your rehearsal dinner and reception so your guests can help you get a real insider's view of the celebrations.

- Have the photographer (or a shutter bug guest) take Polaroids at the reception that can be framed as key chains or magnets and given as keepsakes.

- Frame wedding photographs as thank-yous for your attendants.

- Get extra prints that you can use to make "wedding day" postcards and enclose in your thank-you notes (or have a thank-you note made from a print) and in holiday greeting cards.

- Create a "wedding wall" in your home, a gallery of photographs of your special day.

photographer. A studio may want half on signing of the contract and the other half on delivery. Independents will more often take a smaller amount up front, to hold the date, and then want the balance on the day of the wedding.

TIMING

Arrange for formal portraits (for newspaper announcements) about six months ahead of time, so that you can submit them by the publication deadlines (usually six to eight weeks in advance).

Once the wedding and the reception are over and you've returned from your honeymoon, you'll be choosing the photographs that will commemorate this event in years ahead. Turnaround time depends on whether the photographer develops the pictures on site or uses an off-site lab. You can usually expect to see proofs within two to four weeks. You may have a deadline for making your selection, after which you can usually expect final prints in another six to eight weeks.

Avideotape of your wedding festivities can be another keepsake you'll want and one that can be especially meaningful for family and friends who may not be able to attend the ceremony. "Videography is becoming even more popular than still photography for weddings," say Jim Collier of Collier Video in St. Louis, Missouri. "People can hear what they say and see the whole story of their wedding." There are many different styles of video available—from a simple straight-shot format with no editing to a fully edited tape with music and titles that might even incorporate still photos or footage from your childhood or courtship.

The photographer or studio you hire for your stills might also be equipped for video, in which case they can coordinate the staff and equipment, even the contractual terms for both. If your photographer doesn't offer this service, ask him and your other vendors for recommendations, and check our Resources and your Yellow Pages.

Meet with the videographers you're considering and view samples of their work. Ask them to explain any special effects and features, such as fades (when one scene "dissolves" into another) and animation (moving graphics). Use this video review and explanation process as a chance to see if you get along with the videographer. "I've seen some who come in ordering everyone around like they think they're directing a movie—wanting everything done their way," warns Collier. "They forget it's the bride's day."

In making your final decision, Collier recommends that you take into account:

- The videographer's experience shooting weddings

- The clarity of his product (is the image sharp?)

- The composition of his product (are the scenes well captured?)

- The continuity of his product (is the story coherent and well-told?)

Ask about nonintrusive lighting. With the latest equipment your ceremony site never has to be lit like a football field.

Again, get a contract that specifies all the terms, including special effects, number of tapes you'll receive, fees, and time of delivery. Collier offers three wedding video plans, all of which can be adapted to the client's individual needs and desires. He also asks for a nonrefundable deposit to reserve the date, with the balance due a week before the wedding. These terms will vary from videographer to videographer. Just be sure to get *yours* in a written agreement signed by both parties.

Let your videographer know whether he or she will be working with a photographer. "I always call the photographer before the wedding," says Collier, "and work out everything tactically so we can both get what we need and not trip over each other."

Collier delivers his final words of advice with a laugh: "Don't let Uncle Charlie do your video. Couples always end up coming in to get me to try to fix it."

PHOTOS ON THE BIG DAY

Whether you hire a photographer, a videographer, or both, you are wise to make a list of shots that you know will be absolute musts. (Sometimes the photographer will provide you with a basic list that you can modify and, as stated above, this should be in your contract.) Designate a friend, relative, or member of your wedding party to act as "photo captain" to help identify those special people you want photographs of during the ceremony and reception and to help assemble them for group shots. Make sure your photographer(s) and photo captain have copies of your subject list.

Keep in mind that some ministers don't allow the use of flash during the ceremony; some will allow photographs to be taken as long as the shutter is inaudible; some don't allow photography at all. Give your photographer the name and number of your officiant to find out his or her protocol. Don't be disappointed if you discover that you will have to simulate shots after the ceremony—the restaging will be just as precious (and probably less nerve-racking).

Arrange to have the photographer and videographer arrive an hour before the ceremony (the videographer actually takes longer to set up) and make sure that the decorator is gone so they won't be getting in each other's way. "Don't plan group shots at this time—Black folks tend to run late and you don't need to add to your pre-

Disposable cameras on the tables at your reception give guests a chance to get those irreplaceable candid shots of you and each other.
Camera and table tent courtesy of Heritage Weddings™ mail-order catalog.

Take a few pictures, then pass the camera around. Please leave the camera on your table. We look forward to seeing your pictures of our special day.

A Checklist of Subjects for the Photographer

- View of the church
- Bride's mother adjusting the veil
- Bridegroom and best man looking at their watches
- The bridal procession
- The bride and groom at the altar
- The exchange of rings
- The kiss
- The signing of the marriage certificate
- You and your groom as you leave the church
- You and your groom with your parents and his
- You and your groom with the whole wedding party

- The bridesmaids alone
- The groomsmen alone
- Toasts at the reception
- The first dance
- Cutting the cake
- Throwing the bouquet
- Your getaway as you leave for your honeymoon
- Hands together with rings
- Broom jumping
- Group shot of family and friends who have traveled a long distance

wedding anxiety by waiting for Uncle Joe to show up," advises Ingrum. Instead, allow time for photographs *between* the ceremony and reception.

"Our people love to take shots in romantic locations or the couple may have 'their spot'—a place that has special significance just to them, maybe where they first kissed or went on their first date," adds Ingrum. "I like getting wedding shots in those locations, but I try to only take the couple." If you want to use more than one location, limit the subjects at the second spot to yourself and your groom, so you won't have the hassle of dragging the whole wedding party around town. You don't want everybody to be too tired and irritated to dance at the reception.

Your wedding album and video tell the story of your special day in pictures that you can view again and again in the years to come, share with friends and family, and pass along to your children, grandchildren, and beyond. They are the visual record of your dream come true. And, as Ingrum reminds us, "Wedding photos are an important part of the history and culture of our people."

Flowers and weddings—the seeds of love, full-grown.

SAYING IT WITH FLOWERS,

AND MORE

OU ARE STRUTTING your splendid married stuff up

the aisle on the arm of your groom, past pews draped with

kente cloth tied with cowrie shells and a spray of lilies of the

valley. You get into the waiting limo that's sprinkled with petals of your favorite

flower and emerge at your reception, where you enter through a heart-shaped arch

made of balloons in your favorite colors. You share your first dance under a floating

balloon canopy and are toasted by glasses raised high to an *Adinkra* ice sculpture.

No matter what kind of wedding you have—formal, informal, religious, or civil—the decorations you choose can set the scene and create the right ambience for your ceremony and reception. When asked why flowers continue to be such an important part of African-American weddings, Ruth Oliver, owner of the Black Orchid in Harlem (see Resources), takes us back to our roots in her reply, "Fresh flowers are from the earth, they are grown from a seed and bring forth life. A beautiful new beginning—that's what flowers are and that's what weddings are."

While flowers are the traditional mainstays of wedding decor, many brides today want adornments that are more unusual or more personal. Balloons, ice sculptures, and Afrocentric symbols and fabrics are among the many alternatives available for designing the distinctive atmosphere of your festivities. Vietta Wright of Vietta's Creative Designs in Newark, New Jersey (see Resources), works exclusively with dried, silk, and other fabricated flowers and unusual decorations. "For one bride, I made a bouquet handle that looked like a wand of pearls. She showed me a picture of a wand and I improvised, letting strings of pearls cascade from the bouquet. Then I lit the bouquet using a string of lights operated by a tiny battery we slid into a pocket I made in her satin bridal bag, where it was totally hidden. As she walked, the pearls cascaded and the lights in her bouquet twinkled like starlight. It was a nighttime candlelight wedding, so I lit the whole wedding party—the attendants' bouquet lights flashed, while the bride's stayed on. I even lit the groom's boutonniere."

SELECTING AND TALKING TO YOUR FLORIST

Whatever other decorations you decide on, you will probably at least want to use flowers for your bridal bouquet and your bridesmaids', for boutonnieres for your groom and his groomsmen, and for corsages for special relatives. Start your search for the perfect florist up to a year ahead and place your final order no later than four months before the ceremony, preferably six. As with any other aspect of your wedding planning, finding someone to really "hook it up" means interviewing several prospects. Perhaps you and your fiancé have attended a wedding or party where you really liked the floral arrangements. Maybe a floral window display has caught your eye. Get the name of the florist in each case and make an appointment.

Traditional Wedding Flowers

Apple Blossoms—**for good fortune**

Blue Violets—**for faithfulness**

Gardenias—**for joy**

Lilacs—**for first love**

Lilies—**for purity and innocence**

Lily of the Valley—**for return of happiness**

Orange Blossoms—**for purity and fertility (an orange tree blossoms and bears fruit at the same time)**

Orchids—**for passion**

Roses—**for romance**

Ruth and Vietta give very different advice regarding choosing a florist. Vietta says, "Know what you want. I like a challenge and want to create and even improve on my client's dream, no matter how difficult." Ruth advises, "Let your florist visit the wedding and reception sites and see your dress and make suggestions. The florist is a professional and can use flowers to coordinate the colors of the dress with the locations." But both agree that you have to have "rapport" with your florist.

Bring pictures of your ceremony and reception sites (or, as Ruth suggests, and if the florist is willing, allow for a site visit) and provide as much information as you can about the overall style of your wedding. Give the florist a photograph of your wedding gown and swatches of the bridesmaids' dresses as soon as they're available. The colors you choose for your flowers should be consistent with the general color scheme, season, and degree of formality of your wedding. If you're planning a holiday wedding, ask about specific designs that incorporate associated symbols or motifs.

Look through the florists' portfolios to get a sense of *their* style and whether it will be compatible with yours. Get client references and check them. Be sure to see the whole range of their work, from corsages to centerpieces, and ask questions about the flowers and arrangements you like—what colors are available, what flowers could be substituted, what kind of accents could be used (ribbons on bouquets, garlands around archways, hollowed-out fruits as centerpiece holders), and how styles you like could be adapted to other uses—for example, pew baskets that can double as centerpieces or wreaths that could work as circlets for your hair.

Inquire about the florist's freshness guarantee, their options for substitutions if a flower you order isn't available, and refunds in case of cancellation. As with your other vendors, when you make your final selection, get all the specifics in a signed and countersigned contract. Make sure the delivery schedule is spelled out so everything arrives at your home and ceremony and reception site on time. You should expect to pay a deposit, but never pay the total amount in advance.

Remember, too, that elaborate arrangements and off-season or exotic flowers that are flown in from another location are more expensive. (On the other hand, a single bird-of-paradise or a sprig of flowering ginger might be all you need to make a dramatic statement.) If you're planning an autumn or winter wedding, you might consider using dried flowers at your reception site; they can be less costly than fresh and add a seasonal touch.

Silk and dried floral arrangements are extremely popular in Afrocentric weddings. "Use of the silk flowers themselves is the same in all kinds of weddings," says Vietta. "Orchids, roses, and lilies are the most popular flowers and you can use any fabric with these silk or dried flowers. I add African fabric to the wedding arrangements; that's all that's needed to make them Afrocentric. The client chooses the fabric or brings me a swatch and I find it. Often I mix the dress fabric with Afrocentric fabric to tie the wedding 'look' together."

THE BRIDAL BOUQUET

The bridal bouquet is usually hand tied with ribbon or fixed in an "oasis" (a water-soaked Styrofoam-like substance) inside a plastic holder and is coordinated with the flowers worn or carried by the rest of the wedding party, as well as with other floral arrangements on the site. "Traditionally," the bouquet is white, but as Vietta's comments have illustrated, there are many creative alternatives and various shapes, sizes, and styles to choose from. Some brides select a combination of flowers whose first initials spell out her groom's name or a romantic message.

If you're after fragrance as well as appearance, freesia, daffodils, gardenias, lilacs, jasmine, roses, and lilies are among the most aromatic flowers.

Ruth has found that calla lilies, roses, and orchids, as well as bouquets of field flowers, are the most popular choices for Black brides. She has also observed that "reds, yellows, and blues—the stronger colors—are more apt to be chosen for Afrocentric weddings." Like Vietta, she has observed that Afrocentric weddings use "the same floral styles, but with bolder colors and different ribbons. They [those having Afrocentric weddings] don't like colonial styles," she adds.

Simplicity, freshness—the essence of the bridal bouquet.

Cowrie shells adorn this bridal bouquet, a perfect adornment for the Afrocentric attire.

Styles for Your Bouquet

Arm Bouquet: composed of long stemmed flowers that are hand tied or French braided with ribbon and carried cradled in the arm

Biedermeier: a small, compact bouquet with rings of flowers, one inside the other, each ring consisting of a different flower and often of a different color

Boa: a garland of flowers and greens wired together so that it can be worn draped around the shoulders or "beauty queen" style, diagonally across the bodice

Cascade: an arrangement of flowers and greens that "cascades" down from the holder

Composite: "new" flowers created by gluing or wiring different petals and blossoms together, often one inside the other (for instance, a "glamelia" consists of multiple gladiola blossoms stuffed inside each other to give the appearance of a camellia)

Nosegay: a small, round arrangement, in a holder or hand tied

Pomander: flowers inserted into a globe-shaped oasis to achieve a ball-shaped bouquet that can be carried hanging from a ribbon

Tussie-Mussie: a hand-tied bouquet of flowers (each chosen for its symbolic meaning) whose stems have been cut to a manageable length and trimmed with a ribbon or inserted into a silver cone-shaped holder (popular in Victorian times)

Wired: each flower wired along the length of its stem so that it can be sculpted into an overall design

The arm bouquet.

The tussie-mussie.

The nosegay.

The crescent.

A selection of bridal bouquet styles.

Flowers everywhere—the bouquet, boutonniere, even in her hair—add to the romance.

"Dried field flowers are very popular at Afrocentric weddings, especially for the bridal bouquet," comments Vietta. "In a wedding for an African couple, the bride's bouquet was made of raw rice. It looked like wheat. I wrapped the stems of rice with satin and put on pearls, bugle beads, and appliques. Her attendants carried colored baskets with fruit. For the ring bearer, I created a basket with one kola nut and two cups for wine."

When selecting your bridal bouquet, keep the style of your gown in mind. If the front of your dress is beautifully embroidered, you won't want to carry a cascade arrangement or wear a flower boa that might obscure the detail. If your dress is ornate and colorful, you might want the design of your bouquet to be less complex. On the other hand, if you're wearing an elegant sheath, you might choose a dramatic wired bouquet to offset its simplicity.

Bridesmaids' bouquets—follow the form of the bridal bouquet.

The bride's bouquet is usually larger and more elaborate than those the bridesmaids carry, which can be smaller versions of it, as in Vietta's variation in the lighting of the bride's and bridesmaids' bouquets for the candlelight wedding. Or, bridemaids can simply carry single blossoms.

The boutonnieres for the groom and groomsmen can repeat the bridal motif in miniature or echo just one flower, as can the corsages for the mothers of the bride and groom. Flower girls might carry baskets with loose petals that match the bouquet, pomanders (ball-shaped bouquets) on ribbons, or hoops of flowers.

But the sky is the limit when you work with a creative professional florist—like Ruth or Vietta—using fresh, dried, or fabric flowers. "Bridal bouquets are my specialty," says Vietta, "but I like coordinating all the bridal party pieces to match it. I've used dried and silk flowers and all kinds of other decorations to make pillows for ring bearers, flower girls' baskets, and even special gift bags for the bride to give to her attendants as gifts."

FLOWERS FOR THE CEREMONY AND RECEPTION

I like to go and see what's needed," says Ruth, regarding her visits to the church and reception halls she decorates for clients. "I supply aisle runners, pew bows, arches, altar arrangements—all kinds of spaces can be decorated."

At the Ceremony Site

If you've determined that you can have free reign with your decorations at your ceremony site (see chapter 11, "Your Ceremony, Your Way"), arrange to have your florist visit and ask her to keep in mind your bridal color scheme and any special cultural features of your wedding, as well as the architectural features of the site itself.

Remember that in addition to having flowers on the altar and perhaps the pews, you can also use them to pay tribute to absent or departed loved ones or to acknowledge special feelings for significant guests.

- ✤ Create your bridal bouquet with your late mother's favorite blooms.

- ✤ Leave a bouquet on an empty front pew to honor the memory of your grandmother or stop by her grave to leave flowers on your way to the reception.

- ✤ Hand your mother a flower from your bouquet as you walk down the aisle while your groom pulls one from his boutonniere for *his* mom. (Bouquets and boutonnieres and pew arrangements can all be constructed with pull-out sections that allow you to incorporate the giving of flowers into your ceremony.)

At the Reception

Again, the size and architectural features of your reception site will help determine your use of flowers there. Archways, columns, and bannisters might be trimmed with garlands. If you're having a seated dinner (and you're watching your budget) you might spend less on entryway or lobby flowers and more on centerpieces that guests will be looking at for hours; a door wreath can beautifully, and less expensively, announce that a wedding is going on inside. If you're having a cocktail reception, you might use flowers only on the bar and the cake table.

Elegant centerpieces add charm to a reception and make excellent "take home" gifts for the wedding party.

Centerpiece arrangements can be as simple as single rosebuds in crystal vases of varying heights throughout the room, as practical as edible fruits and sweets, as creative as topiaries in a shape that correspond to the theme of your wedding, as thoughtful as breakaway centerpieces composed of individual potted plants that guests can take with them as living keepsakes.

Combine exotic fruits and foliage, such as pomegranates (symbols of hospitality) and eucalyptus (highly aromatic). If you haven't donated the altar flowers to the church as a token of appreciation, arrange to have them brought to the site, along with the pew ribbons, to decorate the bridal table. Just be sure to keep the centerpiece arrangements small enough so that guests can still see each other!

BALLOON ARTISTRY

Balloon decorating for special occasions began increasing in popularity in the 1980s and has been growing ever since. Today's brides are applauding the use of balloons at receptions, as centerpieces, canopies, and sculptures, and even in church, in the form of balloon releases rather than the traditional birdseed-throwing at the end of the ceremony. Available in every conceivable color and pattern, balloons can be an elegant way to add romance and magic to your wedding. And to add excitement as well.

If you really want your reception to start (or end) with a bang, try a colorful balloon drop as a dramatic kick-off or finale. A large balloon, usually three to five feet in diameter, decorated with ribbons and bows and containing dozens of smaller balloons and confetti, is suspended above the dance floor. At the appropriate moment, the disk jockey or band leader activates a control and the balloon explodes, showering its contents on the assembled guests.

Balloons can be fashioned into columns and archways to define the dance floor, or into freestanding hearts or other shapes that complement the theme of your wedding. Lights can be run through the framework of the structure that holds them or placed underneath for dramatic effect. As centerpieces, balloons personalized with your names and wedding date can be intertwined with candles and tulle, attached by ribbons to bud vases or party baskets, or used as accents for other decorations such as top hats or party horns. If you are considering a floating balloon canopy over your dance floor, be sure the reception room has ceilings at least ten feet high.

If you're going to use balloon decorations, take special care in selecting a designer. Ask the staff at the reception site if they have a professional balloon decor company they've worked with successfully. Ask wedding coordinators—your own if you've hired one—for recommendations. Attend bridal shows where balloon artists will have decorated their own booths, even entrances and fashion show stages. You can also contact the Qualatex Balloon Network in Wichita, Kansas, for a Certified Balloon Artist (CBA) in your area. (See Resources.) In order to be certified by Qualatex, an artist must complete a comprehensive balloon-artistry program.

As with the photographers and florists you've interviewed, check out the designer's background and experience, portfolios and samples, and client references. Make it a priority to see him or her at work on a job, from setup to finished product. Tell him your ideas for color scheme and design in as much detail as you can. If he or she says that something you have in mind can't work, ask why and get alternative suggestions. And again, don't commit yourself or pay any money without a fully detailed contract signed by both of you.

Lighter than air, balloons add elegance and whimsy to your special day.

THE COOL ELEGANCE OF ICE

Ice sculptures are a crowd-pleasing way to add beauty to any decor. The sculptures can be made in shapes that complement the theme of your wedding or have sentimental meaning for you and your groom. They can serve as centerpieces on your buffet or sweets table, accented with flowers, or be placed to the side of the head table and illuminated. You can even serve food out of them—shrimp cocktail from a sculpted shrimp, for instance. They might seem like an extravagance, but they often *look* more expensive than they are—and drip trays and other maintenance needs are usually included in the cost.

You can find ice sculptors in the Yellow Pages or by contacting caterers, who often use them.

AFROCENTRIC DECORATIONS

Afrocentric fabrics and symbols can add special meaning to your wedding and reception, either on their own or combined with other decorations like flowers or balloons, or as decorative accents that double as favors, such as printed matchbooks and cocktail stirrers or African beads and charms. Your florist, like Ruth and Vietta, may have experience with Afrocentric weddings that can save you lots of legwork and enhance your creative vision. Also see our Resources for Afrocentric gift and crafts shops and chapter 7, "Your Invitation" for information on printed favors. Traditional African cloths—kente, *Adinkra,* and *aso oke,* among others—offer an abundance of decorating options (see chapter 4, "Your Signature Fashion"). They can be used as table cloths or runners, decorated with matching ribbons and flowers, as backdrops to the head table, or as a colorful setting for the wedding cake.

In many parts of Africa, bowls, baskets, stools, and cooking vessels traditionally celebrate union, shelter, and nourishment. In Ghana, the bride receives a cooking pot to symbolize her new role as homemaker. Use handsome pots as centerpiece containers that might hold wedding favors for your guests. Or distribute decorated baskets with a boxed slice of wedding cake that your guests can take home. Tie the increasingly popular ritual of jumping

Heavy Afrocentric influence in attire and bouquet make a regal statement.

1. Release butterflies instead of balloons at the end of your ceremony.

2. Line the entranceway to your reception with easels displaying pictures of yourself and your bridegroom as children on through your dating days.

3. Use a "wedding scroll" in place of a guestbook at your reception. Hang it on an easel and have a member of the wedding party collect signatures. It can be a keepsake suitable for framing.

4. Put a wine or champagne glass etched with your names and wedding date at each place setting. Your guests can toast you and keep the glass as a souvenir.

5. In Kenya, swords are given to newlyweds as symbols of marriage and fertility. Use decorated swords as centerpieces for the head table at the reception.

6. Order a pyramid-shaped wedding cake with a fountain that spouts water from "the Nile."

7. Give your guests mugs with your names and wedding date, each containing a packet of African coffee.

the broom into your decor by including a miniature broom tied with kente cloth in each reception centerpiece and giving one to each of your guests as a keepsake.

Whether you decide to send up balloons, simply toss the bouquet, or both, decorations can create the fantasy setting for your wedding celebrations and reflect the new beginning that flowers, fresh or fabricated, so gloriously symbolize.

One of a wide selection of invitations that celebrate our African traditions.

Afrocentric invitation courtesy of Heritage Weddings™ mail-order catalog, design by Carole Joy Creations®, Inc.

SEVEN

YOUR INVITATION

EDDING CONSULTANT AMELIA Montgomery remembers a young Black professional couple, the woman a lawyer and her fiancé a financial advisor, who disagreed on their invitations. "The bride wanted the most inexpensive of the invitations they were shown. The groom tried to tell her that the invitation represented *them*, that it would form the first image of their wedding in their guests' minds and to remember they were inviting business associates and clients. He was so frustrated that he asked me to talk with her privately. When I did, I just handed her the invitation she had chosen. Then I asked her to describe for me the kind of wedding her most important client would think he was being invited to, based on receiving that invitation. She put down that invitation and began leafing through the book of more lavish ones. They made a beautiful selection."

Envision *your* guests receiving an elegant hand-calligraphed envelope embossed with *Adinkra* symbols. When they open it, they first see a gold metallic lining and then pull out an engraved card with a colorful kente cloth border asking them to join you for your wedding celebrations.

Your invitation is one of the first impressions you give of your wedding. It sets the tone; it reflects your personality; it provides necessary information regarding the ceremony and reception. Take time composing and designing the invitation that will say it all perfectly, with your signature style.

PREPARING YOUR INVITATION

Once you've finalized your guest list and booked your ceremony and reception sites (see chapters 3, 11, and 12), you'll be ready to choose the style, wording, and other enclosures for your invitation. Visit stationers, card shops, and party stores, page through bridal magazines and order catalogs and samples to see what's available on the market, even if you think you want to design your own—you may get additional ideas.

The Style

The "Traditional" wedding invitation is *engraved* in black ink on white or ivory paper with a die that cuts the letters into the surface so that you can feel the letters, raised on the front and indented on the back, as you run your finger across them. The die is given to you as a keepsake.

Alternative printing techniques are *thermography,* a less expensive process that applies raised letters to the surface of the paper without cutting, so that you can feel them on the front but not on the back, and *offset printing,* the least expensive, which simply transfers ink to the paper without cutting or raising the letters and is the way most books and periodicals are printed today. All three techniques take about the same period of time and can be used with all the different typefaces, but engraving is the most visually elegant.

Recent technological advances have opened the doors for the production of nontraditional, custom-made invitations that reflect individual style and taste. Aided by sophisticated software, stationers can offer almost endless options for bringing together visual elements and typefaces in a multitude of combinations and colors. From invitations printed on handmade papers, incorporating photographs or other original artwork, cut in shapes to correspond to special symbols or themes, decorated with foils or lace or ribbons, with special enclosures like seeds (for a garden wedding) or sand (for the beach), to invitations enclosed (like the ship) in a bottle or with computer chips that play a tune or convey a spoken message—just about anything is possible these days.

Black brides are going back to their cultural roots when choosing the style of invitations. We may not necessarily plan an exclusively Afrocentric affair, but many are using invitations to add that cultural touch. Invitation houses are increasingly recognizing this, and the market has quickly expanded to include such lines as the Heritage Weddings mail-order catalog, Hallmark's Mahogany line, and Rhapsody Graphics.

Your bridal consultant may have catalogs from these lines that she can show you, or you can ask your other vendors for recommendations and check in your Yellow Pages under Wedding Supplies and Services, and Invitations and Announcements for stationers and card shops near you. Any store that sells invitations will have samples of all the typefaces, symbols, and other graphics, and the varieties and colors of paper, ink, and foil available.

The Wording

Once you've decided on the style of your invitation, give special thought to the wording. What your invitation *says* gives your guests a sense of the emotional and spiritual tone of your wedding as well as providing them with necessary practical information. The basic elements of the wording are:

- ↝ The names of those issuing the invitation

- ↝ The date and time of day

- ↝ The place

- The kind of attire expected of your guests, if you wish ("Black Tie" for a formal evening wedding or "Formal African Attire," for instance)

- A request for a response if the person is being invited to the reception as well as the ceremony and an address to respond to

"Traditional." All the words (with the exception of "Mr." and "Mrs.") and numbers (with the exception of zip codes and street numbers longer than two digits) are "Traditionally" spelled out.

"Traditionally," the bride's parents issue the invitation:

Mr. and Mrs. Joseph Futon

request the honour of your presence

at the marriage of their daughter

Shannon Hope

to

Leon James Crawford

on Saturday, the seventeenth of August

Nineteen hundred and ninety-nine

at four o'clock in the afternoon

North Side Gospel Center

1234 Any Street

Anytown, Anystate

and afterward in

the Church Hall

R. S. V. P.

Street address

City, State zip code

(Note that in this case the reception is being held at the same location as the ceremony and all the guests are invited.)

If you are asking only certain guests to the reception, you'd use a separate reception card and omit the R.S.V.P. from the invitation to the ceremony:

———————

Mr. and Mrs. Joseph Futon

request the pleasure of your company

at the reception

immediately following the ceremony

at their home

Sixty-four Liberty Street

R.S.V.P.

(Note that the invitation now requests "the pleasure of your company" because the occasion is social rather than sacred.)

If your parents are no longer together but still want to issue a joint invitation:

———————

Pamela Austin Futon

(your mother's first, maiden, and married names—

or her new married name if she has remarried)

and

Joseph Futon

request the honour of your presence

at the marriage of their daughter

Shannon Hope

to

Leon James Crawford . . .

If one of your parents is no longer living, the surviving parent issues the invitation in his or her own name:

————————

Mrs. Joseph Futon

requests the honour of your presence

at the marriage of her daughter

Shannon Hope

to

Leon James Crawford . . .

If your surviving parent has remarried:

————————

Mr. and Mrs. Harold Washington

request the honour of your presence

at the marriage of Mrs. Washington's daughter

(or their daughter, if you're close to your stepfather)

Shannon Hope Futon

to

Leon James Crawford . . .

If both sets of parents issue the invitation:

————————

Mr. and Mrs. Joseph Futon

request the honour of your presence

at the marriage of their daughter

Shannon Hope

to

Leon James Crawford

son of Mr. and Mrs. James Crawford . . .

or

———

Mr. and Mrs. Joseph Futon

and

Mr. and Mrs. James Crawford

request the honour of your presence

at the marriage of their children

Shannon Hope

and Leon James . . .

If the groom's parents issue the invitation ("Traditionally" done if they are paying for the wedding but rarely followed today):

———

Mr. and Mrs. James Crawford

request the honour of your presence

at the marriage of

Miss Shannon Hope Futon

to their son

Mr. Leon James Crawford . . .

If the bride and groom issue the invitation:

———

Miss Shannon Hope Futon

and

Mr. Leon James Crawford

request the honour of your presence

at their marriage . . .

African-Inspired Wording. Today, many of us are relaxing the "Traditional" wording and using our invitations to celebrate our ancestry as well as our own special day. Many of the invitation houses now offer a number of wording choices, as well as the option of composing your own. Here are some samples from Heritage Weddings™ mail-order catalog:

Issued by both sets of parents:

What began with our African ancestors,

continues as two families become one.

With joyful hearts the parents of

Shannon Hope Futon

and

Leon James Crawford

invite you to witness

the marriage of their children

on Saturday, the seventeenth of August

Nineteen hundred and ninety-nine

at four o'clock in the afternoon

North Side Gospel Center

1234 Any Street

Anytown, Anystate

Your presence will complete the circle

of family, friendship, and faith.

Invitation wording copyright © 1997 Heritage Weddings™ mail-order catalog.

Issued by the bride and groom:

Shannon Hope Futon

and

Leon James Crawford

invite you to share a day of happiness

as they celebrate their African-American ancestry,

unite their families,

and begin a new life together in love

by exchanging marriage vows

on Saturday, the seventeenth of August

Nineteen hundred and ninety-nine

at four o'clock in the afternoon

North Side Gospel Center

1234 Any Street

Anytown, Anystate

Invitation wording copyright © 1997 Heritage Weddings™ mail-order catalog.

Just as our ancestors

Jumped the Broom

we will join hands

as bride and groom

and pledge our love and faithfulness

We invite you

to share our new beginning

on Saturday, the seventeenth of August

Nineteen hundred and ninety-nine

at four o'clock in the afternoon

North Side Gospel Center

1234 Any Street

Anytown, Anystate

Shannon Hope Futon

and

Leon James Crawford

Invitation wording copyright © 1997 Heritage Weddings™ mail-order catalog.

Verses. Some couples choose to have their invitations printed on a card with the words of the invitation itself on the inside and an inspirational verse on the outside. Again, many of the invitation houses offer a selection of these if you don't have a piece of favorite poetry or lines of your own that you want to use. These verses (Copyright © 1997) are from Heritage Weddings™ mail-order catalog:

On this day
we will become one . . .
in the spirit of our heritage,
the circle of our family,
and the strength of our love

In our ancestry there is strength
In our hearts there is love
In our lives there is joy

Other Elements and Enclosures

Along with the invitation (and envelopes for mailing), you may need to order additional enclosures in the same style—such as an invitation to the reception, a response card, even a map to help your guests get from one site to another.

Protective tissue was once necessary to keep the ink of an engraved invitation from smudging. No longer a necessity with today's production techniques, it has come to have decorative value instead. Some couples use it to add a touch of color to their invitations.

The outer envelope "Traditionally" has the return address embossed (die cut into the paper without ink) on the back flap. You may decide, for practical purposes, to have the return address *printed* instead.

The inner envelope "Traditionally" contains all the elements of the invitation. You may decide to do without it if your invitation has relatively few enclosures and you're willing to depart from "Tradition."

The reception card is a card smaller than the invitation and is used to inform the guest of the time and place of the reception.

The response card and envelope is another small card, which can be either blank or printed (your stationer or invitation catalog will show you the options) so that guests can check off whether they accept or decline—with a stamped and addressed envelope. If you use a response card, do not put R.S.V.P. on your invitation. When you're ready to mail your invitations, it's wise to number the response cards in cross-reference to your master guest list in case you can't read the handwriting when they're returned.

A pew card assigns seats at the ceremony for special guests, if you wish.

These may either be enclosed with the invitation or sent after acceptance and may be handwritten or printed:

Please present this card

North Side Gospel Center

Saturday, the seventeenth of August

Pew number 4

These are called "within the ribbons" cards when special seating at the ceremony is indicated by ribbons on the pews.

Hotel accommodation cards bear the name, address, and telephone number of a hotel where you may have set aside a block of rooms for out-of-town guests, who can then call and make a reservation. The hotel may provide these, although you may want to reprint them to match the style of your invitation.

Parking cards have the name and address of parking facilities that have been reserved for guests and paid for by (including gratuities) the hosts.

Travel cards announce special transportation you may have arranged for getting guests from the ceremony to the reception.

Maps give directions from the ceremony site to the reception site, if you haven't arranged transportation.

At-home cards announce your new name and address (if they're changing) and when the new address takes effect:

Mr. and Mrs. Leon James Crawford

after the seventeenth of August

526 Any Street

Anytown, Anystate zip code

OTHER STATIONERY AND PRINTED MATERIAL

Wedding Programs

It may be helpful for your guests to have a printed "order of service" for your ceremony, explaining any special rituals you may be incorporating. A program also provides a place to name your attendants, musicians, and officiants, to thank those who have contributed to the preparations, and to pay tribute to absent loved ones (see chapter 11, "Your Ceremony, Your Way" for program guidelines). You may wish to coordinate the style with your invitation.

Wedding Announcements

Announcements are sent immediately following the wedding to those you were unable to invite but with whom you want to share your happy news. Again, you may choose to print them to match the style of your invitations. They are issued in the name of the hosts and state the date, year, and location of the ceremony and do not imply the expectation of a gift:

Mr. and Mrs. Joseph Futon

have the honour of announcing

the marriage of their daughter

Shannon Hope

and

Leon James Crawford

on Saturday, the seventeenth of August

Nineteen hundred and ninety-nine

North Side Gospel Center

Anytown, Anystate

Acknowledgments of Gifts Received

If you anticipate that you won't be able to write thank-you notes for all the wedding gifts you receive before your ceremony until *after* your honeymoon, you may order printed acknowledgments to let the givers know that their presents arrived safely and that you will be writing them personally soon:

Miss Shannon Futon

wishes to acknowledge the receipt

of your wedding gift

and will write a personal note of

appreciation at an early date

Stationery

Thank-you notes may be printed with the bride's maiden name for use before the wedding (with a separate set for the groom) and with the couple's names (or joint monogram) for use after the wedding. You may of course use unprinted cards instead.

Personal stationery, for use after the wedding, may be printed with your married name and address, or with your address only, so that you and your husband can share it.

Printed Favors and Mementos

Most stationers and invitation houses can also arrange for printed matchbooks, napkins, cocktail stirrers, boxes for individual slices of cake, and other items that you may wish to have at your reception and offer as keepsakes for your guests.

ORDERING YOUR INVITATION

When you've determined the basic style, wording, and enclosures for your invitation and decided on the other printed pieces you want, get several estimates. In figuring the total number of invitations and enclosures you'll need, allow for a separate set for every unmarried person over eighteen, even if he or she is living with someone who's also invited. Married couples and families with young children receive joint invitations. Order at least fifty extra sets and one hundred extra envelopes as backup for any mistakes made in addressing them and for any late additions to your guest list after you've started to receive regrets. Make sure the estimates of cost include every item in the right quantities. Place your order three to six months in advance of the ceremony, the longer time if you're using special elements—such as handmade paper or an audio computer chip—or if your ceremony is taking place near a holiday.

Check the Copy

Compose and proofread the text of your invitations, enclosures, and other material carefully before you submit your order. (Ask a friend to proofread also.) Even the smallest errors in time or place can cause confusion for your guests and embarrassment for you.

If you order from a stationer, ask if you can see typeset copy before everything is printed so that you can have a chance to correct any mistakes. If you order through an invitation house (one of the commercial lines we mentioned earlier), you will probably not have the opportunity to check the copy again after your initial submission, so make sure it's perfect!

Read all the printed matter as soon as you receive it (and verify the counts) so that you can schedule corrections at that stage if necessary. (If the printer is responsible for the errors, he shouldn't charge for fixing them.)

LETTER PERFECT

To add the finishing touches to your invitation, decide how you plan to address the outer and inner envelopes. The "Traditional" choice is professional hand calligraphy. Today, computer-generated calligraphy is an increasingly popular and less expensive option, and you can always choose to address them yourself (with the help of family and friends) in your own handwriting.

Hand calligraphy is the most costly and the most time-consuming of the methods as well as the most elegant. For knowledgeable referrals, ask your stationer or wedding consultant. Once you have the names of two or three calligraphers, inform them of the typeface of your invitation and request samples to see whose artistry you like best. "You want the style of lettering to match the style of your invitation," says Janet Kaspar, owner of Baltic Studios in Itasca, Illinois. Are the letters in the samples clean, neat, and balanced? Will the calligrapher also stuff and stamp the envelopes? Be sure to ask about turnaround time.

Many stationers and mail-order invitation houses now offer computer calligraphy. (If you're especially computer literate, you might want to purchase the software Perfect Calligraphy and do it yourself.) Again, ask to see samples compatible with the typeface of your invitation and find out whether the store will also stuff and stamp.

Forms of Address

As with the wording of your invitation, the "Traditional" way to address the *outer envelope* is to spell out everything except Mr., Mrs., Ms., Dr., Jr., zip codes, and street numbers.

Double-check the proper names and titles for your guests. If you're addressing an invitation that includes children under the age of eighteen, you may list them by first names under the names of their parents:

Mr. and Mrs. Clarence Austin

Joseph, Mary, and Pamela (in alphabetical order)

If there isn't enough room to name them all on the outer envelope, you may list them instead on the inner envelope. Don't resort to using "and Family." If there are several children of the same sex, you may address them collectively as the Messrs. Austin (boys) or Misses Austin.

The inner envelope, if you're using one, may be left blank on less formal invitations; otherwise it bears only the titles and last names of the guests. If there are children included, they may be addressed here either by their first names or by the more formal "Master" or "Miss."

PUTTING IT ALL TOGETHER

Allow at least a week for stuffing and stamping the envelopes if you're doing it yourself:

1. Put all the enclosures face up directly on top (or inside, if it's a folded invitation).

2. Insert in the inner envelope (or the outer, if you're only using one) with the type facing the back flap.

3. If you're using an inner envelope, it should then be inserted into the outer one with the front facing the back flap so that guests see their names first when they remove it.

Take a fully assembled sample to the post office to be weighed and evaluated for postage. And ask about special stamps that might be appropriate while you're there. The Heritage Stamp Collection honors notable African-Americans and the Love series may have current issues that would look beautiful on your invitation. (Be sure to include stamps for the return of the response cards in your final count.)

Mail your invitations at least four weeks before the wedding, up to eight if

Contemporary Christian graphic on an invitation.
Invitation courtesy of Heritage Weddings™ mail-order catalog.

the ceremony is taking place on or near a holiday or if you want to have extra time to send out additional invitations after you've started to receive regrets. You want to allow enough time for out-of-towners to respond but not so much that local guests forget!

Also address and stamp your wedding announcements, if you'll be sending one, and ask a member of the bridal party to mail them for you immediately following the ceremony.

NO TIME FOR PRINTED INVITATIONS?

f you're having a very small ceremony, or one that is being planned quickly, it is not unusual to handwrite, fax, or even phone invitations up to a week before. And, nowadays, don't forget e-mail. Handwritten, faxed, or e-mailed invitations can use the same wordings given for printed invitations above. Or they can be more homespun or creative—design one on your computer using special typefaces and borders.

If you're phoning, it's still a good idea to phrase the invitation to indicate who's hosting the event—say something like, "Mom and Dad are hoping you can join us . . ."

Once your invitations are in the mail, the word is out and the tone of your wedding, that first impression of your Big Day, is set.

One couple's distinctive choice: "London" dishware by Sasaki.

EIGHT

GIVING AND RECEIVING

WITH GRACE

HERE'S NOTHING LIKE a wedding to put folks in a gift-giving mood. Your family, friends, and associates will probably want to express their affection and best wishes for your future by giving you a present. They'll give you items that will beautify your home, simplify your married life, or help you to make some big purchase, like a home. At the same time, you and your groom will want to show your

Setting Up a Mortgage Registry

Couples apply to a bank that offers mortgage registries, giving their names, address, dates of birth, date of wedding, Social Security numbers, and places of business. (Ask your bridal consultant and married friends for referrals if your bank doesn't offer this service.)

The bank then sets up an escrow account and gives the couple cards to send out with their invitations to let guests know where they may make a contribution:

We are pleased to announce

that we have registered with the

ARBOR HOME BRIDAL REGISTRY

If you would like to assist us in saving for the purchase of our first home

please call the Arbor National Mortgage Bridal Registry

for gift information

1-800-ARBOR-91

Gifts to the account, which is interest-bearing, must be left in the bank for at least six months after the wedding, unless they are withdrawn for the purchase of a house.

appreciation to those whose love and support has been important to you in your lives so far and especially during all the preparations for your ceremony and celebrations. And you and he will probably also want to mark this Day-of-All-Days in your relationship by giving each other gifts that signify your feelings and commitment.

If you're the kind of Sister who has trouble "letting people do for her," try for once to let yourself be on the receiving end. Relax and enjoy being "showered" with gifts. Take advantage of the opportunity to get things you and your groom need and might not be able to afford to buy yourselves. Accept gifts you are given gladly and graciously, while not expecting them. If your man is the "don't give me nothing" type, help him accept gifts by reminding him that while it is more *blessed* to give than to receive, it takes more *grace* to receive. Help him see that receiving gracefully and appreciatively allows others to feel the joy of giving.

In every culture, gift-giving is part of what weddings are for. As we've seen in chapter 3, in Africa families exchange gifts at weddings to maintain balance in the community and to provide for the future of the new couple. Here, too, the community helps newlyweds set up a home, which, in turn, enlarges and strengthens the community.

All this gift-giving can sometimes be challenging. No one deliberately gives you something he or she thinks you won't like, already have, or can't possibly use, but it happens. Not everyone's taste is identical to yours, and you may end up with salad bowls that would scare your dinner guests, artwork that you would only hang in the attic, or objects whose identity and purpose remain an utter mystery. Fortunately, there's a way to cut down on duplication and even disappointment and make it easier for your gift-givers—the bridal registry.

THE REGISTRY

The bridal registry is a practical solution to gift dilemmas for both the givers and the receivers. Here's how it works: You and your fiancé, with the help of a registry consultant, compile a list of items you need and want in as much detail as possible (item number, style, color, manufacturer, even price). This way those who are buying you gifts can select something they can be sure you'll like and that you don't already have. (The store updates the list as items are bought.) This service is free and is especially useful for distant relatives or friends of the family who don't know you well. Even your closest friends, who may want to give you something completely personal, can consult the list as a guide to your preferences and needs.

Once upon a time, brides registered only for their linens, silver, and china and crystal patterns. Today, registry items range from tools and appliances to honeymoons and mortgages. The variety of places offering registry services has broadened to include specialty stores, hardware stores, travel agencies, African art galleries, and banks. It's become the norm for brides- and grooms-to-be to register at more than one store. By doing so, you provide yourselves and your gift-givers with the widest choices and the most convenient locations possible. (If you do register with several stores, though, you may want to divide your list of items among them to avoid duplication of gifts.)

4W Circle of Art and Enterprise in Brooklyn, New York (see Resources), a collective of four Afrocentric shops, offers a popular bridal registry. "All kinds of people are really open to not just buying the traditional wedding items. We see

Registry Checklist

Bridal registry shouldn't be a nightmare! This gift registry checklist has been designed as a guide to help you and your fiancé consider what to register for. No list is ever complete, but this one is meant to give you the basics. We suggest that the two of you review it before going to register.

BAKEWARE

Bundt Form Pan

Cookie Sheet

Loaf Pan

Muffin Pan

Pie Pan

Pizza Brick

Sheet Pan

Springform Pan

BARWARE

Beer Mugs

Coasters

Corkscrew

Highballs

Ice Bucket/Tongs

Irish Coffee Mugs

Pilsners

Pitcher

Wine Decanter

Wine Rack

CASUAL LINENS

Bath Sheets

Bath Towels

Bedspreads

Blankets

Cloth Napkins

Comforter/Duvet

Hand Towels

Place Mats

Sheets

Shower Curtain

Washcloths

CRYSTAL

Brandy Snifters

Champagne Flutes

Cordials

Decanters

Goblets

Pitchers

Wineglasses (red, white)

CUTLERY

Bread Knife

Chef's Knife

Cleaver

Cutting Board

Kitchen Shears

Knife Block

Paring Knife

Sharpening Tool

Steak Knives

DINNERWARE

Accent Plates

Bread & Butter Plates

Buffet Plates

Cereal Bowls

Coffee Cups and Saucers

Dessert Set

Dinner Plates

Egg Cups

Fruit Saucers

Mugs

Salad Bowls

Salad/Dessert Plates

Service Plate

Soup Bowls

Soup Tureen

ELECTRONICS

Camera Equipment

CD Player

Clock Radio

Computer

FAX Machine

Television

VCR

Video Camera Equipment

FLATWARE

Creamed Soup Spoons

Dinner Forks

Dinner Knives

Salad/Dessert Forks

Soup Spoons

Tea/Dessert Spoons

FORMAL LINENS

Formal Napkins

Linen/Lace Tablecloths

Place Mats

GLASSWARE

Everyday Glasses

Juice Glasses

KITCHEN LINENS

Apron

Dish Cloths

Dish Towels

Napkins

Oven Mitts

Pot Holders

Tablecloths

KITCHENWARE

Blender

Bread Maker

Cappuccino Maker

Coffeemaker

Colander

Cookbooks

Cook's Spoon (slotted)

Cook's Spoon (solid)

Cookware Set

Cookware Utensils

Cooling Rack

Electric Skillet

Espresso Maker

Food Processor

Garlic Press

Grater

Gravy/Sauce Ladle

Hand Mixer

Ice Cream Maker

Juicer

Measuring Set

Microwave Cookware

Microwave Oven

Mixing Bowls

Pasta Machine/Maker

Pasta Servers

Pie/Cake Server

Pizza Cutter

Popcorn Popper

Roasting Pan

Salad Servers

Saucepans

Sauté Pan

Serving Utensils

Skillets

Stand Mixer

Steamer Insert

Stir-fry Pan

Stock Pots

Tea Kettle

Thermometer

Timer

Toaster/Toaster Oven

Waffle Iron

Wok

SERVING PIECES

Bread Tray

Butter Dish

Cake Plate

Cream and Sugar Bowls

Gravy/Sauce Boat

Platters

Salt & Pepper Shakers

MISCELLANEOUS

Barbecue

Baskets

Books

Candlestick Holders

Decorative Pieces

Exercise/Sporting
    Equipment

Furniture

Hand-held Vacuum

Luggage

Mirrors

Napkin Rings

Personalized Stationery

Picture Frames

Shower/Bath Accessories

Tools

Vases

OTHER

_____

_____

_____

_____

_____

_____

_____

_____

_____

_____

_____

_____

_____

_____

_____

_____

Meridian glassware

Delphi dinnerware

Leaf cutlery

Your inventory of what the two of you
already own will also help you choose
complementary patterns before you
register for such items as shown here.

Afrocentric Mail-Order Catalogs

Gold Coast Africa, Inc.
P.O. Box 8940
Madison, Wisconsin 53708-8940
800-818-5136 fax: 608-324-6666
wholesale, institutional or custom orders 732-899-4001

Homeland Authentics
122 West 27th Street, 8th floor
New York, New York 10001
800-237-4226 (800-AFRICAN) fax: 212-367-9290
www.homeland-ibn.com

Nu Nubian
132 South La Brea Avenue
Los Angeles, California 90036
800-537-0449 fax: 213-937-5664

friends and relatives of the couple getting married come in with the registry cards
and pick out gifts of African artwork, decorative plates, African fashions, everything!" says Alisha Patterson, a staff person at 4W Circle.

TAKING INVENTORY

Before you register, you and your fiancé will want to take inventory of
the things you will each bring to your new home or that you have now,
if you're already living together. Chances are you may already own many of the basics
(cookware, flatware, microwave, toaster, coffee maker, television, and VCR, for instance), though that's not to say you don't want replacements, additions, or updates.
Decide as a couple what new items you want. (Use the checklist in this chapter as a
guide.)

Go room by room; think about your lifestyle and your dreams for the future. Consider color schemes and general decor, and don't forget smaller accents and accessories you might like, such as picture frames and vases. You and your groom will be making a home together, and this is an opportunity to get a detailed sense of your individual styles and see how they complement each other.

If you share an interest, sport, or hobby, consider making it a gift category. Nikki and Carlos, whom you met in previous chapters, share a love of African art and artifacts and registered at 4W Circle. "We wanted to include a Black-owned store for our registry. We got wonderful things that we both really wanted!" exclaims Nikki. "And we introduced a great store to our family and friends for future patronage." If you have different interests—he's the cook and you're the plant person, for instance—you might want to divide the list accordingly.

Think about present and future needs as you create your inventory. Remember, wedding gifts can last a lifetime, so don't automatically exclude things (such as silverware or fine china) that might seem beyond your present circumstances. And don't be shy about listing things you might think are "too expensive." Several of your guests may pool their resources for a joint gift. This is your ultimate "wish list." Browse through online shopping sites and catalogs (see Resources). Write down all your ideas to use as guidelines when you go to register.

WHERE TO REGISTER

Next you'll need to decide *where* to register. As mentioned earlier, department stores, hardware stores, bath stores, housewares and electronic stores, bookstores, museum shops, and boutiques—even mail-order houses—now offer bridal registries. (See Resources for ideas.) Visit or contact a number of possibilities and browse through their selections or catalogs. You might decide to register by category with specialty stores—for linens at one store, for example, kitchen equipment at another, and tools and hardware at yet another. Or you might divide your list among several department stores. Or you might combine specialty shops and department stores, or choose a single store that has everything you want.

Keep the home locations and convenience of your guests in mind. Either choose shops that offer mail-order service or stores that have nationwide outlets. "We have our store hours—we're open late several nights—and phone number, including an 800 number for out-of-towners, on the bridal registry cards we give out," says Patterson of 4W Circle, "so people can plan to come in and pick out the gift they want to give or call us to select and ship for them. Most people buy the gift and something for themselves, too!" Selma Jackson, co-owner of 4W Circle, adds, "We love working with out-of-state guests of our brides via our 800 number [see Resources]. It's not a question of 'Do you think they'll like it?' because the bride and groom have already made their personal choices. We work with the guests in finding the gift on the registry list that's in their price range. Whatever they spend, they feel they gave a wonderful gift. We always hear, 'The bride and groom loved our gift,' and the giver is pleased that the couple was pleased. We started offering the Afrocentric bridal registry as a service to brides but after four years we see it's a service to the shoppers, too."

The Bridal Registry
Of
4W Circle of Art & Enterprise
Bride _____
Groom _____
Have registered their gift preferences with 4W Circle.
Please stop by or call and let *Ms. Selma Jackson*,
our expert Bridal Consultant, help with your selections.

704 Fulton St. / 91 Hanson Place
(between So. Oxford & So. Portland)
Brooklyn, NY 11217
(718) 875-6500   (800) 227-7392 Outside NY

Open: Tues. – Fri. 11-9   Sat. 10-9   Sun. 1-7

Sample registry card.

Chain stores will usually carry your list at all their national outlets, so out-of-town guests can request your list and purchase gifts at their local branch.

You'll probably find your preliminary list changing as you begin to shop around. You'll see items that are more attractive or more practical than those you had in mind, as well as some you didn't even know existed. Keep notes of brand names and style numbers. There is no end to what you can register for and where. Most stores will keep your list active for a year after you've registered, and you can continue adding and subtracting items as you go.

HOW TO REGISTER

Register at least four to six months before your wedding—even as soon as you get engaged, especially if you're having an engagement party to which guests may want to bring gifts. Let your families and the wedding party spread the news about where you're registered; personal printed announce-

Dinnerware Basics

The typical place setting consists of a dinner plate, salad/dessert plate, bread and butter plate, and cup and saucer. Serving pieces may include serving platters, serving bowls, gravy boat, butter dish, and creamer and sugar bowl.

Registry consultants recommend registering for at least eight or twelve full place settings. Most manufacturers' patterns are "open stock," which means that you can purchase additional pieces—or replace broken ones—individually.

Porcelain (China) is made of refined, high-quality clay that has been fired at 2800 degrees (the clay turns white during the process). The high firing temperature gives porcelain more density than earthenware, making it harder, more durable, and chip resistant. Porcelain is a superb choice for long-lasting, fine dinnerware. It is oven-safe up to 350 degrees, microwave safe up to four minutes, and dishwasher safe. The word "porcelain" is derived from the Middle French word for "cowrie shells."

Earthenware is a clay-based porous ceramic that is fired at low temperatures and often glazed in vivid colors. A good choice for everyday use, it is oven-safe up to 350 degrees, microwave safe up to four minutes, and dishwasher safe.

Stoneware is made of heavy nonporous clay fired at very high temperatures. It has a more textural, handcrafted look and, like earthenware, is great for everyday use and is less expensive than porcelain.

ments make it seem as though you've asked for gifts. Perhaps you are fortunate enough to register at a store that has gift giving and receiving down to a delicate science. At 4W Circle, says Patterson, "When couples come in to register, we ask them how many guests they are inviting to their wedding. We give them that number of registry cards to give to their parents or close friends, who might be planning a shower or know lots of the guests. Those people can distribute the cards—that way it's easy for people to contact us and find out what the couple wants."

When you've narrowed down your choice of stores, make appointments with their registry consultants. Your final decision may be influenced by the courtesy and knowledge of the sales staff. Most registry departments at larger stores schedule an initial one- or two-hour meeting to acquaint you with the process, answer any ques-

From Glassware to Crystal

Consider your china, everyday dinnerware, and flatware patterns when choosing glassware and crystal. Have your registry consultant set up sample place settings so that you can see how everything looks together. Because glass is breakable, you might want to register for more than the standard eight to twelve pieces of each item.

Glassware is made of sand mixed with natural elements. It's for everyday use (dishwasher safe) and includes everything from juice glasses to tall ice-tea glasses.

Crystal is more delicate than ordinary glass but also heavier and more brilliant, with a clarity all its own. It is made from sand mixed with natural elements and 24 to 34 percent lead. Registry consultants classify crystal by its function as either barware (sherry glasses, brandy snifters, and high- and low-ball glasses) or stemware (water goblets, wine, and champagne glasses for formal dining). Crystal is dishwasher safe as long as it is placed carefully and securely in the rack. When you wash it by hand, use a rubber mat on the sink's bottom to cushion the glass and a splash of ammonia to reduce spotting and maintain overall sparkle.

tions, and walk you through the beginning of your selection. You'll usually get either a worksheet or workbook (or even a bar-code scanner) to record your choices.

Smaller stores and boutiques are often more casual and may not require an appointment in advance. "Couples don't need an appointment. They come and we give them a bridal registry sheet where they fill in the items they want," says Patterson. "One of us tours the store with them to explain various items and help them make their selections. People are amazed by the Afrocentric things they can put on their list—art, decorative items for their home, clothing, so much!"

Take as much time as you need. Experiment with the merchandise. Mix and match to see how items work together. If you are not sure how the china pattern you picked will go with the linen tablecloth and the crystal and flatware you've selected, ask to see the pieces together in a table display. Remember, the consultant is there to help you—to offer suggestions and provide alternatives.

Once you've compiled your list, the items will be entered into the store's computer system at all their locations. If a store has more than one location, your list will be available in all of them. Don't worry if you change your mind later, as you can always add or delete items as you shop and get new ideas. All purchases from your list are recorded in the system to prevent duplication. If you register for the same items at two or more different stores, you may have to keep track of purchases yourself, although some stores from different chains are now also linked by computer.

SAYING THANK YOU

It's not enough to *say* thank you. Everyone who has taken the time and thought to select a gift for you (or give a party for you or somehow contribute to your wedding) deserves your time and thought in the form of a prompt, handwritten acknowledgment, even if you've already thanked them in person. No exceptions.

As soon as you've registered, set up a convenient system in your wedding organizer for recording each gift you receive—an index card, notebook page, or computer file. Your system will list:

- The name of the giver

- The date you received the gift

- A description of the gift

- A few words (about its usefulness or attractiveness) that you can use in composing your note

- The date you send your thank-you note

Acknowledge all gifts that you receive before the wedding as they arrive. Thank-you's for all gifts received from your wedding day on need to be sent within three months after receipt. Never send printed thank-you's and try not to put off the actual writing for too long. If you're taking a long honeymoon or know that your post-wedding schedule is going to be hectic, you can send a printed acknowledgment (order these with your invitations) that you've received a gift and will be writing at the first opportunity (see chapter 7, "Your Invitation" for sample wording).

Thank-you notes should be handwritten on informal stationery, which may be printed with your maiden name (before the wedding) or your married name, with your husband's if you wish (after the wedding). In the past, the bride wrote them all, but now the groom shares this responsibility. Men are sometimes weak in the "written-thank-you" department and you may need to take up your man's slack. His not thanking his friends, co-workers, and family for their gifts is no excuse for them *not* to receive a note. It reflects badly on *both* of you. Remind, cajole, perhaps nag, but if he doesn't do the right thing within the time frame given here, do it yourself. You'll both be glad you did.

Thank-you notes with an Afrocentric border.
Thank-you notes courtesy of Heritage Weddings™ mail-order catalog.

What may seem like a chore can be a pleasure if it's an opportunity for the two of you to reflect on the memories of your wedding and to treat yourselves to romantic rewards as the list gets smaller. Divide your list between you (he'll take his friends and you'll take yours, for instance) and schedule time together to write. You'll each sign only your own name to your notes, but mention each other.

> *Dear Eric and Lovis,*
>
> *We were completely wowed by the wall hanging of Adinkra symbols you gave us for our wedding! The colors match our foyer tiles so exactly that it's uncanny. Thank you so much. Ed still can't believe you picked it without having seen our house. We look forward to your visit to our new home when you will see for yourselves how perfect a gift it is.*
>
> *Love, Jan*

Be as sincere and as spontaneous as you can in your writing. The notes needn't be long, but they should be personal. (See Resources for a list of books on letter writing that may be helpful.) Mention a particular detail of the gift that especially turns you on. If you can't be sincere about the gift itself, be sincere about the thought behind it. If you've exchanged a gift, don't say so; give thanks for the one you were given. (And think carefully about exchanges, taking everybody's feelings into account. Maybe you should hang on to that strange plate from Uncle Buddy so that you can bring it out when he visits.) If you're given money, don't mention the amount—just say something about how you're going to use it.

Dear Aunt Argent,

Jan opened the card you sent us for our wedding. She put her head down with a gasp, and when I rushed over to her, all she could say was, "I can't believe I married into a family like this!" We are both overwhelmed by your generosity, which will help make our dream trip to West Africa a reality. You remind us that the meaning of family in Africa is alive and well in our family!

Love, Ed

Don't try to knock off too many notes in one session—your haste will be obvious in your words. A heartfelt written thank-you can be a treasured memento of the occasion, even for your closest friends and family, who won't expect a formal note but should definitely receive one.

DISPLAYING AND PROTECTING YOUR GIFTS

Some couples choose to display their gifts at home before the wedding (during a scheduled gathering, perhaps). Guests like to see what you've received, but be careful to arrange such a display so that it doesn't allow for awkward comparisons of expense. Don't display cards with gifts. Be sure that the display area is secure (you might hire an ununiformed guard and/or alert the local police) and that the gifts are covered under your homeowners or apartment insurance by calling your broker and adding these items to your coverage list.

Make provisions for receiving gifts and keeping them safely at the reception site, since some guests will present them on your wedding day. (We advise against

Formula for the Perfect Wedding

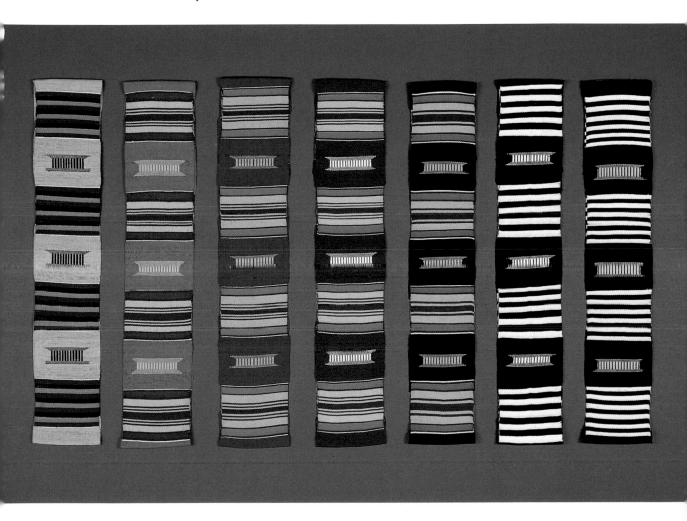

Contemporary reproductions of traditional African woven cloth.

LEFT
Traditional tux, worn with a *style* that makes it distinctly African-American.

RIGHT
African influence on a tux makes formal dressing a whole new "Black thang." Wonderful!

LEFT
Vested tuxedo, made even more formal by the addition of studs on his shirt and a bow tie . . .

. . . although he could have worn a traditional tie . . . or less, and you'd still want to marry him, yes?

In full traditional regalia, a man who knows his history and wears it with style.

*N*ow, add a
woman.

White beads and
lace from head to
toe do not a bride
make. It's the
allure . . .

And nothing is more alluring than gold, here mixed with bridal white.

If you have a notion to get married in a hat . . .

. . . put that notion into motion!

You can accessorize
to the hilt.

"When a bride is well dressed, you
notice the bride. When she's not,
you notice the dress," said Coco
Chanel. Well, not *exactly*. All the
details of preparation come
together in a flawless, relaxed
appearance that allows love and
romance to beam through.

Yes, you can put flowers *under* there,
too. What you wear beneath your dress
(for his eyes only) is almost as important
as your bridal attire.

Or you can also be a barefoot bride. This Afrocentric gown needs no accessory but you!

In full traditional regalia, a woman who knows her history and wears it with style.

If there's one overarching point we hope to prove in this book, it's that weddings are not just white—

—they're dark, sultry, sexy . . .

—they're whimsical,
unforgettable . . .
everything you are.

$\mathcal{N}$ow add the makings of
a great day . . .

Sweets on top of sweets on top of sweets—a cake
to remember, forever.

Flowers—the addition of beads
makes this arrangement formal.

A nosegay of field flowers.

A celebration in African tradition
will immediately follow the ceremony
The Hilton
1548 East Wilshire
Cleveland

Mr. and Mrs. Ernest Tyler Woodson
and
Mrs. Edward Keith Jones
invite you to share in the happiness
as their families are united
through the marriage of their children
Tricia Felice Woodson
and
Darnel Edward Jones
This new beginning will be celebrated
in joyous African tradition
on Saturday, the twenty-fifth of July
Nineteen hundred and ninety-eight
at four o'clock in the afternoon
Belgrade Avenue United Methodist Church
2463 Belgrade Avenue
Cleveland, Ohio

A "shout out" to all the people you love.

Afrocentric invitation courtesy of Heritage Weddings™ mail-order catalog.

A magnificent balloon swan to evoke the mood of elegant celebration.

$\mathcal{M}$ix well for
happily ever after . . .

In full traditional regalia, a man and woman who know their history and wear it with style.

displaying gifts at your reception site for reasons of practicality as well as security.) Assign a member of the wedding party to collect them and put them in a locked room or closet and then get them to your home (or to friends or family who will watch them during your honeymoon) afterward.

Anticipate receiving gifts of checks and cash. Ask your bank in advance how checks should be made out for hassle-free deposit and have your family and friends spread the word. Carry a handbag with you at the reception to collect them (or ask a trusted member of your wedding party to do so) and arrange for their safekeeping (or deposit) while you're off on your honeymoon.

GIFTS TO (AND FROM) THE WEDDING PARTY

It's "Traditional" for the bride and groom to give gifts to their wedding party and other special people as keepsakes and thank-you's for their participation. These are usually the same for each bridesmaid and for each groomsman, although the gifts for the honor attendants are sometimes slightly more elaborate. Often these gifts are engraved with the date of the wedding, the name of the bride and groom, and the initials of the recipient, and are given beforehand so they may be worn during the ceremony (see Resources under Favors/Gifts). Here are some suggestions:

For the bridesmaids

- Lockets or charms engraved with African symbols.

- Necklaces of colorful African beads. In Kenya, these are given in recognition of beauty. The girls with the most admirers have the most strands.

- Cowrie shell earrings. The feminine shape of the shell is associated in many African cultures with attractiveness and fertility.

For the groomsmen

- Silver key chains.

- Monogrammed cuff links.

✎ Cummerbunds and bow ties in African fabric to wear on the day of the wedding.

For all the wedding party

✎ Picture frames engraved with ankhs.

✎ Leather calendar covers embossed with African symbols.

✎ Bottles of wine with customized labels to commemorate the occasion.

Or you can individualize each gift to appeal to special hobbies and interests (though you should make sure they're all within the same price range). The possibilities are endless. The most important thing is to give these people who've shared your special day (and all the preparations leading up to it) something to treasure as you have treasured their participation.

There are others who may not be members of the wedding party but who have been just as instrumental in bringing it all together—your parents, "other mothers," and close relatives, friends who've given you parties or helped with crucial tasks. Arrange to have flowers delivered the day after the ceremony; order extra copies of your wedding photographs, album, or videotape to use as gifts; make a special post-honeymoon dinner date for relaxed recollections of all the festivities. It's especially nice gesture for you and your bridegroom, individually, to give a present to each other's parents—as a thank you for all they've done and as a symbol of your future relationship.

GIFTS FOR EACH OTHER

With so much gift-giving going on, you and your groom shouldn't miss the opportunity to exchange symbols of your love, along with your vows. Your gifts to each other need not be expensive or elaborate; a romantic note inscribed in a book of your favorite poetry, an inexpensive, personal— even quirky—item, such as sexy underwear, can be as meaningful as you make it. Leave each other gifts in places where they can be discovered as you dress for the Big Event. Then later, when the "I do" moment arrives, you will have that private knowledge of your special commitment on this public day of celebration.

Gifts are a way of spreading love. Think of all the love you receive in the form of time and labor for your wedding, and of the love the two of you have for each other multiplied and spread among your friends, families, and associates. Receive with love and gratitude. Give with love and blessedness and you will be blessed in return.

GOOD-BYE TO

THE SINGLE LIFE:

PRE-WEDDING PARTIES

ONE ARE THE days when the last bridal shower you attended was almost exactly like the one before and the one before that. Gone, too, are the days when the women got together over cake and punch while the men did their own separate (often unmentionable) thing. Today, we Sisters are giving our girl-friends unusual send-offs, ones that may even include the men. Popular ways to mark the transition from single-hood to marriage now include a return to older traditions as well as an introduction of new ones.

T"raditional" bridal showers serve the very practical purpose of helping newlyweds set up housekeeping. They are hosted during daylight hours by one or more of the bridesmaids or other good friends who will be attending the wedding. (Parents and other close relatives "Traditionally" avoid hosting showers since it can seem as though they're asking for gifts, but this too is changing.) Guests—usually ladies only—"shower" the bride-to-be with small, often theme-related items to equip the couple's new household. It is most common for bridal showers to be held in the home of one of the hosts. They are "Traditionally" a surprise for the guest of honor, although (*because* they're "Traditional") most brides know what's up when they're invited to their best friend's home on a Saturday afternoon a couple of weeks before the wedding. A "Traditional" shower might be just what you want and need. You might welcome the opportunity for a last "unmarried" gathering with your girlfriends and really look forward to their help in outfitting a new kitchen, bedroom, or bath, stocking the larder, or adding sexiness to your lingerie drawer.

If so, here are some ideas that you can pass along to friends as they plan the shower that's right for you:

A Room-in-the-House Shower. Pick a particular room and ask guests to bring a gift that would be used in that room. If you've chosen the bedroom, for instance, gifts can range from sheets and pillowcases to bedside books and reading lamps. Or you can assign each guest a different room.

Pantry Shower. To stock the cupboards, ask guests to bring canned goods, spices, and other staples, along with storage containers and supplies.

Recipe Shower. Another kitchen-related theme. Each guest contributes a favorite recipe and an ingredient, utensil, or piece of equipment used in making the dish.

An "Outdoor" Shower. For the bride with a "green thumb" and the terrace or backyard to go with it, guests can bring gifts ranging from seeds and bulbs to spades and watering cans to equipment for outdoor entertaining. If weather permits, hold the party outdoors, too!

"Around the Clock" Shower. Instead of assigning rooms of the house, assign hours of the day and ask each guest to bring something appropriate—say, an exotic blend of coffee for 8 A.M., a video for after-dinner entertainment, sexy underwear for midnight.

A Soothing Shower. Not every "Traditional" shower has to be purely practical. Perhaps what you could most use at this stage of the wedding planning is some relaxation and self-indulgence. Bath oils and salts, skin creams, gift certificates for a massage or a manicure, luxurious lingerie—guests can shower you with gifts that calm and comfort you.

Girlfriends' Night In. Relive the good old days of the ever-popular sleep-over. Have the girls pack their overnight cases and head over to the hostess's house for pizza and beer. Dance to old records, get out the old yearbooks, play Truth or Dare and pin-the-tail-on-the-hunk. Gifts might include sentimental items from school or dating days. (With any luck, the boys will crash in on your party in the middle of the night!) Or follow the boys' bachelor party lead and have a *Girlfriends' Night Out,* a bachelorette dinner at a favorite restaurant with reminiscing about all the ups and downs of single life, from first dates to first jobs.

As you can see, "Traditional" doesn't necessarily mean expensive or elaborate or even "sedate"; it's flexible enough to accommodate a wide range of tastes and prices. You can put your own personal spin on any of these ideas to suit your needs and the budgets of your hosts and guests.

CONTEMPORARY ALTERNATIVES

Perhaps you want to put a new spin on the whole idea of "Tradition." *Co-ed "Jack and Jill" showers* are fast gaining popularity and can be a contemporary answer to the "Traditional" tea party/stag party single-sex celebrations. Many of the previous ideas can be easily expanded or adapted to include men. (*He* may be the cook in the household anyway.) Or you can focus less on homemaking and more on mutual interests and activities. If you love music, for example, a great shower might be one where his friends and your friends all bring a CD to add to your soon-to-be-combined music collection. Party hearty during the shower!

Power-Tools-for-the-Power-Couple Shower. A his and hers shower for filling the tool chest and supply cabinet. Scissors, batteries, nails, hammers, screwdrivers, wrenches, light bulbs, brooms, mops, picture hangers, needles and thread—all the basics for maintenance and minor repairs will be on hand when you need them after this shower. Guests can bring their gifts "as they are" in the original bag, tied with either a piece of ribbon or a piece of twine. This is great if you're buying a home, especially a fixer-upper, or even if you're only moving into a new apartment.

A co-ed CD shower is just the practice you need to get your moves together for the reception and to let go of some of your pre-wedding stress.

"Around the World." If the two of you have a passion for travel, enlarge the boundaries of "around the clock" (above) and assign an international destination for each hour. Create a party decor using travel posters and clocks set to different time zones. Serve appetizers from different countries (nachos, tapas, and dim sum, for instance). Gifts could be a cookbook, spice, or travel guide for each destination.

Honeymoon Shower. Instead of going around the world, the event could focus just on your honeymoon destination. Bring out the beach chairs, play reggae music, serve rum punch and roti. Gifts can be as practical as a travel guide and sunscreen or as romantic as a book of love poetry to read to each other in the honeymoon suite.

A Sporting Shower. If you and your fiancé share an interest in a particular sport, your hosts can ask guests to bring related gifts—tennis balls, swimming goggles, ski hats. Or if your interest is as spectators rather than participants, maybe your hosts and guests can pitch in to buy a block of tickets for the next game and you can have your shower in the stands.

Wine Shower. Guests bring bottles of wine from different states or countries or items associated with drinking wine (glasses, corkscrews, ice buckets, wine guides). This kind of shower could also be used as an opportunity to sample wines and champagnes that are being considered for your reception.

Entertainment Shower. If you're both music fans or movie buffs, the perfect shower gifts might be CDs or videotapes for your collection, reference guides for settling those "who-directed-that" disputes, gift certificates to the local theater, or tickets for that upcoming concert.

AFROCENTRIC "RITES OF PASSAGE"

If we look to our ancestors in Africa for pre-wedding customs, we find an emphasis on the spiritual preparations for marriage. The elders of the community advise the betrothed couple—separately, in single-sex sessions—on the meaning and responsibilities of the union they are about to enter into. For Wolof women, this practice is called "Loading the Bride." Many cultures also perform purification rituals to cleanse the body and soul of any impurities that either partner might bring to the relationship. For Zulu women, it's customary for the bride and her female companions to bathe together on her wedding morning. Among the G'wi of Botswana, the bride-to-be fasts in silence for four days outside the village and then has her head shaved and is bathed by the female elders. In Egypt, the young woman collects water from the sacred Nile and washes herself with it before her nuptials.

Why not do as many of our ancestors did and use your pre-wedding party as an opportunity to receive support and guidance from your elders? Invite them to share their experience of getting married, the nuances of family relationships, and their secrets for helping love endure. You'll be surprised at how much you may learn, not to mention how grateful your elders will be for this gesture of care and respect.

Here are some ideas for incorporating African customs of counseling and purification in your own shower:

Loading-the-Bride Shower. The female friends and relatives of one bride we know came up with this "rites of passage" celebration when she said she didn't want the usual lingerie and cookware. They sat her on a chair, covered her breasts with kente cloth and left her shoulders exposed. The room was candlelit. Next to her was a bowl of warm water and a loofah. One by one, her friends gently wiped her shoulders with the loofah and said things such as, "This is to wash away all past hurts," "This is to wash away all past relationships," "This is to wash away all past rejections." Afterward, the Sisters formed a circle around her and posed serious questions about why she'd chosen her mate, how she thought she'd make their marriage last.

Jumping-the-Broom Shower. Guests bring ribbons inscribed with advice and observations about marriage, which are placed in a basket for the bride to draw out, one by one, and read aloud. At the end, all the ribbons are tied to a decorative broom that can be used if she plans to jump the broom in her wedding ceremony.

Kwanzaa Shower. Guests bring gifts related to the seven principles of Kwanzaa. For Self-determination, for instance, they might offer items made by African-Americans; for Creativity, a membership in a Black cultural institution; for Collective Work and Responsibility, the promise to baby-sit for the couple or to volunteer in the larger community by visiting patients in nursing homes or hospitals.

Night of the Henna Shower. This is an ancient African ceremony still practiced by Orthodox Muslims. The women gather a night or two before the wedding to tell stories, give presents, sing and dance. They paint the bride-to-be's hands with henna, a symbol of purity, and dress her hair.

Queh-Queh Shower. A Guyanese custom that has its origins in Africa, the *queh-queh* is usually held a week or two before a wedding. It is a co-ed celebration of the coming ceremony that includes African dancing, drumming, and music, along with traditional songs, often sexual in nature and performed by family elders.

Whatever form of shower you have—"Traditional," contemporary, or Afrocentric—it's wise to hold it at least two weeks before the wedding. You (and at least some of the other guests) are going to be busy getting ready for the Big Day. "Traditionally," everyone who's invited should also be invited to the wedding—mostly so no one's feelings get hurt.

Your hosts should issue invitations, either by phone or in writing, a couple of weeks ahead, specifying the theme and any gift guidelines, as well as the time and place. (Most stationery stores carry preprinted invitations with blanks for the theme and other details.) She may ask you for a guest list. Be sure to find out from the host how many people she can accommodate.

It's perfectly permissible to have more than one shower. If you have friends at church, at the office, in your sorority, etc., many of whom may not know one another, each group may throw a shower for you. Enjoy them all! Be careful if you try to combine their efforts. You may be comfortable with everyone, but they may not feel comfortable with each other. Let friends from different circles have you to themselves if they wish. By all means take advantage of the opportunity to be showered with gifts and good wishes, just be sure to coordinate the times and the guest lists so that no one feels obliged to attend too many pre-wedding parties or give too many gifts.

If you live in one place and are being married in another, having two showers might be the practical way to celebrate with friends in both locations. Those in the town where the ceremony will be could arrange a shower to coincide with a visit when you'll be checking out vendors or supervising fittings.

Your co-workers may want to give you an "office shower" and even buy a group gift. One bride-to-be was rushed into an emergency meeting in the conference room of the large corporation where she worked, only to be greeted by "Surprise!" cheered by all her colleagues and management. From behind the cake, balloons, and a gigantic box wrapped in the classic Tiffany blue, came her fiancé to hug her as she wept for joy. Such an office shower can be the perfect opportunity for your co-workers to meet, if they haven't already, your spouse-to-be and for him to connect faces to all those office-drama characters you've talked about *ad nauseam*. This doesn't mean they'll expect to be invited to the ceremony, but it does mean that you should acknowledge their kindness with a note addressed to the group and posted in the office or sent by interoffice e-mail.

The "Traditional" counterpart to the all-female shower is the all-male *bachelor party*, hosted by his best man and including his ushers as well as other close family members and friends. Though not usually a gift-giving occasion focused on setting up house, it *is,* like the shower, a time for the groom-to-be to enjoy the support of his friends as he makes the transition to married life. We've all heard stories of how that "support" too often turns into encouragement to behave outrageously, drink too much, indulge in at least the idea of a final sexual fling—and turn up with a hangover on the day of the wedding.

It doesn't have to be that way. Many grooms-to-be land in the middle of a big drunken bash that only makes them feel uncomfortable because that's what their friends assume they want, because that's the "Tradition." Just as you've seen that there are meaningful alternatives to "Traditional" pre-wedding celebrations for the bride, grooms can look at other ways to mark this important transition.

Discuss how each of you would like to commemorate this "rite of passage" in your lives. It may never have occurred to your fiancé to define his own idea of a bachelor party. As with so many other wedding preparations, the keys to success are planning and communication. So encourage your fiancé to develop a plan that he can then present to his friends.

Consider "Traditional," contemporary, and Afrocentric options. Perhaps you'll decide on a co-ed celebration, a combination of a shower and a bachelor party that will enable you to bypass some of the drawbacks of either one by itself. If you each want to have a single-sex gathering instead, talk about ways to avoid the drawbacks. He might decide on a "Loading the Groom" party, where his male friends, mentors, and elders share their wedding wisdom.

As with showers, it's a good idea to schedule bachelor parties at least two weeks before the ceremony. Even if it isn't going to be a late night out on the town, many of the people involved will have other pre-wedding responsibilities. Invitations can be given in person, by phone, or in writing.

In the final flurry of activity leading up to the wedding, it can be especially pleasurable to spend some quiet time with those who are going to be playing a special part in your ceremony—your attendants. A bridesmaids' breakfast, luncheon, or dinner can give you a chance to thank them collectively for all their help and give them a chance to calm your prenuptial nerves. If you have attendants who don't know each other, this is the opportunity to introduce them. It's also a good time to present them with gifts that show your love and gratitude for their contribution to your important day—and they may want to give you a group gift in return (see chapter 8, "Giving and Receiving").

The bridesmaids "Traditionally" host the party, but the bride may decide that *she'd* like to, as another sign of her appreciation. Plan a relaxed, no-wedding-work gathering if you can. The timing will depend partly on when everybody can get together, which may not be until just days before the ceremony if you or your attendants are coming from out-of-town. A more formal gathering—which requires much preparation in its own right—should probably be scheduled at least a couple of weeks before the wedding, since other preparations will take precedence closer to the main event.

All the pre-wedding celebrations—showers, bachelor and bridesmaids' parties, whether "Traditional," contemporary, or Afrocentric—are occasions to reflect on preparations for marriage beyond booking vendors and deciding on clothes and food and decor; to focus on the emotional, spiritual, and material preparations for the joint life that lies ahead. Use these opportunities to receive gifts of wisdom from those who have gone before you, as well as the more tangible gifts that will contribute comfort and convenience to the home you make together.

Three very different brides with varying health, beauty, hair-care, and makeup needs—yet all can benefit from this simple prenuptial wedding regimen.

KEEPING YOURSELF TOGETHER:

FITNESS, HEALTH, AND

BEAUTY

HE BIG DAY is fast approaching. You want to look and feel your best, so allow time to get yourself in shape and make a wedding day beauty plan. And even include some much deserved relaxation.

What better excuse than your wedding to start a healthy regime of diet and exercise? Even if you're active and careful about what you eat, you may want to step up your current program in order to shed those last few stubborn pounds, and it's never too soon to begin thinking about that perfect hairstyle and makeup or to get your skin and nails looking great.

Shelley Cumberlander has always been "pleasingly plump." In her early twenties, she wore a size 13/14 and wanted to be smaller. But before she could shed her baby fat, she had one of her own and found herself larger than ever. "I didn't lose any of the sixty-seven pounds I gained with my pregnancy. I tried everything, from the cabbage soup diet to Slim Fast and Dick Gregory liquid diets. If I lost a couple of pounds, they would come right back." When she got engaged, she got serious. "My goal was to lose sixty pounds and I had nine months to do it." With thirty minutes of exercise daily, the help of her doctor, and a prescribed appetite suppressant, as well as the elimination of salty, fried, and fast foods from her diet, Shelley dropped forty pounds and two dress sizes by her wedding.

The best way to lose unwanted pounds is to eat right and exercise regularly. Don't fall for weight loss gimmicks. As Oprah says, you have to "make the connection" and adopt a healthy lifestyle that will keep you looking fabulous long after the wedding. According to the National Center for Health Statistics, about 45 percent of us Black women are 20 percent above the ideal body weight for our height, frame, and age, and as a result are at greater risk for hypertension, heart disease, diabetes, and stroke—other reasons besides "looks" to make a lifestyle change as you make the big move of marriage.

We also tend to exercise less than white women or Black men, even though exercise is the cheapest, easiest, and safest way to avoid serious illness as well as to slow the effects of aging, speed weight loss, and alleviate stress. So buy a book (see Resources) and do it—join a gym or exercise class, hire a trainer. Just get moving! Here are three ideas for getting started:

1. Choose a form of aerobic exercise you like, consult your doctor, and start gradually. For anyone planning a wedding, spare time is definitely at a premium. But you don't need to spend hours and you don't have to buy special equipment to start a fitness program. You can get results by committing yourself to just three twenty-minute aerobic exercise sessions a week. Increasing to five thirty-minute sessions will make a real difference. Statistics now show that moderate activity, like brisk walking, can be as effective as more vigorous exercise. Take advantage of the everyday opportunities to incorporate exercise into your routine. Climb the stairs instead of riding the elevator. Park your car farther from the office and walk. And remember to have fun—you'll be more likely to stick with it. African-inspired dance is an excellent aerobic outlet, perfect for shaking off those extra pounds and many gyms now offer classes.

2. Add two or three sessions a week of light weight lifting, alternating upper and lower body, to tone your arms and legs. Don't be concerned about "bulking up." "Black women worry that they will look like body builders," says Pekti, a personal trainer and owner of Black Market Body in New York. "But two- or three-pound weights won't do that. They'll give you definition." At three months, he says, you should be making rapid progress. "Little cuts in the arms will show, thighs will be firmer. You know the changes are occurring when women start taking off the sweats and putting on shorts and T-shirts."

3. Set your goals in small increments. Think "I'll lose five pounds by . . ." and then "I'll lose five more by . . . ," rather than "I have three months to lose thirty-five pounds." Experts vary, but a two-pound weight loss per month is ideal for *keeping* it off. By setting easily attainable goals, you boost your feeling of "I can do this thing!" Stay positive. Focus on your assets and achievements. Look past the gimmicks and do what feels right for your body and your mind. Don't weigh in every day. Weight obsession is out; fitness is in. Concentrate not only on the size of your wedding gown, but on a long and healthy life with your new partner.

EAT RIGHT

I don't suggest using an event as a goal to lose weight, but it can be done— as long as it's approached as a lifelong change," says Barbara Dixon, a registered dietician and author of *Good Health for African Americans* (see Resources).

A balanced diet includes all the nutrients necessary to keep your body running at its best. Eating well may take some research and planning, but the payoff is worth the effort. Don't automatically assume that you're going to have to give up all the foods you love. "You want to minimize deprivation to keep from backsliding into old habits," according to Fraca Alphin, director of Nutrition for Duke University Diet Fitness Center. You may have to make some changes in preparation and quantities, but eating "right" can be just as pleasurable as eating wrong.

Forget those miracle "crash" diets. A semi-starved body suffers from fatigue and lethargy and actually expends fewer calories. You don't want to crash on your way up the aisle. You need a diet that will *increase* your energy and sense of well being, one that will establish new eating habits for life, not just a short-term fix-it for your wedding day.

If you think you have a chronic "weight problem" and insist on losing a large amount of weight before your wedding, discuss the matter with a doctor or nutritionist. Diet drugs can sometimes be helpful supplements to a program of proper exercise and nutrition, but should never be used without professional supervision. And the support and acceptance you receive from talking about your problem may be all the "drug" you need to make healthy, slimming changes in your lifestyle.

Do your research and develop a game plan. Check your local bookstore or library for books on nutrition and cookbooks with simple, healthy recipes that you can make at home (see Resources). Home cooking isn't just good for the soul—it gives you control over what goes into your body. Here are some general principles to follow:

- ☙ Reduce your intake of saturated fat, salt, refined sugar, alcohol, and caffeine

- ☙ Eliminate nicotine

- ☙ Increase your intake of grains, fresh fruits, and vegetables

- ☙ Increase fish and skinless poultry

- ☙ Decrease red meat

- ☙ Give up snack foods like potato chips and candy bars

As with starting an exercise program, gradual implementation of these principles allows you to set realistic goals and meet them. Remember, we're talking about a permanent change, not an overnight transformation.

Cooking Lean

1. **Eat low-fat dairy products. Use skim milk instead of cream or whole milk when the recipe allows.**

2. **Create sauces and toppings from fresh fruits, vegetables, and herbs instead of butter and oil.**

3. **Cook with nonstick pans to cut down on added fats.**

4. **Dress salads with lemon juice, salsa, fresh herbs, or low-fat yogurt instead of mayonnaise or oil-based dressings.**

5. **Trim the fat from meat and the skin from chicken.**

6. **Brown and sauté with chicken broth or nonstick spray instead of oil, butter, or margarine.**

Start by keeping a "food diary" in which you write down everything you put into your mouth for two weeks. Note when you eat and how you feel at the time. Don't try to make changes during this period. At the end, you'll have a valuable record of your current eating patterns (some of them otherwise unconscious) on which to base your new plan. Pinpoint your major stumbling blocks to a healthier lifestyle and begin the modification process. If you have to have beef, try eating it once a week rather than three times. If you can only drink regular soda, look at your overall diet and find other places to cut those extra calories. Don't be lulled into a false sense of security by just eating fat-free foods. They still contain calories and you can still *over*eat and thus gain weight.

Again, don't allow yourself to get discouraged if you slip back into old habits once in a while. Just try again, and again, until new habits are established. You're working on the best wedding present you can get, even better than that band of gold—the gift of a long life.

Although Shelley Cumberlander didn't reach her initial goal of losing sixty pounds, she was more than pleased with what she accomplished. "I liked the way I

Twelve Steps to a Healthy Lifestyle

1. *Get a vision and make a game plan.* **Decide how much weight you'd like to lose. Set goals for physical fitness.**

2. *Be informed.* **Once you've defined your goals, research and design a program for achieving them.**

3. *Keep a food diary.* **For two weeks, write down everything you eat. Note the time and your mood. Try not to change your habits just because you're keeping track. Once you have an accurate look at your eating pattern, you will know what issues you have to address.**

4. *Figure out the formula.* **To lose stored energy (e.g., fat), you must burn an additional 3500 calories. Figure out how many calories you are eating by taking your current weight and multiplying it by 10. (If you already exercise three times a week, multiply by 13.) Then cut your caloric intake by 500 calories a day to lose a pound a week.**

5. *Commit to a twenty-minute exercise program three days a week.* **Join a gym, buy an exercise video, take daily walks. Incorporate exercise into everyday routines: ride your bike to work instead of taking the bus; use the stairs instead of the elevator; take the dog on a nightly run through the park.**

6. *Hire a personal trainer and custom-design a workout program.* **Without spending megabucks, you can enjoy the benefits of a trainer to maximize your exercise efforts. A good personal trainer can monitor workouts to make sure you're exercising correctly, protecting**

looked on my wedding day," she proudly recalls. "And I was happy with how my pictures turned out."

THE MANE EVENT

Your hair is your crowning glory—especially on the day of your wedding. On ceremonial occasions in Africa, our ancestors—men and women alike—devoted much of their preparations to styling their hair, from the use of special ointments and dressings to elaborate plaiting and weaving to ornamentation with against injuries, and modifying your program as your needs change. Consider having a trainer design a program for you and your fiancé so you can exercise together.

7. *Drink eight glasses of water a day.* **The body is 80 percent water. Water flushes out the system via the kidneys. When you are dehydrated, the liver has to aid the kidneys, taking away the energy it normally earmarks for boosting your metabolism. Water is also very good for your skin, making it less prone to break outs. If water is not your beverage of choice, liven it up with a twist of lemon or sparkling waters—but whatever you do, drink up!**

8. *Hide the salt.* **Research shows that African-Americans harbor some sort of salt sensitivity. While other races excrete excess sodium and water through sweat and urine, Blacks tend to retain it, which may be why we are twice as likely to have high blood pressure.**

9. *Reduce saturated fats.* **Saturated fat is the bad fat. You can see saturated fat form a hard white film on food at room temperature. The majority of saturated fat comes from animals, such as fatty cuts of beef and pork.**

10. *Keep a journal.* **Journal writing can chronicle your challenges and triumphs and provide in sight and inspiration for your new healthy lifestyle. Include positive affirmations as motivational tools to keep you on the right track.**

11. *Make moderate not radical changes.* **You're more likely to stick to your new health regime if you make gradual changes. Start by replacing that afternoon candybar with a snack of fruit. Begin exercising for ten minutes at a time and build up to thirty-minute workout sessions.**

12. *Don't give up.*

beads and precious metals. After you've put all that time into finding the perfect dress, working out, and eating sensibly, you want your hair to be perfect, too. Along with every other detail of your day, having the right hairstyle takes time and planning. Here are some do's and don'ts from the experts to keep in mind:

Do allow at least six weeks before the ceremony to work on achieving your desired look—up to six months if you're thinking of changing your current length, style, or color. "Take your headpiece and go to your salon at least twice before the wedding," advises Ted Gibson, global sales trainer for the Aveda Corp. "It's important to experiment to get a clear idea of the style you want to create for that picture-perfect look."

From cornrows to cascades of curls, your stylist can create an elegant look for your special day.

Think first about how willing you are to experiment on your wedding day. "Some people want to embark on a new frontier with a look they've never tried before," says Wendy, hair stylist for Toss Full-Service Salon in Chicago. "Others feel most comfortable with simply updating or making their classic look more fancy." Define the limits of your adventurousness before you start talking with professionals.

Do make an appointment for a consultation with a good hairdresser—your own, if you already have one you like, or get recommendations from friends, relatives, or co-workers whose hair always looks fabulous. Bring along photographs of your dress as well as your headpiece and pictures of styles you're considering trying. The three key factors to discuss with your hairdresser are:

- Texture
- Color
- Style

"Don't fight natural tendencies," says Darlene Mathis in her beauty book *Women of Color.* "Enhance them, so that your heritage works for you, not against you." Most professionals recommend that you go with the flow of your natural texture. If you want to try something different—either perming or relaxing—ask your hairdresser how he or she thinks your hair will respond. The *health* of your hair should be the primary consideration. Liza Espinoza, chemical specialist and artist for Joico International, warns, "Brides-to-be should be very careful when it comes to chemical services. If the hair isn't healthy, it won't look as good or shine as much and it will be difficult to manage." Again, experiment sooner rather than later, so that you have plenty of time to undo anything that doesn't work.

Do make sure your hair color harmonizes with your skin tone and eye color. If you're curious to see how a new shade would look, get professional advice and then try a temporary dye first or have a plan for correcting any blunders.

Don't choose a hairstyle that's inconsistent with your overall bridal image. If you'll be wearing a gown with simple lines, you probably don't want to have a lot of curls and complications on your head. Also remember that your headpiece will be up there too, competing for space and attention. Generally speaking—whether you opt for straight or curly, long or short—your bridal hairstyle should be simple, comfortable, and compatible with your attire. You'll be facing a long day. It's sensible to choose a style that you won't have to worry about keeping in place.

Some more tips from the professionals:

For short hair: Wendy says, "Consider trying a little color for added richness. Enhance your natural texture with a salon treatment or products to intensify curl and add sheen."

According to Gibson, "Afros are in. Crisp lines and healthy shine make the difference. A fresh trim and a spritz of spray will help give the final gloss and set the style."

"Multi-textured looks are very popular," Espinoza notes, "and can give you a lot of options with your headpiece." She says twisting can work well (with pomade for added shine and control) or try pin curls. Or consider a short Afro with more length in the front or textured around the face for accent. "Ornamentation with flowers instead of the traditional veil is very attractive with short hair," she adds.

For mid-length hair: Wendy suggests the 1960s flip as a fresh, sophisticated alternative if your veil is simple.

If you're growing your hair out and don't want to cut it, she recommends an up-do and a light trim: "You don't have to change the length dramatically to freshen the look when you're between styles."

For long hair: "Wear long hair up for control and polish," says Wendy. "This allows you to look graceful and elegant for the entire day without any stress about falling curls or the dreaded frizzies."

Gibson reports, "Sophisticated, finished, glossy—we are returning to the glamour focus of the 1940s and 1950s—a retro-elegance with controlled wet sets creating soft, subtle waves."

According to Espinoza, very soft feminine looks are back with loose, glamorous curl. "We're also doing a lot of fringing around the face with slight layering for accent."

Weaving and Bonding

For added length, thickness, or color, weaves—by which commercial hair is attached to the natural hair—are perhaps the most popular styling aid among Black brides today, according to Brittanica Stewart of Brittanica and Associates Salon in

Which woman has a weave? They all do.

New York City. And our grooms like the effect, too. "Men have a thing for hair," says Britannica. "They don't care if you beg, borrow, or steal it—they love hair! I did a weave for an administrator at a major recording company who was getting married. She has fairly long hair already. The weave added fullness and a bit more length. When she returned from her honeymoon, she said her husband never knew her hair was a weave!"

Brittanica always asks a bride whether she's considering a weave because of need or desire. "A wedding-day look is very different from an everyday look. It may call for more framing to flatter her face or for extra height or length for an upsweep. Or her natural hair may be too weak to withstand a color treatment and weaving in colored commercial hair is the best option. These are *needs*. *Desire* is when the bride wants to make a fashion statement or simply dazzle!" says Brittanica. When she knows whether a bride is going for a look just for her wedding, needing help achieving a vision beyond the capabilities of her own hair, or wanting a total life change, Britannica can advise her on the most appropriate of the four popular methods of weaving:

Cornrow is the most popular and lasts approximately two months. Natural hair is cornrowed (braided flat along the scalp) and the commercial hair is attached to the braids. The cost ranges from $500 to $1500, depending on the quantity of commercial hair used.

Interlocking extensions are the best choice for glamour "for the day" and last a maximum of forty-eight hours. Natural hair is braided *together* with commercial hair. Priced at Britannica and Associates at $150 for the first hour and $100 for each additional hour.

The Christina Method is the only patented weaving process and is best for long-term live-in looks and the health of the hair. It lasts for two or three months and the natural hair can be relaxed while the weave is in place. The finest quality commercial hair is attached to the natural hair at the scalp with a "weaving machine." Cost ranges from $500 to $2000, depending on the amount of commercial hair required.

Bonding, in which an adhesive solution is applied to the scalp to attach commercial hair, should only be used for up to twenty-four hours to avoid extreme breakage. Although it's least expensive of the four methods (from $50 to $150), Britannica doesn't recommend it because of the damage it can do to the natural hair.

The cost of weaving varies for different salons and regions of the country as well as for the different method used. We've given you these sample price ranges just to let you know that you'll need to allow more room in your beauty budget for a weave than you would for styling your natural hair.

Before you decide on a weave, always consult with a professional who should:

- Never give you a price over the phone

- Look carefully at your scalp

- Match your hair with one of the four commercial hair types—crinkly, curly, wavy, or straight

Brittanica emphasizes that you tell your professional how long you're planning to keep the weave in and under what conditions: "I heard about a bride whose new hair became a ball of muss after she jumped in the pool on her honeymoon." She reminds us that, even with a weave, there's no such thing as maintenance-free hair.

With good professional advice and styling and proper care, you can achieve a perfect wedding-day look that will also survive an active honeymoon intact.

Once you've found the look you like, set up a regular schedule for conditioning and trimming so you can *maintain* the look until your wedding day. And, finally, consider having your stylist visit your home to do your hair just before the ceremony. It's an additional expense but worth it for warding off stress and avoiding last minute problems. It could keep your Big Day from being a bad hair day.

GETTING THAT GLOW

The key to an unforgettable face for your wedding day is strikingly beautiful skin. Consistent care, a healthy diet, and the correct cosmetic products are the essential elements for success.

According to Bradley Stroden, esthetician (beauty service professional) and trainer for the Aveda Corp., the most important thing is to use a balanced skin-care system that works for you: "Many women use a cleanser from one cosmetic line, a toner from another, and a moisturizer from yet another. You can get the maximum benefit in the minimum time with products from *one* line that are designed to work together. Irritation and other problems can result from using products that are *un*-balanced, such as a strong cleanser and toner, followed by a weak moisturizer."

Identify your skin type and condition so that you can choose the system that is best for you. Stroden says, "Women usually know their skin better than they think they do. All it takes is tuning into yourself. Your body is always giving you signs. Just pay attention to what it's trying to tell you."

- ✦ Oily skin is usually shiny all over.

- ✦ Dry skin may feel tight and drawn and appear dull and flaky.

- ✦ Combination skin, as the phrase suggests, is a combination of the two— typically with the oiliness in the "T-zone," beside the nose and across the forehead.

How do you know whether your skin-care system is right? "If you have *oily* skin that feels tight or drawn, you're probably using the wrong system," says Stroden. "Your skin may be *over*producing oil, even though it appears dry. The key in this case is to pare down your routine to the minimum to allow your skin to normalize before correcting your system."

Stroden recommends the same basic skin-care routine for all skin types:

- Cleanse to remove dirt, impurities, and excess oil.

- Tone and exfoliate. It is just as important to remove dead cells from dry skin as from oily and break-out prone skin, so that the natural oil can flow freely.

- Hydrate, to put moisture back into the skin and protect it from the sun and other extremes of weather.

In general, remember the key to preserving your skin is gentleness. Never use Buff Puffs, loofahs, or scrubs on your face. They tear at the skin, causing abrasion, scarring, and discoloration. If you're over forty, Stroden suggests that you consider giving up soap and adding an alpha-hydroxy acid to your routine to whittle away fine lines, firm your skin, and improve its color and texture.

Don't change your routine or try out new products right before your wedding. You never know how your skin will react. Even a facial you're not used to could cause redness or even breakouts. Give yourself six months or so if you're going to experiment.

If you do have an acne flare-up before your Big Day, don't just cover it up with makeup. Visit a dermatologist who takes you and your skin seriously. You may even discover that an esthetician (beauty service professional) who can treat the problem topically is a better alternative. Give any treatment you get time to work.

If you're heading off for a honeymoon in the sun, Stroden reminds you to protect your skin by using one of the many moisturizers on the market that contain a sunscreen, preferably with SPF15: "It's not just the time you spend on the beach that does the damage; it's every single second that your skin is exposed to sunlight, whether you're shopping or simply walking to your car. African-American skin is just as vulnerable as that of a Nordic blonde. The aging effect may be less visible because of higher levels of melanin in Black skin, but the sun is penetrating just the same."

Overall, according to Strodes, "the makeup trend of the nineties is bucking the trends. Find a timeless classic look for yourself a la the makeup of the twenties, thirties and forties, when the face was the focal point. Emphasize your unique features. If you have beautiful eyes or lovely lips, play them up. Look in magazines for ideas and have fun experimenting, but don't feel pressured by 'fashion'—do only what works for you."

YOUR MAKEUP

Until recently the selection of makeup formulated especially for women of color was limited. Now many cosmetic companies offer lines specifically targeted to us or incorporate shades for women of color into their existing lines. Foundations and powders now contain increased pigment levels and use transparent titanium dioxide, which prevents the "ashy" effect these products previously had on Black skin. Cheek and lip colors are bolder and blend more easily to complement darker skin tones.

Supermodel Iman.

With so many choices available today, how do you select and apply the products that will help you appear most radiant on your Big Day (and in the photographs you'll be looking at for years to come)? Byron Barnes, the creative director of Iman Skin Care and Cosmetics, recommends that you visit a makeup counter in a department store for a full face makeup session, which is usually free. Get a chart for placement of the product and the product colors that were used so you can repeat it yourself.

After you are made up, think about the lighting you'll be seen in at your wedding and replicate that lighting as best as you can. Walk outside with a mirror if you need to and see how you will really look. Also, consider that you will be in pictures. You may need to wear a little more foundation to avoid shine, a little more concealer under the eyes, a bit more mascara. Black skin, even when it is not oily, reflects light and will look shiny in photos without a little extra foundation and some pressed powder.

In consultation with the makeup artist, follow these guidelines as you select the combination of products that's right for you:

Determine your skin tone. "Women of color have more of a challenge finding a foundation because they have a wider range of skin tones," says B. J. Gillian, Cover Girl's makeup pro.

With the help of your professional, decide if your skin is dark, medium, or light. "Undertone" is the amount of yellow, red, or neutral pigment in your skin. When you stand in front of a mirror and surround your face with a white cloth, the most prominent shade you see is your undertone.

Use concealer. African-American skin tends to heal more slowly and not as invisibly as lighter complexions. Blemish marks often turn purple. Women of color also tend to have dark shadows around the eyes, nose, and mouth. Before you apply foundation, use concealer in a shade that matches your skin tone and blend evenly.

Choose the right foundation. Gillian stresses the importance of foundation, especially for your wedding photos: "The camera sees more than your friends do."

Test foundation right above your jawline and view the result in natural light. Because many women of color have an oily T-zone, Gillian recommends an oil-free foundation. The Prescriptives line offers a custom-blended foundation and powder created just for your face right at the makeup counter.

Always apply foundation with a sponge for even coverage. For a more radiant look, use a shade that's a bit lighter than your skin tone on the center of your face and one that matches your skin on the sides of your face. For more defined cheekbones, use a darker shade on your nose.

Finish with powder. Gillian recommends using a combination foundation and powder so you don't have to retouch your makeup as often. If you opt for a separate powder, choose one that's translucent and oil-free so you preserve the finish and don't discolor your foundation. Apply with a puff, starting at the center of your face and working your way out. And don't forget your eyelids, neck, ears, and décolletage.

Apply a natural-looking blush. What looks good in person might look garish in photos. Stick to natural colors compatible with the undertones that appear inside your lower lip. In general, Gillian and Barnes agree, neutral colors of the same family work best for bridal makeup.

Apply blush first to the apples of your cheeks and work your way out. You can also use a deeper shade to contour your cheekbones, eye creases, and nose.

Choose eye shadow that blends with your skin tone. Gillian advises against bright, frosty shades on your wedding day. Go neutral for a classic look.

Don't forget eyeliner. Apply a deep, preferably black, eyeliner close to and in between your top lashes, but not too heavily. (Cat-eyes are out!) To give the illusion of long lower lashes, apply a bit of earth-colored or brown eye shadow under your bottom lashes and smudge it.

Use mascara. If your lashes don't curl naturally, use a curler first. Wait two minutes between coats to avoid clumps.

Always use lip liner. Use a brownish shade or, if you're lining inside your natural lip line, a shade that's slightly darker. Fill your lips in with the liner, too, so that your lipstick stays put longer.

Pick a lip color more opaque than your usual shade. Find the color that works best with your undertone and that's opaque enough to show up well in photographs.

Have a makeup "dress rehearsal." Byron Barnes strongly suggests trying out your makeup and testing it in photographs before the Big Day.

Invite your attendants over for a makeup party. (This also gives you a chance to preview the "group look.") Apply the makeup you each plan to wear and try to replicate the lighting you'll be seen in on your wedding day. Take Polaroids of each other and look at the results with honest eyes. As we mentioned earlier, Black skin, even when it is not oily, reflects light and will often look shiny in photographs. You may need to wear a little more foundation to compensate, a little more concealer under the eyes, a bit more mascara—while avoiding applying so much that you look theatrical. (Carry a little pressed powder with you on your wedding day for touch-ups.)

Ideally, says Barnes, "you want to strike a balance between being camera-ready and being able to greet people comfortably face-to-face. 'Less is more,' Iman always tells us. I think she's right, especially for weddings. I've seen some brides that end up looking like the cake!"

Consider hiring a makeup artist. Often, behind-the-counter artists freelance by making house calls. See if the one you've used is available to do your makeup on your wedding day or if she can recommend another professional.

If you do hire a makeup artist, get the terms of your agreement in writing, including a provision for a back-up artist. Spell out

- ✎ The cost of the bride's makeup

- ✎ Additional costs for the bridesmaids, mother-of-the-bride, and even for applying a little powder on the groom and his attendants if you wish

- ✎ Whether the artist will bring the makeup or expect it to be supplied

- ✎ Who pays for the artist's transportation

- ✎ Whether the artist will stay to do touch-ups for the photographs

- ✎ The terms of payment

As a bride-to-be whose hands will be on nonstop display, you don't want to wait until the last minute to take care of them. Starting a simple home-maintenance program at least two months before the wedding will give you softer, healthier-looking hands and nails.

Since hands are often exposed to the elements, it is important to pamper them weekly with an exfoliating treatment to remove dead skin cells:

- Wet your hands with warm water and apply a gentle cleansing product that will remove oil and dirt without disturbing the natural acid balance of your skin. (Don't use a bar soap, which is drying.)

- Work up a rich, foamy lather.

- Rinse and pat dry.

- Finally, to seal in moisture, apply a softening lotion that doesn't leave your hands feeling sticky or greasy.

This bride's beautiful hands make her perfectly ready to "give her hand" in marriage.

Henna Hands

The ancient art of henna painting is practiced in many African cultures and in the Muslim faith. On the night before her wedding—"the henna night"—the bride has her hands decorated with intricate designs applied in the dye from the henna plant. These designs are thought to bring good fortune.

Your nails are probably the first things people notice about your hands. Even if you are fairly accomplished at doing your nails at home, treat yourself to a professional manicure before your wedding. Shelve the neon shades and busy designs in favor of more subdued tints that complement your attire. Bring a swatch or picture of your gown and get suggestions from your manicurist. Keep your nails in a natural shape (round or square) and at a manageable length (about ¼ inch beyond the fingertip).

And while you're at it, treat yourself to a pedicure, too!

The right
routine for
health and good
looks is just as
important for
the groom as it
is for the bride.

FOR YOUR GROOM

Men sometimes say they don't like makeup, and if you usually do not wear much of it, Byron Barnes advises that it's best to let your groom know early on, "I'm going to be wearing makeup. I'm going to a professional." Let him see you the day you go to the makeup counter. If you're going to be using a makeup artist, Barnes advises you show him the look you have achieved and explain what the artist has done and why. Let your groom know early on that you are paying special attention to your wedding day hair and makeup. "This is the perfect opportunity to suggest that he, too, think about allowing himself to be gently dusted with powder before the wedding photos," Barnes points out. "I've seen lots of men, especially those who are balding, look shocked when they get their wedding pictures back

Keeping Yourself Together: Fitness, Health, and Beauty

and see themselves—their heads or foreheads just shining!" Barnes recommends a liquid powder made by Iman, Undercover Agent Oil Control Lotion, for people of color to use to counter just this feature of dark skin. "Men like it because it is invisible and undetectable."

"Make sure that he decides how he wants to wear his hair ahead of time, too," adds Liza Espinoza. "He should get a fresh cut about three days before the wedding for a polished, clean, and well-groomed look. The glossy look of healthy hair is very important for him, too. There are a number of great shine products on the market for men."

Bradley Stroden has some tips for the bridegroom, too. Aside from the fact that men grow much more hair on their faces, male skin is no different from female skin and skin care is just as important:

- Shave carefully and treat your skin well afterward. Ingrown hairs may pose a special challenge for Black men. A skin-care professional can advise about shaving techniques for individual skin type and condition. It may be that an ultraclose shave is not the best choice.

- Alpha-hydroxy acid and sunscreen should also be part of your routine.

- Like Barnes, he suggests a light dusting of powder for your wedding photos.

KEEPING YOUR COOL

Dealing with caterers, photographers, and florists, keeping the guest list down while trying to keep your spirits up—no use trying to deny it, all these wedding preparations can get on your *nerves*. Prenuptial anxieties are normal, but they shouldn't be overwhelming. If you're eating right and exercising regularly, you'll already be building a good defense against stress. But before you start to feel as though everything's turning into an appalling mess rather than an appealing celebration, schedule some time to relax.

Set aside a few minutes a day for prayer or meditation (perhaps just after you get up in the morning and again before you go to bed at night). Your mind needs a break from all the demands of planning your wedding. A simple breathing exercise, where you focus on inhaling and exhaling, can do much to calm you when you feel on edge.

You Deserve a Break for a Day

We're all familiar with the luxurious overnight health spas of the "rich and famous." Day spas condense many of the best elements found in their overnight counterparts into one-day pampering sessions.

A good day spa should offer the following services:

Body Massages: **A therapeutic procedure designed to relieve muscle tension. Often involves the use of scented oils (aromatherapy).**

Body Wraps: **The use of sea algae or mud mixed with oils to soften and detoxify the skin.**

Facial Waxing: **The removal of unwanted facial hair using warm wax.**

Facial Treatments: **Deep-cleansing, softening techniques that have anti- aging effects.**

Paraffin Treatments: **The application of warm wax to the hands, feet or face to deeply moisturize, smooth, and cleanse the skin.**

Manicures and Pedicures: **The spa versions of these may involve the use of sea botanicals, oils, and paraffin.**

Hydrotherapy/Vichy Showers: **Gentle water massages from underwater bath jets or overhead shower sprays to invigorate the circulatory and immune systems.**

Make a preliminary visit to the spa to check out their services and get a feel for the facilities. Have your first session seven or eight weeks before the ceremony to allow time for follow-ups. You can even select and test your wedding makeup at a spa.

Compose a few simple affirmations to repeat to yourself when those doubts start to nag. Most of our anxieties tend to focus on what other people will think of us and how we look, whether we'll live up to the demands (usually *self*-imposed) of the occasion. Here are some suggestions for affirmations from Byron Barnes, who's soothed many a bridal nerve, to inspire you:

Wedding Day Checklist

↪ **Confirm with your makeup artist (again, be sure to have a backup) and your hairdresser the night before.**

↪ **Schedule a half-hour nap before beginning on hair and makeup.**

↪ **First do your hair (so no hair spray goes over your makeup), then your makeup (so no makeup will stain your gown), then get dressed.**

↪ **Prepare a "wedding rescue kit" that includes**

 Tissues

 Q-tips

 Lipstick

 Face powder

 Lens lubricant and lens case if you wear contacts (it never fails that they fall out at weddings!)

 Needle and thread in the color of your gown

 Band-Aids ("I've seen a bride sewing a tear in her gown stick herself and drip the blood on her dress!" warns Barnes.)

 Safety pins

↪ True beauty is within.

↪ There is a light in me. My inner gifts will shine through.

↪ My physical appearance is only part of me.

↪ Clothing and makeup just enhance what is already inside me.

Pamper yourself occasionally. Go for that manicure and pedicure. Get a massage. Better yet, sign up for the full treatment at one of the many day spas that have been cropping up across the country. (And encourage your fiancé to sign up, too—many of them now have facilities for men.) If you still have trouble "letting go" of wedding concerns, consider really getting away by taking a weekend trip (with your fiancé, of course) to a place where no one's going to ask you who's on your guest list or what you'll be serving at the reception.

Make a wedding day schedule. Organization and preparedness are the main keys to relaxation. "People always ask why Iman is so relaxed," says Byron. "She's relaxed because she's prepared. She leaves no stone unturned."

Allow at least four hours before your ceremony, if you can, to do your hair and makeup and get dressed, and ask a member of your wedding party to be your special assistant during that time. Delegate as many of the other day-of preparations as possible. Barnes confirms, "The brides who are most relaxed have a friend to help them dress. She handles all the things the bride can't do while she's in the makeup chair—like worry about why one of the groomsmen's boutonnieres wasn't delivered on time, the kind of thing that stresses a bride. She can't jump up out of the makeup chair to resolve a problem!"

Barnes also advises brides to take a short nap before starting on their hair and makeup: "Anywhere she can lie down and put her feet up on a pillow is fine. We recommend using Iman's Eye Firming Cream and putting a slice of cucumber over each eye."

As you follow your health and beauty plan for your wedding, keep before you your vision of yourself in your dream scenario from chapter 1—looking and feeling your very best. Exercising, eating right, caring for your skin and hair, taking regular "time outs"—all the attention you pay to yourself during the pre-wedding preparations will pay off in your radiant, relaxed appearance on the Big Day.

YOUR CEREMONY,

YOUR WAY

E DEBATED ABOUT whether we should even have a big wedding," Carlos Webb remembers. "We thought we could use the money for a car or put it toward the down payment on a house. But we wanted to share our happiness with everybody, and have no regrets. The ceremony we had, the site where we held it, the drummers, the rituals—

everything met our cultural and educational goals. I felt so happy and proud of the outcome!"

You'll recall from chapter 3 that Carlos and his fiancée Nikki planned their own Afrocentric ceremony, inspired by the "perfect site" they found when they attended an open house for Kwanzaa at the Akwaaba Mansion in Brooklyn, New York.

Your ceremony is at the heart of your wedding festivities. By asking the right questions of yourselves and your officiant(s)—to get the right combination of information and inspiration—the two of you, like Nikki and Carlos, can meet your own goals in expressing your love for each other and in sharing your happiness with your guests.

FOLLOW UP ON YOUR FIRST CALLS

Turn back to Ceremony Sites and Key Decision #6 in chapter 3 and to the Ceremony section of your planner. Review the information you recorded during your "first calls" to your short list of possible sites when you asked about:

- ✎ Cost

- ✎ Capacity

- ✎ Availability

Those calls may have enabled you to make your final decision. Or perhaps there were two or three places that suited your budget, choice of date, and estimate of size. In either case, you'll now need to follow up with more detailed questions.

A Sacred Place

As we mentioned in chapter 3, if you've chosen to hold your ceremony in a house of worship, in your first calls you determined:

- ✎ The basic cost for the site and other fees for additional services

- ✎ The number of people it will seat

- ✎ Its availability on your date(s) of choice

- The possibility of including an outside officiant (if you're planning a ceremony that incorporates other spiritual or cultural traditions)

Your next step is to make an appointment with the site's officiant to discuss:

- The requirements for marriage

- The elements and protocol of the ceremony

- Any restrictions on access to and use of the space

If you've hired a wedding consultant, ask if she may also attend. Amelia Montgomery has sometimes met with initial resistance from clergy members who have performed ceremonies for couples whose weddings she's planned. After they've seen that she's not there to take over but rather to support them and make their role easier, she's usually found their resistance turns to appreciation and gratitude.

Write down the three main areas listed above in your planner and use them to help you formulate a list of questions to ask at your appointment (or to phone, fax, or mail if you're planning from a distance). Keep your dream ceremony scenario at hand as you make your list to be sure that you cover any special features that are essential to your vision. If a representative from another denomination, faith, or spiritual tradition will be participating, for instance, include a question about how to coordinate his involvement. Should you be the one to call him or should the site's officiant? Should you all have a joint meeting? Here are some general guidelines to follow as you develop your own list:

Requirements:

- What documents do you need from us? (You may have to submit proof of baptism, for instance, or of divorce or widowhood.)

- Do we need any special permissions or dispensations? (Some faiths require these in the case of remarriage after divorce, or if a member of the faith is marrying someone who is not.) What is the application process and how long will it take?

- Do you recommend or require premarital counseling? How many sessions? How should we prepare?

The Ceremony:

- What is the standard order of service? (Ask for a copy if you don't already have one.)

- Is it permissible for us to write our own vows? If so, do you have guidelines or samples that other couples have created?

- At what points in the ceremony may we incorporate ethnic rituals—an African libation prayer or bitter herb tasting, for instance? Again, do you have guidelines to follow or sample programs from other similar ceremonies?

- May we choose our own readings from the scripture and include other readings, from African or African-American literature for example?

- May we ask members of the wedding party or the congregation to participate in the service by giving a reading, saying a prayer, or having some other special role?

- When do you usually schedule the signing of the marriage license? Is it possible to sign it during the service? How many witnesses do we need?

- May we choose our own music and hire musicians or must we use the church organist and follow his or her suggestions? Are members of the church choir available? Are there any fees for the use of the organist and choir?

- May we decorate the site as we wish? What items for the ceremony, such as candles and aisle runners, does the church supply? Is it permissible to throw rice or birdseed after the ceremony?

- May we have a receiving line at the site?

- Will there be a rehearsal for the ceremony? When? Who should attend?

Restrictions:

- Does the church have a dress code or (if you'll also be holding your reception on church property) any restrictions on types of music, dancing, or the use of alcohol?

↦ What is the protocol concerning photographers, florists, wedding consultants, and other vendors who might need access to the church in advance and be present during the ceremony?

A Secular Place

You may have decided to have a civil ceremony or a religious one in a nonreligious setting. If so, your questions will be slightly different from the preceding ones and you may need to make *two* appointments—one with your officiant and one with the management of the site you've chosen (or the two or three you're considering), but you'll follow the same general guidelines. You'll still ask about marriage re-

A place of splendor you will always remember.

quirements, the form of the ceremony, and how it can be modified to fit your vision, and restrictions that apply to the use of the site.

If you're going to have a civil ceremony in city hall, you can find out the requirements, including any documents you'll need, by calling your local marriage license bureau. Ask what the ceremony consists of (get a copy, if you can) and whether you can incorporate your own readings or write your own vows. If you'll be married outside a municipal office, discuss these things with the officiant who will be performing the ceremony and make sure that your plans are acceptable at the site you've chosen.

Record all the answers to your questions in the Ceremony section of your planner.

The additional information you've gathered will either confirm your earlier choice of site or, if you were still considering several options, help you make a final decision. At most houses of worship you'll now simply ask the officiant or his staff to put the date and time of ceremony on the church calendar and make your next appointment for counseling or further planning. If your ceremony site is a secular one (where you may also be holding your reception), you'll probably need to reserve it by signing a contract and making a deposit. See chapter 12, "Celebrating Your Union in Style" for guidelines on booking by contract.

PREMARITAL COUNSELING

You may have learned during your meeting with your officiant that premarital counseling was strongly suggested, if not required. Nearly every religious and spiritual tradition has a long, wonderful history of this practice. In Africa, the elder women counseled the young woman and the elder men counseled the young man. Through a series of discussions, the elders passed on their wisdom and assessed the maturity of the couple. Only if they felt that the couple was ready to take on the responsibilities of marriage did they give their permission for the wedding to take place.

Today many faiths continue this practice. You and your fiancé meet over a period of time with your clergy to discuss your families, your upbringing, education, community activities, personal interests, careers, and aspirations. In a spiritual context, these discussions give the two of you a special opportunity to discover just how you feel about life—its challenges and triumphs—and about each other. They also

I t may help for you and your fiancé to think of sharing your spiritual selves as unwrapping a package. You have to go through a lot of layers to get to the gift inside, but reaching it is worth the work.

> *Start small.* Talk about the little things first, in everyday terms. Traditional religious words can make people uncomfortable. It may be easier to talk about "screwing up" than about sin, or about "feeling on the right track" than about inner peace. Don't change your style just because you're talking about your spiritual self.

> *Take risks.* Be prepared to let your partner see your spiritual side. To start a conversation, speak for yourself and listen for his reaction.

> *Be flexible.* Don't get locked into thinking you have to talk about things at a certain time or in a certain way. Give each other both scheduled and unscheduled opportunities to discuss important spiritual issues.

> *Be accepting.* This is especially important if your beliefs or ways of expressing them are very different. Both you and your partner need to know that you are loved for who you are. Within that trust and acceptance, there is security in talking about your differences.

> *Serve together.* Teaching a class together or reaching out to those in need can draw you closer together spiritually.

> *Pray together.*

give your counselor a chance to assess your true compatibility as a couple and to offer you guidance in building your life together. If you and your fiancé are of different faiths, you may find it especially helpful to define your common areas of belief before you are joined together as man and wife. Even if neither of you practices a particular religion or the church you're going to be married in doesn't "require" counseling, you might consider seeking it from an independent organization (see Resources) or at least sitting down together to talk about the spiritual aspects of your lives.

Be prepared for your counselor to ask some searching questions, especially if you're marrying outside your faith or have been married before. Among the basic issues he'll want to explore are:

Keeping the Faith You Share

by Revs. Henry and Ella Mitchell

In fifty-four years of marriage we have evolved a pattern of prayer together as the very first activity of each day, before we even leave the bed. First, one of us reads several pages from a book on spiritual discipline, often a devotional classic. Then, quite often, we share responses to the reading, followed by moments of silence. Then Ella prays, followed by Henry. Like our Lord's Prayer, we both begin with praise and thanks. Although there is no fixed formula, we usually focus on the blessings of the previous day or so. We then move to admitting things we have said and done wrong and on to requests for others (by name), followed by personal requests. The following prayers are very typical of the one each of us offers each morning:

ELLA: O Thou in whose presence our souls take delight, on whom in affliction we call, our comfort by day and our song in the night, our joy, our salvation, our all, we thank you and praise your name for all the joys and privileges which you have so abundantly bestowed on us. We can never forget or take for granted the enduring pleasure of just living and serving together. How we praise you for calling us together and making us one.

When I call to remembrance your care, I pray your forgiveness for my anxiety from time to time—the way I seem momentarily to forget your sure and merciful provision for all our needs—the way I get uptight in the midst of what looks like a crisis. Lord, you know my heart and my habits. Please, I pray you, help my habits to yield to my highest ambitions.

- What will be the ethics, philosophy, or spiritual foundation of your life as a couple?

- How will you resolve conflicts as they arise? By whose set of beliefs or guidelines?

- In what spiritual tradition will you raise your children?

Different traditions recommend different premarital practices—from fasting to sexual abstinence—to strengthen the couple physically and spiritually in preparation for their commitment to each other. Nikki and Carlos's officiant, the Rev. Philip Valentine, who adheres to the ancient Egyptian sacred sciences of the Khamit, advises

And now we lift in prayer others of our kin, whoever they may be, we pray also for our students and our ever-growing extended family, and all whose lives we touch.

We pray you this day, O God, to lead and guide us—to help us stay in the very center of your creative and fruitful will. May your name always be glorified, and may we always serve you to the very best of our ability. This is our prayer in the spirit of our servant, Savior and Lord, Jesus Christ. Amen.

HENRY: Gracious God, how we continue to thank you and glorify your holy name. How hard it is to find new words to express our gratitude for all the new mercies you bestow on us. We thank you for your awesome acts, the trusted advice of your servants, and the amazing ways you arrange for our needs and our labor—the ways that telephones and finance, dates and planes, insights and obligations all fall together for our good, day after day. We thank you Lord, for growth, for the spiritual surprises that our morning meditations and readings bring forth, pushing us to ever higher heights.

And now, Lord, I pray forgiveness and help as I struggle with a sharp tongue. Help me to be on guard and warned, that I may speak the truth, but only in love. Help me to write my words and express them only if they are likely to be received with benefit.

We bring before you our special concerns: a student as she struggles with an unjust and insensitive person in authority, a lifelong friend as he mourns the loss of his wife.

And, now, we give ourselves to you this day, in joy and hope, in the precious name of our Lord and Savior, Jesus Christ. Amen.

couples to undertake celibacy and a twenty-one-day program of fasting and purification before their ceremony and again before they try to conceive a child. "They purify their bodies and become stronger and more in tune with themselves as a result," he says.

Winston and Lateefah, both practicing Christians, decided on their own to cease sexual activity and became celibate for the year and a half of their engagement. "I got to know her in ways you could not imagine," Winston testifies. "To go through that celibate time made us a lot closer. When something happened, we couldn't just go home and 'break up the place'—we had to express things by talking, not through physical contact. Now we can talk about anything. I can honestly say I *know* Lateefah. We would not have reached that level if we had decided to *sleep* our way through our engagement. By the time it was all said and done, we knew how to do it—be married—the right way."

Listen to your counselor's recommendations and answer his questions as thoughtfully and honestly as you can. And listen to each other. Your counselor's experience may help you and your fiancé address issues that haven't arisen in your courtship but that might play a crucial role in your marriage. He may also be able to help you handle questions and dispel doubts that your families have expressed about your union.

If your counselor has concerns about your relationship, he may suggest further counseling or even decline to act as your officiant. "If I think a couple isn't ready, I refuse to marry them," says Chief Priest Nana Kwabena Brown of the Temple of Nyame, an African centered congregation in Washington, D.C. "I'm not in the wedding business, and I'm not here to say what people want to hear. Marriage is a sacred institution, the foundation of our communities. If a couple isn't ready to represent our communities, I cannot give my blessing."

Act prayerfully on your advisor's concerns. Spirituality is one of the great strengths of Black life. Our elders and advisors possess a wisdom that is worth regarding as you prepare to take your wedding vows, but know that the two of you are the ones to make the final decision.

THE ORDER OF SERVICE

Most wedding ceremonies—"Traditional" and Afrocentric, religious *and* civil—contain the same key elements and follow the same basic structure:

The Charge to the Congregation: The officiant asks the assembled guests to act as witnesses to the marriage and to its "lawfulness."

The Charge to the Bride and Groom: The officiant asks the couple if there is any "impediment" to their becoming husband and wife.

The Declaration of Intent: The officiant states the meaning of marriage and asks the bride and groom, individually, to acknowledge their understanding of the vows they are about to make.

Muslim Marriage

Marriage is not a "sacrament" in Islam, but it is considered an extremely important step, said to be perfecting half of one's religion and given the same weight in the Holy Qur'an as the blood relationship.

The ceremony consists of the signing of the marriage contract, or *Nikah,* which may take place in a mosque, in someone's home, or even in a rented place and is usually performed by the *iman* (the spiritual leader), although any adult male Muslim may officiate. The couple may be separated in the customary way at the mosque, or they may sit facing each other, or the bride may be represented by a male or female relative (*wali*). (If the bride is absent, it usually means she is getting ready for the *walimah,* or reception party.) If the bride is present, she wears festive clothing, though still in accordance with the standards of the Qur'an.

Before the contract is signed by the groom and the bride (or her representative) and two witnesses, several verses of the Qur'an are read and a prayer is said. Both parties are asked three times if they accept each other in marriage according to the terms of the contract. If they agree, the contract is signed and the marriage is completed.

The Exchange of Vows: The bride and groom each make a public promise to abide by the "laws" of marriage.

The Exchange of Rings: The bride and groom exchange rings as a symbol of their vows.

The Pronouncement: The officiant declares the couple "husband and wife."

The language of the service varies from religion to religion and culture to culture, as does its length, with the addition of prayers, readings, and rituals belonging to each tradition.

Study your copy of the service that your ceremony will be based on. See if you can identify its key elements. Mark any parts that you don't understand or that don't speak to your own thoughts and feelings about your marriage.

The Wedding Ceremony of
Nikki and Carlos
Saturday, July 12, 1997
3:00 p.m.
Akwaaba Mansion

ORDER OF CEREMONY

CHIMING OF THE HOUR

POURING OF LIBATION (TAMBIKO)

BLESSING OF ELDERS (MUSUKEBA)

CHARGING OF GUESTS AS WITNESSES

PROCESSIONAL

TASTING OF FOUR ELEMENTS (AFOSHE)

PRONOUNCEMENTS

FEEDING OF IMMEDIATE FAMILY
Poetic Tribute to our Mothers .... Rory Scott
Musical Selection .... Joe Malloy

EXCHANGE OF KOLA NUTS

EXCHANGE OF VOWS

STATEMENT OF INTENT

RECESSIONAL

WEDDING FEAST (KARAMU)

Officiating Minister...................... Reverend Philip Valentine

Drummers .... Kwabena Colon Olaniyan
Kwaku Siaca Bey

Saxophonist .... Steven Clark

THE WEDDING PARTY

Maid of Honor .... Daphne McFarland
Best Man .... Stanley Fogg

Mother of Bride .... Lora Davis
Mother of Groom .... Mable Webb

Grandmother of Bride............................ Martha Malloy
Grandmother of Groom .... Mollie Ramsey

Ushers .... Andre Taylor
Chaz Malloy
LaQuette Taylor
Araya Taylor

We are proud to announce that our ceremony is inspired by the Yoruba traditions of Africa, which offer the tasting of spices representative of the emotions of marriage. A Libation will be poured to call on ancestral spirits and the Supreme Being to take part in the ceremony. There will be music, drumming and poetry. And as in African-American ceremonies, call and response is an integral part of the celebration. Feel free to respond "ashe" (ah-shay) where you might say amen. We hope you feel the spirit that moves through us on this blessed day.

Special Thanks to Joyce McMillan, Anthony Birchette, Carolyn Gilchrist, Michael Morris, Joni Gross, Bernard McRae, Mike King, Aeola Bakr, Belinda Green, Everay, Daniel Cooper, Bola International, Sharon and Mark Grotevant, Martha Malloy and Monique and Glenn Greenwood-Pogue for all the patience, support and creative energy extended to us to make this day perfect and complete.

A Very Special Thanks to our mothers who have given us their blessing, continued love and support. In our shining moments we reflect the beauty and brilliance you have bestowed upon us. We love you.

You may feel that the "Traditional" ceremony best conveys for you the sentiments and sacredness of matrimony, and that by following it as it stands, without modification, you not only make a pledge to each other but join the spiritual community of all those who have had "Traditional" ceremonies before you. That is the truest meaning and power of "Tradition."

On the other hand, its words and rituals may not give full expression to *your* sense of tradition or the nature of your individual commitment to each other. If your officiant has indicated that he's flexible about changes and additions and has given you guidelines, start to explore your options. Turn again to your dream scenario. How do you begin to make that dream happen?

Nikki and Carlos, who envisioned an *Afrocentric* ceremony, began their planning in what might seem like an unusual place. "We started at the library," says Nikki. "We read about African family value systems and wedding customs. This helped us to better understand the true meaning of joining two families in African tradition. My advice to couples who want to have an African inspired wedding that goes beyond using African fabrics in the decor is to do your own research and find African customs that are significant to you personally. Not every custom will appeal to everyone." The following African rituals were meaningful to them and corresponded to the key elements of a "Traditional" service. In consultation with their officiant, they incorporated the rituals into their ceremony.

Pouring of Libation for the Ancestors and Blessing of the Elders. Belief in the guidance of ancestral spirits and respect for the wisdom of the elders are integral parts of life in many African cultures. The ritual pouring of a libation calls on the ancestors to join the assembled guests in witnessing this sacred occasion. The blessing of the elders honors those who have passed along the lessons of their experience to the younger members of their community.

At Nikki and Carlos's wedding, the Rev. Valentine poured the libation and gave the blessing immediately before the Processional and the Charge to the Congregation, so that the living and the dead, the young and the old, were all symbolically gathered together at the beginning of the ceremony. "I pour a Libation [vodka, a "spirit" that represents stimulation and energy] in the four directions—north, south, east, and west—the four gates that the spirits guard, to open the way for our ancestors to attend," he explains. "I call on Menes, who united upper and lower Egypt, and others such as Harriet Tubman. I invite the congregation to call out the names of ancestors who are dear to them, members of the family who have just passed. I also charge the

> ### A Libation Prayer
>
> **All praise to God Almighty**
> **Praise to our African ancestors and roots**
> **God gave his power for the roots of**
> **the trees to spread its branches wide.**
> **If man does not know his roots, then he does**
> **not know his God.**
>
> **Let the spirit of God and our ancestors**
> **bring us closer in unity.**

guests as witnesses, telling them that they, too, are responsible for the two people who are coming together on that day to be married, and, by their very presence they have promised to do their best to maintain this relationship and family structure. And I seat the two eldest members of the families—one on the bride's side and one on the groom's—in aisle seats nearest the couple, to remind them that their elders' wisdom is always close at hand."

Tasting of Four Elements (also called Bitter Herb Tasting or Tasting of Four Temperaments). This ritual dramatizes the "Traditional" promise to love "for better or worse, for richer for poorer, in sickness and in health." The four elements that the Rev. Valentine uses—lemon, vinegar, cayenne pepper, and honey—represent the sour, the bitter, the hot, and the sweet times of marriage. He places each in a crystal bowl, which he then positions to correspond to the four directions. (Four is also the number associated with the base of the pyramid, a symbol of a strong foundation.) He then has the couple taste each, beginning with the lemon: "I let them know that marriage involves individual sacrifice, so that two people can harmonize as one. But sacrifice can cause sour feelings (the lemon) and bitterness (the vinegar) and eventually a heated explosion (represented by the cayenne). When they taste the pepper, they are *cooking,* their eyes are watering . . . and the guests are having a good time watching. But then I say that if they can weather all of this, all the difficult times, and still be friends and lovers, they will come to understand the *sweetness* that's in all the previous three flavors. That is when I give them the honey."

Feeding of the Immediate Family. After Nikki and Carlos tasted the four elements, they demonstrated the African belief that they were joining not only their own lives but those of their families, by each feeding the other's family from baskets of unleavened bread.

Exchange of Kola Nuts. In Africa, the kola nut is a symbol of healing and used for many medicinal purposes. In Nikki and Carlos's ceremony, they exchanged kola nuts with members of their families and each other right before they exchanged their

Nikki and Carlos chose African rituals that held deep personal meaning for them.

Herb tasting.

vows, to symbolize that they would always be able to heal their differences, that no adversity would ever prove greater than the love they have for one another. "People still ask me if we kept our kola nuts—in African tradition you are to use them to soothe any friction . . ." Nikki laughs, "We haven't needed them so far! But the kola nuts are very meaningful keepsakes from our wedding."

An increasingly popular revived tradition—jumping the broom.

Cutting the Cord or Jumping the Broom. At the end of their ceremony, the eldest members of each family (who you remember were seated at the front at the beginning) held a ribbon across the aisle for Nikki and Carlos to walk through, symbolizing the "cutting" of their primary ties with the families who had raised them and their readiness to raise a family of their own. Some couples choose to jump the broom instead, a custom that has its roots in Africa and also symbolizes the beginning of making a home together.

Affirmation of Vows by the Congregation

MINISTER: **We have been privileged to witness a special event in the lives of this couple, in the lives of [name] and [name]. They have made their covenant in our presence and indicated their intention to move through life together. We are now given the opportunity to indicate our support of their decision.**

Do you, as a congregation, commit yourselves to providing all of the encouragement and support possible to help them in their marriage?

CONGREGATION: **We do.**

MINISTER: **And do you agree to do all in your power to assist them in the struggles that they may encounter?**

CONGREGATION: **We do.**

MINISTER: **And do you give yourselves to the ideal of living out a life of commitment that they may see in you that toward which they too should strive?**

CONGREGATION: **We do.**

Combining Key Elements and Adding Your Own

If you're of different faiths or want to pay tribute to a different tradition or culture, find the key elements of each service by using the list at the beginning of this section. You can incorporate African rituals by inserting them alongside the key elements of a Christian ceremony. Or you could use the key elements of one service as the foundation for your ceremony but take the prayers and readings from the other. Consider all the alternatives and find the one that's right for you. Write it down so that you can discuss it with your officiant(s).

Whatever form of service or combination of key elements you choose, there are many ways to add personal touches. Some couples encourage the active involvement of their guests by including an "Affirmation of Vows," in which the congregation pledges their support for the marriage.

Even without altering the language or order of the service, you can make statements about what's important to you. If you want to *honor your ancestors,* for instance, consider dedicating flowers on the altar to their memory, reserving an empty

At the beginning of the ceremony, two candles are lit on the altar—one on the bride's side and one on the groom's—by a member of each family, to represent the couple as individuals. A single candle remains unlit at the center until the two have been pronounced man and wife, at which time each takes their individual candles and together light the center one, to symbolize the joining of their lives and their families.

pew with a bouquet of flowers to indicate their spiritual presence, or making a special tribute to them in your wedding program. If you want special guests to participate, ask them to read a lesson from the scriptures or give one of the prayers. To *symbolize your union,* have your officiant join your wrists with a garland of flowers or a string of cowrie shells (symbols of fertility) after he has pronounced you man and wife. Or light a "unity candle" after your vows to represent the merging of your two lives and your two families.

Again, write down your ideas and make a note to ask your officiant for further suggestions.

Your Vows

The most "Traditional" as well as the most personal moment of every wedding ceremony is the exchange of vows. Many couples today are choosing to make it more personal than ever by modifying the wording—or composing their own—to reflect their individual beliefs and circumstances.

Read the vows for the ceremony you've chosen thoughtfully. Discuss them with your fiancé to see how closely they conform to both of your ideas of the marriage you're making. The decision about the words you will use to express your commitment to each other may be the most important of all your ceremony planning.

"Traditional" Vows. "I take thee to be my wedded husband, to have and to hold from this day forward, for better for worse, for richer for poorer, in sickness and in health, to love and to cherish, till death us do part." If these "Traditional" words, or their counterparts in the service you'll be using, are what you've always imagined yourself saying—if they mean "marriage" to you as no other words would, even your own—by all means say them, as have generations of couples before you.

Family Vows. ". . . And here, before God, we vow to cherish and honor our new family, accepting one another's children as our own. To raise them to be true men and women of God, to nurture their bodies, minds, and spirits with unconditional love." If you, like Darlene and Walter Hunter who spoke these words, are among the many couples who will bring children into your marriage, you may want to add a commitment to your new family to your vows. Try drafting your own, or see if your officiant has an example you can follow. You might even ask the children themselves to participate by making their own vows to honor the new relationship.

Personal Vows. While they consulted several books for ideas, Nikki and Carlos felt that only *their own* words could fully express what was in their hearts on their wedding day:

   Carlos: In the presence of God, our family, and friends, I intend to offer you, Nikki, a husband who is faithful, strong, and kind. I am committing to giving you unending support, unconditional love, and a lifetime of dedication. I will continue to grow spiritually and emotionally and will share with you all the fruit of my labor. I will not waver from the responsibility of being your partner for life.

   Nikki: On this day, I take you, Carlos Matthew Webb, to be my husband and partner for life. Though our commitment to each other does not begin today, I am blessed to have this opportunity to share with our friends and family how much I have loved and admired you for years.

   Since that day in December of 1990 when I finally found the courage to admit my ten-year-old crush on you, I have experienced more support and love from one man than ever imagined.

   Our years together have been filled with teaching and learning from one another, encouraging and comforting each other, laughing and crying together, struggling and supporting one another, and I have loved every minute of it.

   Sometimes I truly wonder where I would be without you in my life. And now that you have invited me to share your life with you, I know that I am blessed.

You inspire me, you challenge me, and you move me with your poetic words, with your thoughts and acts of kindness, and with your intellect and your strength.

I vow to let my heart be ever open to your beauty, your sorrows, your needs, and your love. I intend to lose myself in building a solid family and future. I promise to successfully fulfill our life's goals and purposes.

I will make every effort to forgive you of your faults and hope that you will overlook mine so that each of us can remain equals in the unity of love.

Carlos, I rejoice in our love and I promise to walk by your side with a constancy that only comes from unreserved commitment. And it is this commitment I make to you now as I take you as my husband, from this day forward.

If you want to write your own vows, this is an opportunity for the two of you to focus explicitly on your vision of your future life together. Set aside a time to talk about what you'd like to include in your promises to each other. Some of the areas to consider are:

- Your expectations of marriage and each other

- Your individual strengths and weaknesses

- Your goals for yourselves and for your relationship

Make notes as you talk to refer to when you begin writing. If your feelings, expectations, and goals are completely in sync, you might compose a single set of vows together that you can repeat to each other at the ceremony, as in the "Traditional" service. Or, like Nikki and Carlos, you might want to write yours individually.

Practice saying your vows aloud to each other or a friend, to make sure that they're clear and that you can read (or recite) them comfortably and audibly. And bring a copy of them with you to the ceremony!

Readings

Most wedding ceremonies—whether "Traditional" or Afrocentric—include readings from the sacred texts that belong to the religion or culture in which the marriage is being celebrated. These readings further remind the couple and the congregation of the beliefs and values they share and that provide the spiritual context

A Selection of Readings from the Scriptures

When you make your selections, compare different translations of the Bible (the King James Version, the New International Version, the Revised English Bible, the New Jerusalem Bible, among them) to decide which one speaks most clearly and meaningfully to the two of you. Read them aloud to each other and reflect on what they say in relation to the vows you will exchange.

Old Testament

Genesis 2:18–24—on God's creation of marriage

Song of Solomon 2:8–17—a song to the beloved

Psalm 33—a psalm of rejoicing

Proverbs 5:15–19—man's joy in marriage

Hosea 2:16–21—on betrothal and marriage

New Testament

John 2:1–11—the miracle of the wedding feast at Cana

I Corinthians 13:1–13—the well-known meditation on "faith, hope, and love"

Galatians 5:22–26—on love as the "fruit of the Spirit"

Philippians 2:1–5—on love and Christ and your fellow man

for this occasion. They also give the bride and groom another opportunity to involve family and friends in the ceremony, asking them to participate as readers.

Today, many couples choose "secular" readings—from literature that has special meaning to them—in addition to, or even instead of, the "Traditional" readings from scripture. Talk to each other about the kind of readings you want to have and who you might like to participate. Make a list to present to your officiant, who can offer suggestions or help you find passages that you remember but can't locate.

Music

"We had two drummers playing African drums and a saxophonist. I hadn't planned to dance down the aisle, but the music just affected everyone," Carlos recalls. "My best man started dancing as he went down the aisle and when it was my turn I danced, too. The whole thing was impromptu. I was just moved. The music lifted my spirits."

Music is an important and integral—as well as "Traditional"—part of most wedding ceremonies. Music lifts spirits, moves the body and soul, and brings people together, sometimes more than words do. Spend some time thinking about the kind of music you want to set the mood and create the ambience for your wedding.

The "Traditional" times for music at a wedding are before the Processional (the "Prelude"), during the Processional and the Recessional, and after the ceremony (the "Postlude"). Most officiants are willing to incorporate music at other points, too—after a reading, for instance, or during the lighting of a unity candle. Also consider choosing a hymn or a song that all the congregation can sing together in celebration of your vows.

If your ceremony site has a music director on staff, arrange a meeting to discuss your ideas and find out what the director suggests. (She may have sample tapes for you to listen to and choose from.) If you want to bring in other musicians and determined during your interview with your officiant these things are acceptable at the site, you may still need to coordinate your plans with the director. (See chapter 12, "Celebrating Your Union in Style" for guidelines on hiring outside musicians.)

After you've developed a plan for your ceremony, submit it to your officiant(s), in person or in writing, for review. Their knowledge and experience can help you shape the final details.

YOUR WEDDING PROGRAM

Once your ceremony plan is finalized, think about printing a wedding program for your guests to follow during the service—especially if you're departing from "Tradition"—and to have as a keepsake. If your site doesn't have the facilities to produce a program, you can design and print one on

Ceremony Music

Processional

The Arrival of the Queen of Sheba/Handel

Choral Song/S. S. Wesley

Concerto in G, 1st Movement/J. S. Bach (also used for the Recessional)

Crown Imperial/Walton

March from *Poppea*/Claudio Monteverdi

Music for the *Royal Fireworks*/Handel

"Sinfonia" (from *Wedding Cantata*)/Bach

Trumpet Tune in D/Henry Purcell (also used for the Recessional)

Trumpet Voluntary/John Stanley (also used for the Recessional)

Trumpet Voluntary (Prince of Denmark's March)/Jeremiah Clarke

Recessional

"Allegro" from *Water Music*/Handel

"Bridal Chorus" from *Lohengrin*/Wagner

Fanfare/Jacques Lemmens

Jesu, Joy of Man's Desiring/Bach

"Le Rondeau" (*Masterpiece Theatre* Theme)/Mouret

Rejoicing/Telemann

"Wedding March" from *A Midsummer Night's Dream*/Mendelssohn

Wedding March/John Hodgson

your computer or order it from the stationer who will be printing your invitations. It's a nice touch to coordinate the program's style, color, paper, and typeface with your other printed pieces (see chapter 7, "Your Invitation").

A wedding program usually includes the following information, in the order listed:

- The names of the bride and groom and their parents

- The date and location of the ceremony

- The order of service, with explanations of any unfamiliar rituals and, if you wish, the texts for any special prayers and readings

- The titles of musical selections

- The names of the members of the wedding party

- The name(s) of the officiant(s)

- The names of the organist, choir members, and other musicians and vocalists

You may also give thanks to others who have helped in the planning, pay tribute to departed loved ones, reprint your vows (if you're writing your own), or make a personal statement.

Have your ushers distribute the program as they greet your guests.

THE REHEARSAL

If you're having a religious ceremony, your officiant will usually schedule a rehearsal at the site at least a day ahead. (You may want to ask him to schedule it another day or two earlier to allow more time for all your other last-minute preparations.) You and your groom, all your attendants, and any other participants—including ushers, readers, musicians—attend this rehearsal to run through the order of the service and find out who does what when. (Appoint stand-ins who can brief any out-of-town members of the wedding party who may not have arrived.)

If your officiant is agreeable, your wedding consultant may conduct your rehearsal. Or, if your wedding will be very small and simple or you're having a civil ceremony, you may have your rehearsal just a little beforehand on the day itself.

Your officiant will instruct each of you on your individual roles in the ceremony, as well as on general procedure.

Seating the Guests

The ushers greet guests at the entrance to the ceremony site and escort them to their seats. "Traditionally," the bride's guests sit on the left side as you face the altar or the front of the site, the groom's on the right. (These "sides" correspond to where the bride and groom stand during the ceremony.) The best man should appoint a head usher who will be responsible for seeing that the others arrive at the site an hour before the ceremony begins. He will supervise the seating plan and assign one or two ushers to escort the immediate family.

The usher offers his right or left arm to female guests and leads them up the aisle to the appropriate side, with their male companion (if they have one) following just behind. The first few rows of seats (pews) are "Traditionally" reserved for immediate family (parents in the very first) and other special guests and are sometimes designated by flowers or ribbons. You may send guests who will be seated "within the ribbons" pew cards with their invitations to indicate their seats (see chapter 7, "Your Invitation").

The mothers of the bride and groom are not escorted in until just before the ceremony begins, the groom's mother first (with the father right behind) and then the bride's mother (who takes the second seat in from the aisle in the first row on the left, leaving the aisle seat open for the father of the bride, who will join her after he has given their daughter "away"). After the mothers are seated, "Traditionally" two ushers unroll the aisle runner, from the front of the site to the back, to prepare for the Processional. Alternatively, you may wait for the unrolling until just before the flower girl's entrance, so that the runner remains fresh for the bride.

If you're having a small ceremony or one group of guests outnumbers the other— or if you simply want family and friends from both sides to mix and mingle—a contemporary alternative to "Tradition" is to seat everybody who's "outside the ribbons" together.

The Processional

Just before the start of the "Traditional" Christian ceremony, the officiant, the groom, and the best man enter from the left of the site, and stand to the right of the altar, facing the congregation, as illustrated on p. 243. Their entrance is the signal that the Processional is about to begin.

The *groomsmen* lead, entering from the back of the church singly or in pairs, depending on their number, in order of height—with the either the tallest or the shortest first. When they reach the front, they form a line on the right, behind the groom and the best man, with their sides to the congregation.

Then come the *bridesmaids,* also singly or in pairs and in order of height. They take their places to the left at the head of the aisle, in a line like the groomsmen.

If there are *junior bridesmaids,* they proceed next, in pairs if there are two or more. They also turn to the left and join the line beside the bridesmaids.

The *honor attendant* comes right before *child attendants* (in the order of *pages, ring bearer, and flower girl*) if there are any, or right before the bride. She also turns to the left, and stands in front of the bridesmaids, opposite the best man. The male child attendants turn to the right and stand beside the best man. The female child attendants stand beside the honor attendant.

Then the *bride* makes her entrance, on the right arm of her escort, "Traditionally" her father. When they arrive at the head of the aisle, they remain standing there, in the center, facing the officiant.

The *train bearers,* if any, bring up the rear (and the bride's train).

Contemporary alternatives: If you want to "mix it up," you may have the groomsmen and bridesmaids alternate in the Processional or even walk in pairs (although they shouldn't link arms until the Recessional, when doing so symbolically indicates that the marriage has taken place) and alternate at the altar, with the honor attendant still standing next to the bride and the best man next to the groom.

The bride may choose to be escorted by both her parents, one on each arm, or by her father *and* stepfather, if they're willing. An older bride, or one whose father is deceased, may walk alone or ask her mother or another close relative (even a child from a previous marriage) to escort her.

Positions During the Service

In a Protestant service, the members of the wedding party remain in the positions they take at the end of the Processional for the course of the ceremony. In a Catholic service, which is longer, they may have chairs arranged in the front of the church so they can be seated at certain points; if it's a full mass, the bride and groom may also be seated. In either service, child attendants may go to sit with their parents in the congregation or remain with the wedding attendants.

The bride's escort(s) may remain with her until the moment when the officiant asks, "Who gives this woman to be married to this man?" at which point they take their seats in the congregation. Or they may take their seats at the end of the Processional and then stand to answer from there.

The Recessional

At the end of the service, the bride and groom and all the members of the wedding party turn in place (so that they all remain on their "side" of the aisle) to begin the Recessional, led by the couple, who are now "husband and wife." Everyone walks in pairs, shortest to tallest if possible, to emphasize the pairing that has taken place with the marriage.

The bride takes the groom's right arm, followed by the flower girl with the ring bearer on her left, then by the honor attendant who takes the right arm of the best man, and by each bridesmaid, paired with a groomsman. (If there are more female attendants than male, a groomsman can escort two bridesmaids. Extra males pair up with each other.) If there are junior attendants, they recess immediately behind the honor attendants.

The Receiving Line

Although not technically a part of the run-through at the rehearsal, you may wish to have a receiving line at the ceremony site after the service and this is a good time to coordinate it with your officiant or wedding consultant. You'll need to ask

about the best area for assembling the line and include the signing of the marriage license at a time in the wedding service other than immediately following the ceremony. Also be sure to schedule any photo sessions at the site so as not to conflict.

The "Traditional" order for the members of the receiving line is:

- **The announcer (large informal reception)**
- **The mother of the bride: She is the first person to receive the guests**
- **The father of the groom (optional)**
- **The mother of the groom**
- **The father of the bride (optional)**
- **The bride**
- **The groom**
- **The best man (optional—only if groom requests it. Male attendants do not stand in the receiving line.)**
- **The honor attendant**
- **The bridesmaids**

*Note: If the couple already lives together or they are marrying for the second or third time, they are the only ones to receive their guests.

The main purpose of the receiving line is to give the bride and groom and the hosts of the wedding an opportunity to greet all their guests and "receive" their congratulations. At a large wedding it can be difficult for you to get a chance to speak to everybody unless you have a receiving line. On the other hand, your line shouldn't be so long that it takes a lot of time away from the rest of the festivities. Use your good judgment in deciding who to include.

If your parents are divorced, your father may take the option of not standing on the line. If either or both of your parents have remarried, and you want to include your stepparents, position them so that they won't feel awkward: Your mother should still head the line; perhaps your father and stepmother could stand to the left of the groom. Children are not included in the line. They wait along with the groomsmen on the opposite side in an orderly fashion.

Make sure that anyone who will be playing a special role in the ceremony has a chance to rehearse the movements, if not the words, of his or her part during the rehearsal. Even if a child performs well during the rehearsal, it's wise to make provisions for sudden attacks of stage fright during the ceremony itself. Younger children can freeze—or, worse, start hollering—when they see the assembled crowd. Don't try to force them to go on with the show, but also ask parents ahead of time not to go rushing down the aisle to the rescue. Assign an usher or host or hostess to lead the child quietly to where the parents are sitting.

Keep yourselves from second-guessing your officiant at this stage by thinking of ways to "improve" on procedure or by getting last-minute inspirations about changing the order of the service or adding new material. Remember that you've devoted a lot of time and thought to planning your ceremony and that what may now seem like "inspiration" could just be those "Traditional" (and normal) last-minute jitters. Trust the judgment of your officiant, who's had much more practice at this than you have.

THE REHEARSAL DINNER

Traditionally," the rehearsal is followed by a dinner for the bride and groom, hosted by the groom's family and including the officiant(s), all the members of the wedding party, the consultant, and even out-of-town guests who may already have arrived. Another reason to schedule the rehearsal more than a day in advance of the ceremony, if possible, is to allow the dinner festivities to go on without the pressure of knowing you have to get to the church on time the next morning.

TRANSPORTATION

The logistics of getting the bridal party and other special guests to the church on time on the day of the wedding (and then on to the reception) is as important as planning and rehearsing your ceremony. Discuss the options for transportation well in advance, six months ahead if you can, in order to have plenty of time to arrange for any rentals. One of the best man's responsibilities is to help with these arrangements, so bring him into your discussions early on.

First, decide on how many vehicles you'll need, which will depend on the size of your wedding party and immediate families. The main groups traveling to the ceremony site are "Traditionally" formed as follows:

- ↝ The bride, her father (or whoever will be escorting her up the aisle), and honor attendant

- ↝ The bride's mother and the bridesmaids

- ↝ The groom and his best man

- ↝ The groom's family

The rest of the groomsmen and ushers should already be at the church receiving the guests. However, if they do not have transportation, the couple will then arrange for them to get there at least one hour before the ceremony. Also be sure to consider any elderly relatives or close friends who may need help getting to the site, as well as out-of-town guests.

See how many cars are available to you and who's willing to drive. Friends and relatives who aren't participating in the wedding may be glad to offer their services (and their vehicles), although you also want to be sure that none of your guests end up spending the whole day on the road.

Assess your needs and make a master plan, including a schedule, for all the stages of transportation—from homes and hotels to the ceremony site, from the ceremony to the reception, from the reception to the final destinations for the day.

If you decide to rent cars or hire a limousine service, whether out of necessity or for the style and convenience, ask your friends who've had experience with rentals for business or social occasions to make recommendations. Consult your local Yellow Pages under Automobile Renting and Limousine Service.

Over the phone you can compare available kinds of vehicles, services, and prices (including any wedding packages). Pay a visit to the agencies you're considering before you make a final decision and ask:

- To see their license and insurance policy

- To see the vehicle(s) you'd be renting

- To meet the driver, if you're hiring one

Before you reserve your date and put down a deposit, which most limousine services require, get all the details of the deal in a signed, countersigned, contract that includes:

- The total cost and terms of payment.

- The date, times, names, and locations of the sites.

- The exact specifications of the vehicle, including color, accessories (aisle runner, radio, VCR, bar), and license number.

- The name of the driver, his responsibilities (will he wait at each site or come back), any restrictions on how he will be dressed.

- Will the company decorate the car or can you?

- Policies for cancellation and refund.

The quiet of God's spirit fills the church, ready to bring blessings to the impending union.

THE BIG DAY

Having everything run smoothly on the day of your ceremony is largely a matter of planning ahead, scheduling all the preparations and events realistically, and communicating clearly with all the other people involved.

If you've hired a wedding consultant, she'll coordinate everything and everybody for you. You'll only have to concentrate on getting dressed and made up according to the schedule she'll give you, and trying to stay calm. Some of Amelia Montgomery's clients refer to her affectionately as "The General," in recognition of her ability to deploy the "troops" to accomplish every last detail. Here is a Wedding Day Schedule she developed for one couple for the hours leading up their ceremony at 3:30 in the afternoon:

7:00 A.M.	Breakfast for the bride and her attendants at the home of the matron of honor
8:00 A.M.	Bride's beauty parlor appointment
10:30 A.M.	Bride returns to matron of honor's house to get dressed with attendants
11:00 A.M.	Wedding consultant arrives
11:30 A.M.	Makeup artist arrives
12:00 noon	Flowers for the bridal party arrive
1:00 P.M.	Photographer arrives at the bride's home (or wherever she is dressing) to photograph bride and her attendants
1:30 P.M.	Assistant to the wedding consultant arrives at the church to receive altar flowers, aisle runner, pew ribbons, one boutonniere, and two corsages
1:45 P.M.	Photographer leaves to go to the church to take photographs of bridegroom and his attendants and await the bride's arrival
2:00 P.M.	Limousines arrive at the matron of honor's home to pick up the bride and her attendants
2:00 P.M.	Groomsmen, ushers, and hostesses arrive at the church to begin greeting and seating guests
2:45 P.M.	The groom and the best man arrive at the church
3:00 P.M.	The bride's mother and the groom's parents arrive at the church
3:15 P.M.	Prelude music begins
3:20 P.M.	The bride, her father, and her attendants arrive at the church
3:25 P.M.	The groom's parents are seated The bride's mother is seated
3:30 P.M.	The Processional begins

Use this as a model for making your own pre-ceremony schedule if you don't have a consultant. You'll notice that there were "hostesses" at the ceremony site as well as groomsmen and ushers. Several of your family and friends who've been begging to contribute in some way will probably be happy to assist you in this capacity—especially if you don't have professional help. They can arrive at the site early enough to receive flowers or greet the photographer/videographer, as well as joining ushers in greeting and seating guests.

If you plan your ceremony with care and contemplation, in open and honest consultation with your officiant(s), you'll participate in it with full hearts and look back on it in the years to come with the deep pride and satisfaction with which Nikki and Carlos still speak of theirs. "I was *fully* present for every moment," says Nikki. "We didn't just go through the motions. We said how we honestly feel about each other. Many of our guests later told us they were intrigued and touched by the ceremony. Many were shedding tears of joy for us. To see the effect on others was so touching. As I walked down the aisle I could see the love in everyone's face."

The bride enjoying her first moments of married life.

T W E L V E

CELEBRATING YOUR

UNION IN STYLE:

THE RECEPTION

OUR MOTHER'S FRIEND Melda, a wedding consultant, handled everything at our reception," Lateefah recalls gratefully. "She told me later there'd been problems with the maître d', the wine had run out . . . I can't even remember what else. We never felt a thing! She deflected all the questions so that nobody bothered me. Because she's so picky, everything was extra good!" Even if you haven't hired a wedding consultant, the right planning will allow you to handle the inevitable last-minute snags and let you really *celebrate* at your reception—the first dance, cutting the cake, tossing the bouquet and garter, dashing off to a romantic honeymoon!

And these "Traditions" are no longer the only ones. Black couples are increasingly mixing and matching them with traditions that have special meaning for us and our families and friends. We of the African Diaspora have the advantage of being able to draw on a wide selection of practices from around the world.

As you plan your reception, turn back to your original vision and remember, most of all, a wedding is an occasion to get everybody you love together, to celebrate family and the ties that bind us as a community. Use the opportunity to honor those who came before you and to make your own contribution to tradition.

THE PERFECT PLACE TO PARTY

Turn now to the Reception section of your planner. Whether you made a final decision based on the answers to your "first calls" in chapter 3 or are still considering several possibilities that suit your style and price range and are available on your date, it's time to make an appointment to visit the site(s). Seeing a place—and seeing it in use, if possible—will either confirm your earlier decision or help you choose among the locations on your short list.

Don't worry about having a complete guest list at this stage. Most sites ask for a final count just a week or two before the wedding. You *will* need to have made some basic decisions about the style of reception you want and to have composed a list of questions about the particular services and facilities available and the restrictions that might apply when you follow up on your first calls.

Style

The reception of choice still remains the one held in the evening with a full meal, a big wedding cake, music, and dancing late into the night. "If you're gonna do it, do it right," is the "Traditional" wisdom that many couples still follow. Today, doing it "right" has taken on new forms to suit many different tastes and budgets while retaining the age-old sense of joy and celebration that marks this Day of All Days.

Breakfast Reception. Generally smaller (fifty to seventy-five guests) and less formal than an evening reception. Breakfast is a fresh as well as practical alternative—your guests can feast happily on elegant, delicious omelettes, bacon, and sausages (or biscuits and grits and fried apples—the whole Southern shebang!) for a fraction of the cost of dinner and drinks. Preparation is far easier and less time-consuming, too—a buffet line with an omelette chef will do the trick. Decorations can be simpler and, if you choose to have alcohol, a mimosa toast (champagne and orange juice) may be all the send-off you'll need. And where's the rule against dancing in the morning? (Although perhaps you'll opt for soft background music instead.) The beginning of the day seems an appropriate time to celebrate the beginning of a new life. And you'll be able to make an early getaway for your honeymoon.

Brunch or Lunch. Usually about the same size as a breakfast reception and about the same degree of formality, with a menu that may shift to include sandwich-makings and accompaniments. A carving station with several selections (turkey, ham, and beef, for instance), a salad bar, cake, and a champagne toast can more than satisfy midday appetites, midrange budgets, *and* the celebratory spirit.

Cocktail Reception. Fifty or more guests, informal to formal. The cocktail-and-hors-d'oeuvres reception is a new creature, gaining in popularity. Many couples want a big party to celebrate their nuptials without all the planning and expense involved in a full meal production. Lasting about two or three hours (instead of the usual four to six), with tasty tidbits instead of dinner and still plenty of music to dance to—for the right couple and the right crowd, this style of reception can be a big success. Cutting the cake is the culminating event. (Serve coffee, tea, and soft drinks during the last hour to promote safe driving!)

Evening Reception. Fifty or more guests, informal to formal. When you choose the evening reception, you're going along with about 95 percent of all marrying couples (and your costs will be commensurate). Nowadays, serving stations and buffets are far more common at this style of reception than before and usually far less expensive than the "Traditional" table service. If you're going to go for evening and a full meal on a limited budget, think about serving chicken or turkey instead of beef or seafood, hiring a DJ instead of a band, supplying your own alcohol or having a "closed bar," where you pay for a limited number of drinks per person—a cocktail, glass of wine, and glass of champagne, for instance—rather than an "open" one.

Services

Most reception facilities offer catering and many require that you use their caterer for everything including the wedding cake, to avoid legal liability for any mishaps that might occur. (Ask to see insurance documents and deal only with facilities that are licensed by the local board of health.) Meet with the catering manager when you visit the site, present your plan for the style of your reception and any ideas you may have for the menu, and ask about the services they provide.

- Do you have an in-house party planner who will help us? May we use our own wedding coordinator or at least have her act as our liaison?

- What are your standard menus for our chosen style and the relative costs? Are you open to suggestions for different dishes? May we have a menu-tasting session?

- Do you offer both buffet service and table service? What are the comparative costs? If we're planning a cocktail reception, will you pass the hors d'oeuvres?

- What is the ratio of staff to guests for each serving option? May we have some wait staff dedicated to the bridal table?

- What are the options for serving alcohol (e.g., open bar, closed bar, punch instead of individual mixed drinks) and comparative costs?

- Are costs based on the length of the reception? Are there additional charges for overtime?

- Do you provide all the flatware, dinnerware, and glassware? Is it included in the cost? If we must rent our own, what are your recommendations for sources and quantities? Can you estimate the expense?

- What are the choices for decorations for the hall and the tables and the costs?

If you're hiring an outside caterer, you'll need to ask the same questions and then arrange to have them visit the reception site, inspect the kitchen facilities, and coordinate their work with the site's management. Even if they'll be preparing the food elsewhere and bringing it in, they'll still need to discuss the logistics of delivery and set up. (See chapter 13, "Feeding the Body and the Soul" for more on planning your menu.)

Facilities

Be sure to see the rooms you will be using for your reception, preferably when a party is in progress, so that you can get a sense of the acoustics and lighting and the arrangement of tables and serving stations and the traffic flow between them. Check out the decor and cleanliness of the rest rooms. Depending on the style you're planning, also ask:

- What equipment and facilities are available for bands or DJs?

- Do you have separate facilities for children or could we arrange them?

- Where are all the entrances and exits, stairs and elevators, and rest rooms?

- Are other parties scheduled for the same date? If so, what facilities might we have to share? Will there be sufficient "buffers" (hallways or empty rooms) between other events and ours?

Ask whether the site has any restrictions on such things as smoking, the use of open flames, electronic music.

Signing the Contract

When you're sure you've found the right site and are ready to book, get all the terms in a written contract that specifies *every single* detail you've worked out. Beware of hidden costs, such as parking fees, valet service, or gratuities for rest-room and coat-check attendants. If you don't want your guests to be burdened with these charges, make sure that the prices quoted are inclusive and ask when costs that could fluctuate—the food, for instance—will be finalized. The contract should spell out:

- The terms of payment

- The provisions for last-minute substitutions on the menu

- The policy regarding late changes or adjustments if you decide on extra services or the facility has to alter those you originally agreed upon

- The penalty for cancellation

- The deadline for you to submit the final head count (usually a week or two before the event)

Take time to review the contract thoroughly and question any terms that you don't understand or that seem unreasonable before you sign. It's wise to have your wedding consultant or some other third party review it, too.

MUSIC TO YOUR EARS

You close your eyes and pull your new husband closer as you rock gently to your favorite song. Your first dance as man and wife. You knew that few things would shape the mood of your reception as much as the music you chose. As your guests join you on the dance floor, you can see (and hear) that you made the right decision.

Music can *make* your reception—whether it's a soft, classical accompaniment to your conversation after a morning ceremony, a jazz trio or quartet in the background at brunch, African drummers, or a big band filling the ballroom with dramatic sound for your after-dinner dancing. For many of us, a wedding reception means

Popular First Dance Songs

- "Try a Little Tenderness" by Otis Reading
- "Vision of Love" by Mariah Carey
- "At Last" by Etta James
- "With You I'm Born Again" by Billy Preston and Syreeta
- "Always" by Atlantic Starr
- "Endless Love" by Lionel Richie
- "Inseparable" by Natalie Cole
- "Is This Love" by Bob Marley
- "When I Fall in Love" by Nat King Cole
- "When a Man Loves a Woman" by Percy Sledge
- "Someone Like You" by Van Morrison
- "For You" by Kenny Lattimore
- "All My Life" by K-Ci and JoJo
- "When I'm With You" by Toney Terry
- "You Are My Friend" by Patti LaBelle
- "A House Is Not a Home" by Luther Vandross
- "For the Love of You" by the Isley Brothers

boogying! The memories and pictures of everybody out on the floor will be part of your wedding lore for years to come. ("Who knew Uncle Joe had those moves in him?") Others, out of personal preference or religious belief, may want only background music or accompaniment for singers. Some may want to provide entertainment in the form of a musical program or by hiring a DJ who also acts as the master of ceremony, introducing the bridal party and other guests and putting on a show of his own. Whatever your style and preference, start looking at possibilities up to a year ahead.

The first step is to decide on the kind of music you want. You and your fiancé may share the same taste and be in absolute agreement that you have to hire a rhythm and blues band that can play all your old favorites. It's more likely that your tastes differ at least a little. In either case, it's probably best to plan a mixture of music so that all your guests will hear something that gets them up onto the dance floor.

Hold a "tune-tasting" session with each other one night. Listen to CDs, tapes, and old records and compile a joint list of songs you'd like played at your re-

Top Ten Artists for Love Songs

1. Luther Vandross
2. Anita Baker
3. Barry White
4. Mariah Carey
5. Roberta Flack
6. Marvin Gaye
7. Isley Brothers
8. Peabo Bryson
9. Stevie Wonder
10. Whitney Houston

Top Ten Artists for Dance Songs

1. Rick James
2. George Clinton
3. Aretha Franklin
4. Cameo
5. Earth, Wind & Fire
6. Smokey Robinson
7. Boyz 2 Men
8. James Brown
9. Frankie Beverly and Maze
10. Patti LaBelle

ception, along with the names of the artists and versions you like best. Reminisce about special times in your life that bring certain tunes to mind. Include some standards as well as current hits. This list is a useful tool when you starting talking to musicians or DJs.

Live Music

How do you begin your search for a band? Maybe you've heard a good group at a recent party or another reception you've attended. Ask your friends, wedding consultant, caterer, and photographer for recommendations. Look in the Yellow Pages under Bands and Orchestras and Entertainers. See Resources at the back of this book.

Call and arrange to get a sample audio- or videotape or attend a performance. When you evaluate the performance, judge the structure of the program as well as the style and technical competence.

- Is the band versatile? Can they play selections "from tango to techno" or are they strictly R&B? (If you know you want a mixture of styles, some entertainment agencies offer packages that include, say, a classical ensemble for the cocktail hour and a rock 'n' roll band for dinner and dancing and will arrange for scheduling and set up.)

- Do they have a balance between fast and slow songs?

- Do they make smooth transitions from one song to the next to keep dancers on the floor?

- Are they presentable and personable?

If you like what you see and hear, be sure to meet the musicians personally and check their references as you would for any other vendor. Show them your list of songs (including any you *don't* want played) and discuss the order of the program.

- Do you want the first dance to take place before dinner or between courses?

- Would you like the music to be softer while guests are eating and then work up to a celebratory crescendo?

- Have they played for wedding receptions before and at your site in particular? (Make sure that their equipment will be compatible with the electrical system at your facility.)

The price for live music is usually determined by the length of the performance and the number of instruments. (The size of a band can range from a solo performer to a sixteen-piece orchestra.) Even if you'd heard the band perform and met the musicians, be aware that some professional bands have interchangeable members and the lead vocalist you liked so much might be booked elsewhere at the time of your reception. Get the names of the members you want to perform so that you can specify them in the contract.

Create your own tradition for your reception, drawing from history and culture.

African Drummers

Visit Afrocentric cultural centers and ask for names of drummers who teach there or who accompany dance classes. "I am always happy to play for weddings,"says Madou Dembele, who plays for classes at the Djoniba Dance and Drum Centre in New York City. (See Resources.) "I played for weddings at home [Ivory Coast] and here, also," he laughs, adding, "It's totally different!"

Be sure to discuss with the drummers the style of drumming you want, or at least ask them to describe their conception of wedding accompaniment so you will be sure what to expect at your reception. "In my country we play right next to the bride and groom. Here, when I played at my friend's wedding, they wanted us to play soft, in the background. They had a flute playing with us," said Dembele.

If you want a combination of African sounds and other music during the course of your reception, consider hiring drummers to play while you're eating and a band or DJ for dancing later on.

A Disk Jockey

If you want to hear a wide variety of songs in their original versions, a DJ may be the right choice for your reception music. Most of them have large eclectic collections and are usually willing to add special requests. DJs are often "performers" in their own right, with costumes and routines they develop for the occasion. They can function as MCs, preside over karaoke contests, and generally keep the party going.

It's wise to see them at work and arrange a meeting in person before you make your final decision. (Use the same criteria as you would for evaluating bands, above.) One DJ may be too mellow for you and another too talkative. Go over your song list with them to get a sense of how willing they are to accommodate your wishes.

In general, DJs are less expensive than bands, though the ones who have elaborate acts may end up costing just as much.

Signing the Contract

Whether you decide on live music or a DJ, you should specify all the terms of the deal in a signed, countersigned contract.

Muslims around the world celebrate marriage with a *walimah*, a party following the ceremony. Traditionally, the men and women celebrate separately with festive food (provided by the husband), song, and dance. This is an opportunity for the normally covered women to dress in special clothes, do their hair, and wear makeup. They sing traditional songs from all the cultures represented, a cappella, and dance in every style from Western to African, accompanied only by a drum. The men have a similar party elsewhere, and at the end the groom comes to collect the bride (at which point all the women must re-cover themselves).

Contemporary Muslim practices vary widely, however, and couples may opt for a mixed party. (In some cases that may preclude pretty clothes and makeup for the women, and singing and dancing.) Many African Muslims and African-Americans drawing from those traditions enjoy mixed celebrations with drumming and dancing.

- The names of the performers (including backups should someone be unable to attend)

- Price, including any overtime fees

- Arrival and departure times

- The number of breaks

- Equipment the performers will supply

- Proof of insurance coverage (your site may want a copy, too)

If you'd like to have tapes or CDs played during breaks, make sure there's a clause to that effect. Some bands can liven up their act with bubble or fog machines and special lighting. If such elements are part of the deal, they too should be specified.

At least two weeks before your wedding, give the band or DJ directions to your site and its phone number and make sure you have a way of contacting them on the day of the event. If you've communicated clearly with them along the way, all you'll have to do at the reception is grab your new spouse and dance the night away!

I f you take time now to organize the basic details of your reception—a receiving line (if you didn't have one at your ceremony site), seating arrangements, and an order of events—and delegate some of the on-location responsibilities, you and your groom and all your guests can really relax and celebrate.

Receiving Line

"Instead of greeting guests on a receiving line, we preferred to spend a lot of time visiting guest tables and handing out favors," said Nikki Davis-Webb. "However, that did not leave us much time to dance." A receiving line is the most efficient, if not most personal, way to be able to speak to all your guests. (See chapter 11, "Your Ceremony, Your Way" for guidelines.)

Seating Arrangements

Seating arrangements are an integral part of making a reception a happy social occasion. It's customary for the wedding party to be seated at a head table facing their guests, with the bride and groom at the center and the bridesmaids and groomsmen alternating on either side of them. The parents of the bride and groom are seated at a nearby table, with other key relatives and participants, such as the officiant. You need not follow the custom, especially if you have only one or two attendants. The most important thing is to seat yourselves and your guests in groups that will be socially compatible and conducive to conversation. Although you may be tempted just to let people sit where they want, you can avoid awkwardness and unintentional exclusion if you assign places.

If there are children in the wedding party who will be attending the reception, it's best to seat them with their parents—unless there are going to be a lot of other children in attendance, too. Some of your older guests—even some of the younger ones—may find the presence of children disruptive or inappropriate. Couples often decide to have "adult only" receptions. (If children will attend the wedding but not the reception, you may want to state this on the R.S.V.P. card for the wedding: "Accommodations for children under twelve are not available at the reception.") If you

Dozens of items are available to enhance your reception, from place cards to favors.
Favors courtesy of Heritage Weddings™ mail-order catalog.

want to include children, however, consider making special arrangements for them—a separate "children's area," for instance, where they can play under the supervision of a sitter. Parents who arrive at receptions with small children in tow are one of the most often reported problems at sites where African-American couples hold receptions. Often invitations do not make it clear whether or not parents can bring children or do not realize how the presence of children can change the tone of a reception. Make a plan to handle this situation, so that no feelings are hurt and your invited guests are able to enjoy the reception.

You may use either *escort cards,* which are usually set out and distributed at the entrance of the reception and assign a table number, or place cards on the tables themselves—or both at a very large reception—to seat your guests. Either may be printed (see chapter 7, "Your Invitation") or handwritten, which again may depend on the number of your guests. Ask your groom, a member of your family, or a member of your wedding party to help you work out a seating plan. Try to achieve a good mixture of personalities at each table that will spark conversation as well as to give people who may not get a chance to see each other often the opportunity to have this time together.

Hosts and Hostesses

If you haven't hired a wedding consultant or coordinator for the day and didn't recruit hosts and hostesses for your ceremony (see chapter 11, "Your Ceremony, Your Way"), consider asking for volunteers for your reception. They should arrive at the site about an hour ahead of time, familiarize themselves with the layout— including the location of rest rooms, stairs and elevators—and set up an area for escort cards (table assignments) and the safekeeping of gifts that guests may bring. They may even put place cards on the tables and attend to last-minute decorating details. In general they see to it that everything has been arranged as planned.

Appoint a head host or hostess to assign duties to the others and handle any complaints that don't need to be referred to you. During the reception, hosts and hostesses greet guests, make introductions, get signatures in the guest book, oversee seating, and generally make sure that everybody is comfortable. At the end, they can assist the best man and groomsmen in packing gifts for transportation and collecting any rented items for return. Their help may be one of the nicest gifts you'll receive— the freedom to enjoy your own party.

The Order of Events

The average reception lasts from four to six hours. There are certain "Traditions" you may want to observe during that time—being toasted by members of the wedding party, dancing the "first dance" with your groom, cutting the cake, tossing the bouquet and garter—as well as other family or cultural rituals you'd like your guests to participate in. Most of us have been subjected to toasts that ramble on and on, first dances that got delayed until the bridal party was too laid out to make it to the floor, cakes that didn't get cut until long after dinner when many of the guests had given up and gone home. Just as your ceremony follows an order of service, so should the events of your reception be scheduled in such a way that everything you planned gets accomplished. You don't have to "go by the book" or adhere to a rigid timetable that allows only so many minutes per toast or restricts conversation to the interval between the appetizer and the entree. By the careful timing and placement of events, you can have your cake and make sure that everybody gets to eat it, too.

It can be practical to schedule the *first dance* before dining so that the meal won't be interrupted and people who may have to retire early will still be on hand. Have the band leader or DJ announce it so that guests can clear the floor if dancing has already begun. The "Traditional" order of partners is:

- You and your groom alone.

- Your father cuts in to dance with you while the groom dances with your mother.

- The groom's father cuts in to dance with you and the groom dances with his mother.

- The best man dances with you and the groom dances with the honor attendant.

- The whole wedding party joins you on the dance floor.

- All the guests join you.

If there are difficult relationships or absences that would make such an order awkward, you can have the band leader invite everyone onto the floor after you and your groom have had your own private spin.

Just before food is served, it's "Traditional" for the officiant to bless the occasion as well as the meal that is about to be received. Then the toasting begins. Try to get a sense ahead of time about how many toasts there will be. "Traditionally," the best man makes the first toast to the couple, then the groom toasts the bride and her fam-

Unity Wafer Toast

Bread is a symbol of life, and sharing bread together is an ancient tradition. When we share bread today, we will join our hearts in love and unity for [name] and [name], who have chosen to make this special act part of their wedding day. We are honored by their invitiation to be here with them and share their first meal as husband and wife. As we join with them in breaking and sharing this special bread, we are united by the love we all share for [name] and [name].

Lord, an assembly of family and friends is a precious gift, and we thank you for this opportunity to gather together. It is with pleasure that we are united here today to break bread together in Your name. As [name] and [name] share bread as a symbol of their love and unity, we will share bread with one another for all our hearts are united in joy as we celebrate this special day. In love and support for [name] and [name], we ask all Your blessings be upon them as we break this bread together.

On this very special day for [name] and [name] we ask that everyone join in sharing this bread as a symbol of love and unity. As the hearts are united on the bread, so too are our hearts united in joy for [name] and [name] as they begin their new life together. [Name] and [name], we wish you every happiness.

ily, and the bride toasts the groom and his family. In some cultures that's the end of it; in others it's only the beginning. Not until your Uncle Joe and your groom's Aunt Belle and everybody in between has had their say does anybody get to eat. If you know this is going to be the case, *plan* for it. Maybe you should schedule a toasting time instead of the usual cocktail hour. Also consider placing wafers and the text "unity toast" at each place so that your guests can join together to salute your happiness.

The wedding cake usually serves as dessert in a dinner reception, but you may offer other selections as well or choose to have a Caribbean black cake that is traditionally sliced and distributed to guests as a "take-home" wedding favor rather than eaten on the spot. You may want to have a groom's cake and even bridesmaids' cakes too (see chapter 13, "Feeding the Body and Soul"). Just be sure to have a plan for cutting and serving them before guests have begun to leave.

"Traditionally," the bride holds the knife (a beribboned silver cake knife) to cut the first slice of the cake and the groom puts his hand over hers. They feed each other from that slice, then distribute pieces to their new families. Usually the catering staff or a host or hostess then steps in to cut the rest, having removed the top tier to be frozen for use on the couple's first anniversary. You may provide special napkins or boxes (sometimes printed with your names and the date of the wedding) so that your guests can take a slice home. (Young girls "Traditionally" sleep on these wedding napkins and dream of their husbands-to-be.)

The bouquet and garter toss are "Traditionally" the last events of a reception, signs that the festivities are winding down and the bride and groom are close to making their getaway. All the single bridesmaids and female guests gather for a chance to catch the bridal bouquet that will mean she's the next to walk down the aisle. If you're reluctant to give up your bouquet, you can have a smaller "double" made to throw instead or a pull-out section built into the arrangement.

Then the single men gather for the garter toss. If you're following "Tradition" in this, make sure to wear the garter in an easily accessible place (close to your knee), so your husband doesn't have to grope for it. If you'd rather not reveal your legs, wear a wrist garter!

Other Reception Rituals

All around the world, marriage is an occasion for celebration. For the Xhosa people in South Africa, wedding festivities last five days. In some islands of the Caribbean, family and friends hold a second reception—"Second Sunday"—when the couple returns from their honeymoon.

"A reception is a celebratory event," says Linnyette Richardson-Hall, founder of the Association of Minority Wedding Professionals and president of Premiere Event Management. "African-American traditions are a way of binding family and friends together following your ceremony." She suggests a variation on the Loading-the-Bride and Jumping-the-Broom showers we proposed in chapter 9: having an "Elders Corner" at your reception, where older, long-married guests can write down advice to help ensure a long and happy marriage. Their wise words may be written on ribbons that you can tie on a broom and take with you into your new life.

There may be traditions of your own creation that you'd like to incorporate into the festivities. One couple we know staged an African-inspired "courtship pantomime" at the beginning of their reception. The bride entered separately, completely veiled and escorted by her attendants, and was seated. Then the groom appeared, es-

A Sample Schedule for an Evening Reception

6:00–7:00	**Cocktail hour**
7:00	**Reception begins**
7:00–7:10	**Introduction of the bridal party**
7:10–7:20	**First dance**
7:25	**Seating of the bridal party**
7:30	**Prayer and blessing of the couple**
7:30–7:35	**Toasts**
7:35	**Dinner is served**
8:00–8:30	**Dancing**
8:30–8:40	**Bride and groom cut the cake**
8:40	**Dancing continues**
9:15	**Throwing of the bouquet and garter**
9:30	**Dancing continues**
9:45	**Bride and groom circulate to thank guests for coming and to give out favors**
10:30	**Bride and groom change to street clothes for departure**
11:00	**Reception ends**

corted by his groomsmen. The best man gave the groom a handful of cowrie shells, which the groom then offered to the maid of honor. The maid of honor refused the offer. The best man returned to the groom for further negotiation—and another handful of shells. This time the maid of honor accepted, the bride was unveiled, and she and the groom embraced. Together they then poured a libation for their ancestors.

Invent your own pantomime. Add African drums and dancers. Or put together a family video using old photograph albums to honor *your* ancestors. Your creativity is your only limit.

Toasting and eating and dancing with your loved ones—you may still feel like it's all a dream. With the right planning and the right music in the right place, it's your dream come true.

The taste of love . . . very, very sweet.

THIRTEEN

FEEDING THE BODY

AND SOUL

OR ANY STYLE of reception, the menu depends on your crowd," says Jane Smith, of Jane's Distinctive Catering in New York. "Because we are such a mixed society, working and socializing with such diverse groups, a wedding is no longer a gathering of relatives only. We must include a little bit of every culture in the food—not just African or Caribbean or American."

Smith, who started out by catering church banquets and parties, specializes in helping couples choose the right menu for their wedding feast—one that will suit their budget and the size and diversity of their guest list, as well as their own tastes.

PLANNING YOUR MENU

The key is flexibility," she says, and we heartily agree. When Smith first meets a couple, she asks the basic questions every couple should be ready to answer, whether hiring a caterer (see chapter 11 for full information on choosing and contracting with a caterer), getting help from the kitchens of friends and family, or doing the cooking themselves.

- What do *you* like to eat?

- What are "celebration foods" to you?

- How much can you spend?

- How many people are invited and what are their cultural backgrounds?

- Are your co-workers and employers coming?

Turn to the Food section of your planner and use these questions to begin your own planning.

Budget

As we mentioned in chapter 3, most couples spend at least a third of their total wedding budget on their reception, not including music. If you won't be using a facility that provides catering, subtract the cost of the space from your reception allotment and decide how much of the remaining money you want to put toward food and beverages. For many couples, after the site itself, food is the most important element of their reception and thus the second largest expenditure.

Size

Once you've determined your food and beverage budget, you can divide by the size of your guest list to get a preliminary figure for what you can afford to spend per person, which is the way most caterers charge. Some couples have friends and family who offer to prepare their wedding feasts, and the dollar amount of the food budget (after subtracting what you will spend on beverages) may be allocated among those who will cook for the purchase of food. In this regard, Jane cautions, however, "For a guest list over seventy-five, it's best to hire a caterer. Most people—unless they're in the business—don't have the experience and know-how to cook for that many guests at once or to store the food safely."

Sit-down Meals

The most formal way to serve food to your guests, it also usually offers the least choice. All guests are served the same meal, generally a meat, fowl, or fish (or perhaps a choice between two) with a starch and vegetable. A soup or salad is commonly served before the meal. (A nice touch at a formal dinner is a printed menu card coordinated with your other printed wedding pieces.)

Buffets

You can offer your guests much more variety, although lines and waiting may be a trade-off. Linnyette Richardson-Hall, founder of the Association of Minority Wedding Professionals, also advises couples to keep presentation in mind with a buffet: "A buffet should have visual appeal, have foods placed at different heights—someone with design expertise should be involved in the setup. A contemporary buffet style uses 'food stations,' with different types of food served in separate areas rather than all in one place."

Jane's Distinctive Catering offers three similarly priced buffet plans that reflect the kinds of choices and trade-offs you will find at most caterers. (Buffet prices usually reflect food choice and the amount of service. They can be just as expensive—or more—than a sit-down meal.)

Buffet Plan A

Starters

Fruit or fruit cocktail

1 salad

Choice of cheese plates or crab meat salad

Main courses

3 meats

2 starches

2 vegetables

with punch and cornbread or dinner rolls

Linen, china, and servers

Lace Bridal table

Silk flowers centerpiece

Buffet Plan B

Starters

Fruit or fruit cocktail

2 salads

4 hot hor d'oeuvres

Main courses

3 meats

2 starches

2 vegetables

with punch and cornbread or dinner rolls

Linen, china, servers, and waiters for bridal

party and two family tables

Disposable plates, knives, forks, table covers,

and napkins for guests

Silk flower centerpieces

Jane charges an additional 25 percent for these same menu plans when she uses them in sit-down dinners.

Selecting the Dishes

"I encourage my clients to choose what they and their guests *like*," says Jane. "There's no point in paying for food and having three quarters of it left over at the end of the evening. Because I cater for a lot of cross-cultural marriages, I do a lot of 'mixed' menus. I guide my clients according to the composition of their guest list."

You may not feel yours is a cross-cultural marriage if, say, one of you is African-American from St. Louis and the other is of Jamaican parentage, born and raised in Brooklyn. But there is nothing like food to remind us that there are many

Sample Wedding Breakfast Menu

(from Linnyette Richardson-Hall)

Beverage Service

Fruity mimosas

Bloody Marys

Champagne punch

Sparkling cider

Imported bottled waters and juices

Fruit Tree

Pick your own favorites from an assortment of fresh ripe melons and berries

Made to Order

Omelettes—your choice of Western, Three-Cheese, or Seafood

Crepes

With a selection of fillings

Belgian Waffles

With your choice of toppings

At the Station

Country ham or bacon

Finishing Touches

A wide array of gourmet muffins and breads to complement your meal

cultures within our great African Diaspora. Imagine her family picking over the deep-fried, cornmealed catfish or his folks pushing the jerked pork around on their reception plates. Even if your palates are similar, plan the reception menu with Jane's sound advice in mind.

Here are some of her suggestions for each style of reception, including some of her most popular dishes:

Sample Evening Wedding Feast

(from Linnyette Richardson-Hall)

A p p e t i z e r s

An assortment of fresh California and Florida seasonal fruits

A selection of the finest imported cheeses: cheddar, havarti, muenster, Swiss, hot pepper, and port wine

Your choice of gourmet crackers and cocktail breads

O n   t h e   B u f f e t

Nigerian oven rotisserie chicken

African curried beef

East African yams

Seasoned Southern greens

Mombasan brown rice

Senegalese cheese and pasta salad

A c c o m p a n i e d   b y

Harvest fresh gourmet rolls with sweet creamery butter

Tropical punch

Coffee and herbal teas

T h e   C r o w n i n g   T o u c h

A fruited and spiced carrot wedding cake topped with a nutmeg-laced buttercream icing

---

Breakfast. Eggs and omelets are international. Serve them with ham, home-style potatoes, sausage, and peppers, and for a Caribbean touch, fried dumplings (sometimes called fried bread or johnny cakes), fish, and plantains. Consider a basket of assorted American breads, rolls, and danishes, maybe some hot and cold cereal, and a display of fresh fruits.

Brunch or Lunch. A salad bar with four or five choices (for example, Waldorf salad, carrots and pineapple, seafood, macaroni, and potato); a platter of cold cuts and a nice assortment of breads. Also include a selection of light entrees—chicken, fish, and pasta, for instance—and a steamed vegetable combination.

Cocktail. According to Jane, some of the more popular hors d'oeuvres are fish cakes, beef patties, small quiches, and chicken wings, which can be made several ways, including lemon and pepper, jerk, and barbecue.

Dinner. Dinner for a wedding is more elaborate. Consider serving hot and cold hors d'oeuvres, assorted fruits or a fruit cup, a selection of salads, and usually a choice of three entrees (jerk chicken, broiled salmon, and oxtails, for example), vegetables, rice, dinner rolls, and dessert.

Unless the food is prepared on-site, Jane advises clients to avoid baked potatoes, broccoli, and zucchini—none of which travel well. Prepared fruits will dry out if left uncovered and unrefrigerated for more than an hour. Appetizer sandwiches such as country ham with mayonnaise or tomatoes on biscuits will get soggy if prepared too far in advance. It's usually best to serve condiments separately. Fried foods such as fish and batter-fried okra should be served as soon as they're cooked.

Remember that the presentation of the food is almost as important as the taste of the food. "Every wedding I cater must be a showpiece," says Smith. "I have couples who come to me because they were guests at one of my receptions and promised themselves that they'd hire me when they got married. It gives me great satisfaction to serve people food they enjoy!"

YOUR WEDDING CAKE

For today's couples, the wedding cake is as much a statement of personal style as it is a symbol of love and marriage. Brides and grooms look for pastry chefs who can deliver quality, value, and artistic flair. (Look in your Yellow Pages under Wedding Cakes or Bakeries or ask your caterer or favorite baker for recommendations.) The "Traditional" many-tiered pound cake with white butter cream icing has been joined by cakes with exotic flavors and fillings and cakes that reflect a couple's heritage, such as the Caribbean Black Cake.

Today's cakes are often works of art in themselves. Think about the imagery you want on your cake. You can replace the "Traditional" Caucasian bride and groom figurines with ones with brown skin, but that is only the beginning. Your cake can be decorated with your special colors or renderings of your special theme, edible art that looks almost too good to eat!

For Patty Cakes,
cake decorating
is an art, almost
too awesome
to cut!

Caribbean Black Cake

The plentiful fruits of the Caribbean islands find a festive use in the "black cake" customarily served at weddings. Steeped in sherry or wine (or the local rum) and combined with a dark batter, the resulting confection can be enjoyed by the happy couple and their guests long after the Big Day itself.

1 pound raisins

½ pound prunes

4 ounces cherries

4 ounces finely grated lemon rind

wine of your choice to cover fruit

8 ounces butter or margarine

8 ounces sugar

1 teaspoon vanilla

2 tablespoons browning (a dark brown food coloring available in most supermarkets and specialty stores)

8 ounces (1½ cups) flour

1 teaspoon baking powder

½ teaspoon salt

½ teaspoon cinnamon

4 eggs

1 cup sherry, brandy, or milk

Soak all the fruit in the wine for one or two months ahead of time.

Cream the butter, sugar, vanilla, and browning together until soft and fluffy. Sieve the dry ingredients together. Beat the eggs and sherry, brandy, or milk together and add the mixture to the creamed butter and sugar. Fold in the fruit and then the flour. (Do not overbeat.)

Bake at 350 degrees for 1½ hours or steam for 2 hours.

BRIDAL BUBBLY

The wine you choose for your reception can be among the highlights of the whole spectacular production. When deciding whether to serve red or white wine with your meal and what champagne to use for that special wedding toast, it can help to understand some of the basic classifications and terminology.

White Wine. In white wines, flavor is a balance of sweetness and acidity, a result of the way the grapes are handled during the wine making process. Ideally this balance keeps the wine from being either too sweet or too tart ("dry"). "Traditionally," white wines are served with fish, chicken, turkey, and light meats, such as veal and pork.

Red Wine. Like white wines, red wines are also the product of the interplay between sweetness and acidity, with the addition of a third element, tannin, the substance found in the woody parts of the grapevine as well as in the grape's skin and pips. Most tannin makes its way into red wine during the pressing of the grapes, when the juice is allowed to remain in prolonged contact with the skin and the stalks. (In white wines, this contact is kept to a minimum.) Red wine is "Traditionally" served with meat and game.

Champagne and Sparkling Wines. Champagne (or sparkling wine) is the "Traditional" beverage of choice for the wedding toast. Sparkling wines differ from "still" wines by being fermented twice. It is the second fermentation, which takes place in a closed container that traps the resulting gases, that adds the sparkle. In the champagne method, practiced in the Champagne region of France, the second fermentation occurs in the bottle in which the wine is sold, a much more labor-intensive and expensive process. Beginning in the 1970s, many champagne companies began establishing vineyards in California to make less-costly sparkling wines by using the same techniques used in France. Compare champagnes from France and California with sparkling wines to see if the differences in taste are worth the differences in price.

Ask your caterer, the party planner at your reception site, or your local wine merchant to make suggestions for wine that will complement the food you're serving and to advise you on quantities. Have a tasting session before you make your final decisions.

Nonalcoholic Beverages. More and more couples are opting for alcohol-free receptions. Whether for religious reasons, concern for the safety of guests who must drive home after the festivities, or simply for personal preference, you may decide against serving liquor. If you do, your reception need not feel "tea-totaling." Choose from a wide variety of sparkling beverages sold in elegant "wine" bottles—ciders, juices, even waters that will put fizz in your toasts without getting your guests "toasty."

Bar Service. Should you decide to serve cocktails, your caterer can arrange for an open bar with or without waiters circulating to handle requests for drinks. *Cost* and *control* are two important considerations in deciding whether to include bar service at your reception. A fully stocked bar with unlimited service can easily add 20 percent to the cost of your reception. (A cash bar is inappropriate at weddings.) As a way to keep this cost down, Linnyette Richardson-Hall suggests couples arrange to "bring your own," if the caterer allows. "Leftover alcohol can often be returned to the liquor store for a refund," she says. "Be sure to work with the caterer or a professional liquor salesperson to calculate how much to buy. Remember that you will have to hire barware and bartenders, too, if the caterer is not supplying them, and these costs add up."

It only takes one or two overindulgent guests to affect the mood of your celebrations. If you have an open bar, ask your groom's attendants to be mindful of any excesses and to handle such situations early, firmly, and discreetly.

THE MORNING-AFTER BRUNCH

An intimate, mouth-watering brunch is a wonderful way to show gratitude to your long-distance guests on the day after your wedding. Whether your style is American (eggs and bacon), continental (croissants and coffee), or soul (liver pudding and grits), the menu can be simple as well as delicious.

A typical brunch is usually held in a restaurant, hotel dining room, or club, lasts no longer than three hours, and is usually small, no more than fifteen to twenty guests. It's a perfect way to relax and catch up with those you don't see often enough, especially if you are not dashing off right away on your honeymoon. If possible, arrange a special screening of your wedding video!

"Weddings are such happy occasions," says Jane Smith. "Everybody gets all dressed up and they look forward to eating together. I love it when they all come back to the buffet table with their plates empty, asking for more!" With the right planning and consideration—and the help of an involved caterer—you can give your guests sumptuous food they will enjoy as part of your wedding festivities and remember happily for years to come.

"I love you more today than yesterday. . . ."

FOURTEEN

HAPPILY EVER AFTER

HEN YOU STOOD side by side to exchange your vows, you made a commitment to continue to stand by each other wherever and whenever necessary to make your marriage strong, happy, and successful. That commitment deserves everything you have to offer.

"A relationship is a fragile and precious gift," emphasizes Pat McGinn, a Chicago-based marriage and family counselor who is also a wife and mother of two. "There is no such thing as an unbreakable bond that will survive only because of a sincere promise. It will survive because of the boundaries set around it by partners who make themselves say 'no' to whatever robs too much time and too much energy from the intimate relationship. It will survive when a real investment is made in the life two people share."

"Extracurricular" activities—social clubs, night classes, volunteer work, team sports—can also take time away from each other. Both of you have such interests you will want to explore, and it is excellent for you both to maintain your individuality. Just make sure that you also allow enough time to be with each other.

Establish a practice of spending time alone together, away from work and other responsibilities. "Protect fiercely and nourish carefully your relationship," urges McGinn. "Your boss, your professor, your thesis advisor is not going to say, 'Listen, knock off for a weekend and get in some long hours of quality time with your beloved.' You have to do that yourselves."

TALK, TALK, TALK

Marriage counselors all agree that good communication is the key to sustaining a relationship and to making your home a place of comfort rather than conflict. Letting each other know what your expectations and limits are *before* problems arise can turn potential disagreements into productive learning sessions. Create an environment—even set aside a regular time—to discuss your feelings and to address any issues that may require changes in behavior.

Annica, an editor married for four years to Mitchel, finds that just keeping each other informed can protect their marriage from the sometimes excessive demands of work and other outside commitments. "During the times when I know I'm going to have to put in extra hours, if I apprise Mitchel of my schedule and say, 'This is going to be a hard week or month for me,' it helps a lot. It lets him know that although there's work I must do, he's still the most important thing to me and his feelings matter," she explains.

Couples find great sustenance in a common faith or spiritual belief, and shared faith unifies individuals in marriage, providing practical guidelines for resolving those inevitable differences and keeping the routines of day-to-day life fresh.

"My transition from singlehood to married man was definitely not easy," says Michael McCarter of Los Angeles. "We lived together for four months before the wedding and looking back on it, I was playing house," recalls the twenty-six-year-old groom.

After saying "I do" Michael began to ask himself, "'Did I do the right thing?' I loved her, but something inside me was not sure if marriage was what I wanted right now. I was scared. I was young."

A year later the couple separated for nine months. Though he loved his wife, Sherry, Michael was torn—he missed the comfort of the home the two built, yet he was struggling with understanding whether or not he was ready for the commitment.

"I did a lot of soul searching. The church and God helped me. I let God take control to guide me and to help me to understand what I wanted and what I was afraid of," Michael explains. "I realized that I loved Sherry and that love scared me. God helped me to see that I wanted to make a home and a life with Sherry."

The couple reunited and soon thereafter renewed their faith in God by being resaved. "By rededicating our lives to God we were making a commitment to the Lord and to ourselves. It was the foundation we needed and live by today," he says. "We pray together and encourage each other to pray separately. The church and God have taught us that we need to understand each other more, not just think about ourselves individually. I think about Sherry's needs and try to give her what she needs and wants from me."

The couple renewed their vows on Feb. 24, 1998, in Jamaica. "Believe it or not, I was nervous! I don't know why. As we said our vows all I thought about was how much I loved this woman and how far I had come as a man and in this relationship. I saw my present and future in her eyes. I've definitely grown up, matured, and we are having a fantastic time! I can say with confidence that we will be married for as long as we both shall live. I wouldn't have been able to say that three years ago."

JOINING YOUR NEW FAMILIES

We spoke in chapter 2 about welcoming each other's children into your marriage. During your engagement you will also have come to know each other's parents, siblings, and extended families. All these new ties now need to be nurtured, just as you'll nurture your relationship as husband and wife.

"Be involved as much as possible in each other's family," advises Dana, a free-lance writer married for eight years to William. "I've found that one of the things that pleases my husband the most is the fact that I'm truly interested in getting to know his people. I've really come to love them. I know this wouldn't have happened if I didn't take the initiative."

If they're nearby, ask each other's families over for occasional meals or plan activities that you can all enjoy together. If they're farther away, try to schedule regular telephone conversations or make holiday visits so that you can stay in touch. By building these relationships you will also be strengthening your own. Our families are our first source of unconditional love, a love that in turn supports the new families we form.

You may have to overcome some difficulties as you all settle into your new roles. Talk to each other about your family traditions and the part you expect them to play in your new life. "Keep your perspective," recommends Janice McMullen, a marriage counselor in New Orleans. "When conflicts arise, let your families know although you value their opinions and want them to be happy, your commitment to each other is now first and foremost." You will generally find that you are all seeking a common ground of love and respect.

If you nurture your marriage, establish good communication with each other, and cultivate strong spiritual and familial relationships, a year from now, when you unwrap the top tier of your wedding cake, you will be celebrating just the first of a lifetime of happy anniversaries. We at *Signature Bride* wish you many more!

Bride's Calendar

Twelve Months Before

- Buy a wedding planner or date book
- Determine budget with fiancé
- Determine the date of the wedding
- Choose the location for the ceremony and reception (make reservations)
- Determine style—Afrocentric or European-American, formal or informal, and select colors (which can also be your theme)
- Select your attendants and ushers
- Hire a wedding consultant (optional)
- Book photographer and videographer
- Book musicians (if Afrocentric—dancers and drummers)
- Book florist

Nine Months Before

- Make appointment to visit clergy or judge with fiancé
- Begin development of guest lists: Four separate lists are prepared to determine who is invited. The bride, her parents, the bridegroom, and his parents each compile lists of relatives and friends, without consulting each other.
- Select and order bridal gown, headpiece, and accessories
- Register for wedding gifts with fiancé
- Visit travel agent to make honeymoon plans

Six Months Before

- [ ] Hire a bakery chef
- [ ] Book limousine service
- [ ] Order invitations, announcements, and stationery
- [ ] Hire calligrapher (optional)
- [ ] Complete honeymoon plans with travel agent
- [ ] Select and order bridal attendants' dresses, headpieces, and accessories
- [ ] Select bridegroom's wedding wear
- [ ] Select groomsmen's wedding wear
- [ ] Order wedding rings and engraving

Three Months Before

- [ ] Complete master guest list and start addressing invitation envelopes
- [ ] Think about attendants' gifts
- [ ] Plan recording and display of gifts
- [ ] Reserve a block of rooms at a local hotel for out-of-town guests
- [ ] Get a physical (although not a prerequisite in many states, a good idea anyway)
- [ ] Book hairdresser and discuss a particular hairstyle
- [ ] Confirm with dress shop or seamstress the delivery date of gown
- [ ] Select and purchase your trousseau

Six to Eight Weeks Before

- Mail invitations
- Pick up wedding rings
- Buy wedding gift for groom
- Select and purchase attendants' gifts
- Have final dress and bridal veil fitting
- Sit for portrait
- Send announcement to newspapers
- Submit special request list to photographer and videographer
- Submit special music list to band or DJ
- Plan party for bridesmaids
- As wedding gifts arrive, send thank-you notes

Two Weeks Before

- Get marriage license with fiancé
- Finalize honeymoon reservations
- Address wedding announcements for mailing on wedding day
- Start packing and prepare going-away outfit

One Week Before

- Give final count of guests to caterer
- Purchase traveler's checks and foreign currency if necessary
- Give bridesmaids' luncheon or party
- Move clothing and other items to your new apartment (or house)
- Finalize details with florist, photographer/videographer, chauffeur, etc.
- Confirm rehearsal date and dinner details, which should take place two to three days before ceremony (allowing time for other last minute details). Give attendants their gifts on that night.

RESOURCES

BRIDAL REGISTRY

Carson Pirie Scott/
        Boston Store/Bergner's
Ph: 800-374-3000

The FHA Bridal Registry
(Wedding gifts of cash can
be applied toward your down
payment on a home)
Ph: 800-CALL-FHA

4W Circle of Art &
        Enterprise/Selma Jack-
        son
Brooklyn, New York
Ph: 800-227-7392
718-875-6500

Nationwide Gift Registry
Service Merchandise
Nashville, Tennessee
Ph: 615-660-GIFT

PNC Bank Matri-Money
        Wedding Registry
(Money market account can
be applied toward your down
payment on a home)
Ph: 800-488-8560

Target
Ph: 800-800-8800

CAKES

Cake Man Raven/
        Raven P. D. Dennis III
New York, New York
Ph: 212-283-3438
212-283-3612

Confectionary Artistry
Chicago, Illinois
Ph: 773-285-0282

Daniel Cooper
East Elmhurst, New York
Ph: 718-467-8954

Designer Cakes and Catering
Chicago, Illinois
Ph: 773-239-CAKE

Isn't That Special—Outra-
        geous Cakes
Hoboken, New Jersey
Ph: 800-945-6810
212-722-0678
201-216-0123

Patty Cakes, Inc.
Annandale, Virginia
Ph: 703-354-0677

Polly's Cakes
Portland, Oregon
Ph: 503-230-1986

Sylvia's Sweet Sensations
Oak Park, Illinois
Ph: 708-366-9309

CATERING

Cee Vee Catering Company,
        Inc.
Albuquerque, New Mexico
Ph: 505-242-3533

Emerson
Inwood, New York
Ph: 516-239-6715 (office)
718-574-6898 (home)

Jane's Distinctive Catering
        Inc./Jane Smith
Bronx, New York
Ph: 718-994-8175

Katherine's Catering and
        Special Events, Inc.
Ann Arbor, Michigan
Ph: 734-930-4270

Londel's/Londel Davis
New York, New York
Ph: 212-234-6114

National Caterers Associa-
        tion
Staten Island, New York
Ph: 800-NCA-0029

Tasteful Touch/Anthony
        Birchette
Elmhurst, New York
Ph: 718-476-8436

CLERGY

Reverend Alvin T. Durant
Reverend Cecil G. M.
        Muschett
Reverend Nina M. Neely
Mother African Methodist
        Episcopal Zion Church
New York, New York
Ph: 212-234-1544

Reverend John Harrison
Greater Cooper African
        Methodist Episcopal
        Zion Church
Oakland, California
Ph: 510-444-2672 (church)
510-638-7304 (home)

Baba Keino (Yoruba)
New York, New York
Ph: 212-862-8929

Reverend Phillip Valentine
(Yoruba)
The Temple of The Healing
Spirit
The Self-Healing Education
Center/Institute for
Self-Mastering
Brooklyn, New York
Ph: 718-756-1122

COSMETICS

House of Cosmetics
San Diego, California
Ph: 619-278-2462

Iman Cosmetics
Ph: 800-366-IMAN

Mary Kay Cosmetics
Ph: 800-MARY-KAY

Philosophy
Ph: 888-2-NEW-AGE

Vincent Longo, Inc.
New York, New York
Ph: 212-777-0316

CRYSTAL AND TABLEWARE

Lenox China
Ph: 800-225-1779

Sasaki
New York, New York
Ph: 212-686-5080

DANCERS/DRUMMERS

Djoniba Dance and Drum
Centre
37 East 18th Street
New York, New York
Ph: 212-477-3464

Kwabena Colon
Olaniyan/Kwabena
Bronx, New York
Ph: 718-733-5901
or
Kwaku Siaca Bey/Kwabena
Bronx, New York
Ph: 718-733-5901

The Weusi Ensemble/Abdul
Rahman
Brooklyn, New York
Ph: 718-467-3848

DECORATORS

A Whimsical Expression
Arlington Heights/Chicago,
Illinois
Ph: 847-818-1781

Balloons by Norma
Atlanta, Georgia
Ph: 770-808-9214

Balloon Wishes
Atlanta/Macon, Georgia
Ph: 404-753-6230

Celebration House/Belinda
Green
New York, New York
Ph: 212-749-8222

Every Bloomin' Thing
Miami, Florida
Ph: 305-573-6961

Fresh Ideas
Baltimore, Maryland
410-484-1057

Qualatex Balloon Network
Wichita, Kansas
Ph: 800-356-0901

Rainbow Magic Balloons
Westchester, Illinois
Ph: 708-344-6110

Vietta's Creative Designs/
Vietta Wright
Newark, New Jersey
Ph: 973-923-3824

FASHIONS

Alfred Angelo
Boca Raton, Florida
Ph: 800-528-3589

Anyiam's Creations Interna-
tional/Thony Anyiam
Langley Park, Maryland
Ph: 301-439-1110

Bola International/Bola
(Bridegroom's attire)
New York, New York
Ph: 212-831-7199

Cassandra Bromfield Designs
Brooklyn, New York
Ph: 718-398-1050

Christina's Fashion
(Bridesmaid's attire)
Chula Vista, California
Ph: 619-420-1553

David's Bridal
Ph: 1-888-399-BRIDE

Elegant Brides/Jacqui Scott
Hallendale, Florida
Ph: 954-458-0229

FATOU'S
New York, New York
Ph: 212-926-1661

Ferandun Fashions/June
  Terry
Manhattan, New York
Ph: 212-689-6389

Franklin Rowe International
Manhattan, New York
Ph: 212-967-8763

Images of Royalty Interna-
  tional, Inc./Reverend
  Doris Tongo
The Bronx, New York
Ph: 718-328-5484

Ites International
Atlanta, Georgia
Ph: 770-916-1142

Laurie's Fashions
Queens, New York
Ph: 718-217-2899

McMillan Fashions
New York, New York
Ph: 212-740-3103

Mario Uomo
Chicago, Illinois
Ph: 312-829-UOMO

Michael Joseph Designs
Chicago, Illinois
Ph: 708-388-7435

Modern Tuxedo/Chuck
  Remley
Chicago, Illinois
Ph: 312-357-6000

Nigerian Fabrics and Fash-
  ions/Jonathan Adewumi
Brooklyn, New York
Ph: 800-ADEWUM6
718-260-9416

Only VanEssa!
  (Bridal designs in hand
  crochet)
Brooklyn, New York
Ph: 1-888-MY TOUCH

Phenomenal Women Design
Charleston, South Carolina
Ph: 803-769-4927

The Private Stock Collection
  (Wedding night and
  honeymoon wear)
St. Louis, Missouri
Ph: 314-426-7761

Shades of Color/Joy Stanley
Newark, New Jersey
Ph: 973-596-1006

Shirley's Bridal and
Pageants, Inc.
Elgin, Illinois
Ph: 847-468-0337

Suädé
Newark, New Jersey
Ph: 973-639-1083

TMF Designs, Inc.
New York, New York
Ph: 212-714-8058

FAVORS/GIFTS
African Treasures
St. Louis, Missouri
Ph: 314-867-7400

Artistic Hands Bridal/Babu
  O. M. Shyaam and
  Veronica Decoteau
Brooklyn, New York
Ph: 800-464-7603

AYANA-NANA/Niambi
  Davis
Centreville, Maryland
Ph: 410-758-2878

Beads of Paradise
New York, New York
Ph: 212-620-0642

Cultural Center African
  Art/Gwendolyn Meade
Newark, New Jersey
Ph: 973-282-1982

Flowers to Remember/Deryl
  Wallace
Vallejo, California
Ph: 707-746-9380

Gee's Potpourri/Brenda B.
  Gee
New York, New York
Ph: 212-491-3301

Heritage Weddings™
  Mail Order Catalog
Lumberton, New Jersey
Ph: 1-888-218-8158

Louise's Bridal Works/
  Louise C. Osborne
Hempstead, New York
Ph: 516-483-7186

Nubian Creations/Vicki R.
  McGill
Washington, D.C.
Ph: 202-726-0447

FLORISTS

Black Orchid Florist/Ruth
   Oliver
New York, New York
Ph: 212-662-1121

Bukiety/Tony Polega
Chicago, Illinois
Ph: 312-243-4519

Flowers and Flowers
Miami, Florida
Ph: 305-534-1633

Flowers to Remember/Deryl
   Wallace
Vallejo, California
Ph: 707-746-9380

FlowerWorks/Angel & Mar-
   cia Melendez
Brooklyn, New York
Ph: 718-875-6464

FTD Flowers
Ph: 1-800-SEND FTD

1-800 Flowers
Ph: 1-800-FLOWERS

Vietta's Creative
   Designs/Vietta Wright
Newark, New Jersey
Ph: 973-923-3824

FLORAL PRESERVATION

Keepsake Floral Inc.
Orlando, Florida
Ph: 800-616-KEEP

GOWN PRESERVATION

Heirloomed Memories
Williston, Florida
Ph: 800-822-6911
904-486-3223

GRAPHIC DESIGNER/CALLIGRAPHY

E. Russell Payne
New York, New York
Ph: 212-281-5278

HAIRSTYLISTS

Brittanica and Associates
   Salon/Brittanica
   Stewart
New York, New York
Ph: 212-879-7030

FATOU'S
(African hair braiding)
New York, New York
Ph: 212-926-1661

Turning Heads Beauty and
   Barber Salon/Shannon
   Ayers
New York, New York
Ph: 212-491-5544

HEADWEAR

JRH Millinery
Plainfield, New Jersey
Ph: 908-753-7214

Manika's Designs
Chicago, Illinois
Ph: 312-337-7755

Tammy Darling
New Providence, New Jersey
Ph: 908-771-8971

INVITATIONS/PERSONAL STATIONERY

For Every Occasion
Chicago, Illinois
Ph: 773-324-2875

From the Earth to You
Westbury, New York
Ph: 212-614-5015

Heritage Weddings™
   Mail Order Catalog
Lumberton, New Jersey
Ph: 888-218-8158

Your Creative Link
Chicago, Illinois
Ph: 630-483-0791 ext 3

JEWELERS

The Black Cameo
New York, New York
Ph: 800-4-CAMEO-5

The Gold Connection
St. Louis, Missouri
Ph: 800-290-9792

Studio of Ptah
New York, New York
Ph: 212-343-9706

LIMOUSINES

Academy *Platinum Service*
Hoboken, New Jersey
Ph: 201-420-7000
212-964-6600

APEX Limousine, Inc.
Miami, Florida
Ph: 305-271-7477

First Class Car & Limo
   Service
New York, New York
Ph: 212-304-1111

Golden Touch
Flushing, New York
Ph: 718-886-5204

Las Vegas Limousines
Las Vegas, Nevada
Ph: 888-696-4400
702-736-1419

Limousines by Teddy
     Daniels
New York, New York
Ph: 212-862-6782

Lucky Limousine Service
Albuquerque, New Mexico
Ph: 505-836-4035

Marathon Lines, Inc.
Mount Vernon, New York
Ph: 800-763-8418
914-667-8418

Regal Limousine Service,
     Inc.
Springfield, Virginia
Ph: 703-440-3651

MUSICIANS

Complete Music Disc Jockey
     Service
Albuquerque, New Mexico
Ph: 505-275-7800

Cunning Music Company/
     Bob Cunningham
Brooklyn, New York
Ph: 718-282-8672

DJ Carol/Carol Elfton
White Plains, New York
Ph: 914-948-8246

Fine Entertainment/Elegant
     Affairs
Hallandale, Florida
Ph: 954-458-1229

Jazmyn/James Farley
North Tarrytown, New York
Ph: 914-366-6628
800-341-1889 (beeper)

M&M DJ/Mel
Long Island, New York
Ph: 516-665-3876

Mike King (DJ)
Brooklyn, New York
Ph: 718-498-4295

Milt Harris/C. W. Hamlett
White Plains, New York
Ph: 914-946-8159
914-328-9656

The New York Connection
     Band/Frank Dell
Queens, New York
Ph: 718-262-0259

Rhapsody Productions/
     Delores Major
Atlanta, Georgia
Ph: 404-981-9453

The Sound Pipers
Ph: 201-674-8593/Stan
     Andries
718-589-4067/Connie
     Questell
718-671-0313/Ike Bradley

Steve Clarke (Saxophonist)
Bronx, New York
Ph: 718-563-0945

Versatile Entertainment
D.J.'s
Aurora, Colorado
Ph: 303-680-1384

ONLINE SERVICES

Bridal Gown Search Site
www.bridalgown.com

Bridal Net
www.bridalnet.com

The Knot
www.the knot.com

The MelaNet
www.melanet.com

Wedding Bells
www.weddingbells.com

Wedding Central
www.weddingcentral.com

Wedding Channel
www.weddingchannel.com

Wedding Circle
www.weddingcircle.com

Wedding Gallery
www.weddinggallery.com

PHOTOGRAPHERS/VIDEO-GRAPHERS

David Brenowitz Photogra-
     phy
Golden, Colorado
Ph: 303-279-6562

Collier Video/Jim Collier
St. Louis, Missouri
Ph: 314-868-3903

Creative Eye Media
Hollywood, Florida
Ph: 954-929-5035

52 Shades Photography and
     Video/Michael Morris
Hollis, New York
Ph: 718-217-0200 ext1

Focus-On-Video/Bernard &
     Joni
Flushing, New York
Ph: 718-359-2122

Furla Photography and
Video
Glenview, Illinois
Ph: 847-724-1200
Chicago, Illinois
Ph: 312-755-9900

Garrett's Photography and
Video
Baltimore, Maryland
Ph: 410-523-2411

Lois Daniels Ingrum
Photography
St. Louis, Missouri
Ph: 314-454-1344

Mirage Photography
Atlanta, Georgia
Ph: 404-305-9196

Myers Photography and
Video
New Haven, Connecticut
Ph: 203-785-8444

Payton Studios
Chicago, Illinois
Ph: 888-764-2081

Photography by Trevor
Bitter
Ft. Lauderdale, Florida
Ph: 954-973-0421

Photo Sensation by Sassoon
Miriman, Florida
Ph: 954-894-6611

Scott A. Nelson Photogra-
pher
Alta Lona, California
Ph: 909-822-4700

Spada Photography
Chicago, Illinois
Ph: 312-329-9110

Tony Rose Studios
Baltimore, Maryland
Ph: 410-664-6705

Tyrone Rasheed
New York, New York
Ph: 212-491-2891

Video Perfection, Inc.
Atlanta, Georgia
Ph: 404-822-9031

Vince Cowan Photographer
Washington, D.C.
Ph: 888-442-3499

Wallace Lee
Allentown, Pennsylvania
Ph: 610-437-0600

Wedding Plan Plus Inc./
Carolyn Faulkner
Brooklyn, New York
Ph: 718-272-3705

TRAVEL AND TOURISM

Air Jamaica
Ph: 800-LOVEBIRD

BWIA Airways
Ph: 800-538-2942

Club Jamaica Beach Resort
Ocho Rios, Jamaica
Ph: 800-818-2964

EZ Tours
New York, New York
Ph: 800-348-7200

Greater Fort Lauderdale
Convention and Visitors
Bureau
Fort Lauderdale, Florida
Ph: 954-765-4466

Greater Miami Convention
and Visitors Bureau
Miami, Florida
Ph: 305-539-3084

Greene Travel Unlimited,
Inc./Mildred Greene
New York, New York
Ph: 800-435-0962
212-283-0274

Jamaica Tourist Board
Ph: 800-JAMAICA

Native Weddings, Honey-
moon and Resorts
Tamarac, Florida
Ph: 954-726-7122

New Orleans Metropolitan
Convention and Visitors
Bureau
New Orleans, Louisiana
Ph: 504-566-5011

SATOUR-South African
Tourism Board
New York, New York
Ph: 212-730-2929
Los Angeles, California
Ph: 310-641-8444

U.S. Black Travel and
Tourism Associates
Washington, D.C.
Ph: 202-544-9455
New York, New York
Ph: 212-283-3315

WEDDING CONSULTANTS

A Small Affair, Inc.
Jersey City, New Jersey
Ph: 201-432-7133

A Special Event
Los Angeles, California
Ph: 213-295-6002
Beverly Hills, California
Ph: 310-275-2136

Association of Bridal
    Consultants
New Milford, Connecticut
Ph: 860-355-0464

Atina Productions
Lansing, Illinois
Ph: 773-264-9137

Beautiful Occasions/Lois A.
    Pearce
Hamden, Connecticut
Ph: 203-248-2661

Ingrid Graver
Coral Gables, Florida
Ph: 305-448-1195

Nubian Generation
Brooklyn, New York
Ph: 718-346-7519

Premiere Event Management,
    Ltd./Linnyette
    Richardson-Hall
Baltimore, Maryland
Ph: 410-277-3870

RSVP Wedding and Event
    Planning
Issaquah, Washington
Ph: 206-313-3012

Signature Events
Bothell, Washington
Ph: 425-488-8171

Special Occasions & Cele-
    brations/Edith Foster
El Sobrante, California
Ph: 510-235-5940

Wedding & Party Prepara-
    tions/Ivy Singletary
Wheatley Heights, New York
Ph: 516-643-9750

Weddings by Amelia/Amelia
    A. Montgomery
New York, New York
Ph: 212-283-2106

**WEDDING/RECEPTION
SITES**

Akwaaba Mansion
Brooklyn, New York
Ph: 718-455-5958

Bianca's on the Park/Jennifer
    Scott
New York, New York
Ph: 212-665-1212

Djoniba Dance & Drum
    Centre
37 East 18th Street
New York, New York
Ph: 212-477-3464

Doubletree Hotel
Alburquerque, New Mexico
Ph: 505-247-7000

The Museum for African
    Art/Johanna Cooper
New York, New York
Ph: 212-966-1313

Nassau Inn
Princeton, New Jersey
Ph: 609-921-7500

Regency Plaza Hotel
San Diego, California
Ph: 619-291-8790

Wave Hill
The Bronx, New York
Ph: 212-549-3200

**WEDDING RESOURCE
BOOKS**

African American Historic Places
National Register of His-
    toric Places
Washington, D.C.: The
    Preservation Press,
    1994

*Basic Black: Home Training for
    Modern Times*
Karen Grigsby Bates and
    Karen Elyse Hudson
New York: Doubleday, 1996

*The Hippocrene USA Guide to
    Black America*
Marcella Thum
New York: Hippocrene
Books, Inc., 1991

*In Their Footsteps: The American
    Visions Guide to African
    American Sites*
Henry Chase
New York: Henry Holt &
Company, 1994

Women of Color
Darlene Mathis
New York: Ballentine, 1996

Photos pages xii, xvi, 18, 78, 79, 80, 91, 94, 106, 107, 110, 111, 190, 209, 216: Courtesy of Dorothy Shi.

Photo page xv: Courtesy of Linnyette Richardson-Hall.

Photos pages 3, 231: Courtesy of Michael Morris/52 Shades Photography and Video.

Photo page 5: Courtesy of Furla Photography and Video.

Photo page 5: Courtesy of Lateefah Fleming-Williams and Winston Williams, photography by Dean Rivera of Golden Touch Photography.

Photos pages 6, 7: Courtesy of Michelle and Frank Reid, photography by Ed Porter.

Photos pages 25, 137: Courtesy of Tony Rose Studios.

Photos pages 35, 36: Courtesy of Lee Bradley of The Gold Connection, photography by Frank Sciolino of Concept Creations.

Photos pages 40, 127, 161, 175, 266, 267: Courtesy of Heritage Weddings™ mail-order catalog, ©1997, all rights reserved.

Table page 45: Adapted from information supplied by the Association of Bridal Consultants.

Graph page 59: Adapted from information supplied by the Association of Bridal Consultants.

Photos pages 60, 122, 221, 262: Courtesy of Myers Photography and Video.

Photos pages 76, 102: Courtesy of Cookie Washington of Phenomenal Women Design, photography by Stephanie Harvin, Charleston, South Carolina.

Photos pages 78, 79, 81, 91, 114, 118: Courtesy of James Spada.

Photos pages 78, 87, 95, 113, 135, 138: Courtesy of Reginald Payton of Payton Studios.

Photos page 80: Gowns by Alfred Angelo.

Photos pages 87, 135: Courtesy of Nigerian Fabrics and Fashions; photography by Anderson Ballantyne, Brooklyn, New York; flowers by Ethnically Yours, Brooklyn, New York; accessories by Cellestine Collection, Brooklyn, New York.

Photos pages 100, 103: Courtesy of Debbie Vyskocil.

Photo page 112: Courtesy of Anyiam's Creations International, photography by Raph, male model courtesy of Gloria Forbes.

Photos pages 112, 130, 211: Courtesy of Charles Hodges.

Photos pages 115, 232, 262: Courtesy of Garrett's Photography and Video.

Photos pages 139, 249: Arrangement photo provided by FTD.

Photos pages 141, 180: Centerpiece by Natasha Dahline, Balloon Haven; bunch of balloons by Pioneer® Balloon Company; photos courtesy of Pioneer® Balloon Company, maker of Qualatex® balloons.

Photo page 142: Courtesy of Anyiam's Creations International.

Photo page 144: Courtesy of Heritage Weddings™ mail-order catalog, ©1997, all rights reserved; design by Carole Joy Creations®, Inc.

Photos pages 162, 168: Courtesy of Sasaki.

Registry card page 171: Courtesy of 4W Circle of Art and Enterprise

Photo page 184: Photo provided courtesy of the Greater Miami Convention and Visitors Bureau.

Photo page 198: Courtesy of Turning Heads Beauty and Barber Salon, New York, New York; photography by Eric Von Lockhart; makeup by Daniel Green; stylists: Lee Marieme Priestly, Debra Wilson, Angela Mayo.

Photo page 201: Courtesy of Brittanica Stewart.

Photo page 205: Courtesy of Matthew Jordan Smith.

Photo page 210: Courtesy of Waheedah Bilal.

Wedding program page 228: Courtesy of Nikki and Carlos Webb.

Photo page 233: Courtesy of Vince Cowan Photographer.

Photo page 252: Courtesy of Jerrice and Anthony Epps, photography by Dabney N. Montgomery of Weddings by Amelia.

Photo page 272: Cake created by Charmaine Jones of Isn't That Special—Outrageous Cakes.

Photo page 280: Wedding cake designed and created by Patty K. Collette of Patty Cakes, Inc., in Annandale, Virginia; photography by Bryan Blanken of Blanken Photography Studio in Bethesda, Maryland.

Photo page 284: Courtesy of The Philip Lief Group, photography by David Kelly Crow.

Color Illustration Credits

Photo page I1: Courtesy of African Treasures, photography by Frank Sciolino of Concept Creations.

Photos pages I2, I6, I7, I11, I14, I15: Courtesy of Dorothy Shi.

Photo page I2: Courtesy of Anyiam's Creations International, photography by Raph, male model courtesy of Gloria Forbes.

Photo page I3: Courtesy of Anyiam's Creations International.

Photos pages I4, I7, I10, I14, I15: Courtesy of Reginald Payton of Payton Studios.

Photos pages I5, I8, I9: Courtesy of James Spada.

Photo page I7: Courtesy of Debbie Vyskocil.

Photos pages I12: Courtesy of 1-800-FLOWERS.

Photo page I12: Cake created by Charmaine Jones of Isn't That Special—Outrageous Cakes.

Photo page I13: Courtesy of Heritage Weddings™ mail-order catalog, ©1997, all rights reserved.

Photo page I13: Balloon swan by Pat Skistimas, CBA, and Jim Skistimas, CBA, The Balloon House Design Studio; photo courtesy of Pioneer® Balloon Company, maker of Qualatex® balloons.

Photo page I16: Courtesy of Nigerian Fabrics and Fashions; photography by Anderson Ballantyne, Brooklyn, New York; flowers by Ethnically Yours, Brooklyn, New York; accessories by Cellestine Collection, Brooklyn, New York.

INDEX

Page numbers in italics indicate illustrations.

Flowers for wedding, 131–43, 295
Formal engagement announcements, 27–28
Formal weddings, 10
    dress for, 84, 86
    men's attire, 109–10
Four Elements, tasting of, 230, 232
4W Circle, 165–70, 171, 172, 173
Fragrant flowers, 135
Friends, help with wedding, 64, 68–69

Garter, tossing of, 268, 270
Gele (head wrap), 101, *102*
    for bridesmaids, 116
Ghana, wedding customs, 142
Gibson, Ted, 197, 200
Gifts, 163–74, 267, 294
    acknowledgment of, 157, 174–76
    display of, 176–77
    engagement parties and, 31
    to wedding party, 177–78
Gillian, B. J., 206–7
Glassware, *168*, 173
Gloves, 103–4, 115
Gold rings, 36
Groom
    boutonniere for, 138
    gifts, 178
    wedding attire, 84–85, 88
    wedding costs, 51
Groom's family, and wedding costs, 49, 51
Groomsmen, 71
    boutonnieres for, 138
    gifts to, 177–78
    wedding attire, 84–85
Guest book, *40*
Guests, 72–74
    participation of, 234, 238
    seating of, 242
    wedding costs, 51
Guyanese customs, 186
G'wi people, wedding customs, 185

Hair styles, 196–203, *198, 201,* 295
    of men, 212
Hands, care of, 209–10, *209, 210*
Handwritten invitations, 161
Headpieces, *91,* 91, 99–102, *100, 102,* 295
    for bridesmaids, 115, 116
Health concerns, 191–97

Heirloom gowns, 93–95, *94*
Henderson, Eleanor, 14
Henna Hands, 210, *210*
High blood pressure, 197
Historical sites, 54, 55, 57
"Honeymoon" weddings, 2, 6, 6–7, 54, 58
Hosiery, 104
Hosts and hostesses
    at ceremony site, 250–51
    at reception, 267
Hotel accommodation cards, 155
Hotels, receptions at, 57
Houses of worship, 66, 218–21, *221*
Hunter, Darlene, 24, 236
Hunter, Walter, 236

Ice sculptures, 132, 141–42
Iman (model), *205,* 215
Individual expression, 1–2, 8
    in dress, *76,* 77 78–80, 81–104
    in wedding ceremony, 234–37
Informal engagement announcements, 29–30
Informal weddings, 10
    dress for, 85
Ingrum, Lois Daniels, 120–22, 124, 128
In-laws, relationship with, 288
Innovative decorating ideas, 143
Insurance of wedding gifts, 176
Interfaith ceremonies, 13–14, 54–55, 234
Interlocking hair extensions, 202
Internet, 75
    engagement announcements, 30
Inventory of possessions, 169–70
Invitations, *144,* 145–61, *161,* 295
    to bridal showers, 187
    ordering of, 158–61
Islamic weddings, music, 264

Jackson, Selma, 171
Jewelry, 295
Jumping the broom, 4, *5,* 142–43, 233, *233*
Jumping the Broom Shower, 186
Junior attendants, 69, 71, 72

Kaspar, Janet, 159
Kenya, wedding customs, 143, 177
Kohl, Tammy, 36

Kola nuts, exchange of, 230–31
Koro people, Africa, 21
Kwanzaa, life principles, 52
Kwanzaa Shower, 186

Libation, pouring of, 229–30
Lifestyle, healthy, 192, 196–97
Lifestyle photographs, 28
Lighted bouquets, 132
Limousine service, 248, 295–96
Live music for reception, 260–63, 262
"Loading the Bride," 185, 186
Lobolo (bride price), 47
Location of wedding, 13, 53–58, 65–67
Long-distance planning, 2
Long hair, styles for, 200
Lunch receptions, 255, 278

McCarter, Michael and Sherry, 287
McGinn, Pat, 285
McMullen, Janice, 288
Maid of Honor, role of, 70
Makeup, 205–9
Manicures, 210
Maps, 156
Marriage, Muslim, 227
Marriage counselors, 286
Marriage license, 37–38
    signing of, 220, 245
Mathis, Darlene, *Women of Color,* 199
Matron of Honor, role of, 70
Meditation, 212–14
Mementoes, printed, 158
Men
    and makeup, 211–12
    and thank-you notes, 175
    wedding attire, *106, 107,* 107–12, *110, 111, 112*
    and wedding plans, 8–9, 15, 64–65
Menu, for reception, 273–83
Mitchell, Henry and Ella, 224–25
Mixed-race weddings, 14
Money, gifts of, 177
Montgomery, Amelia, 11, 15, 45, 61, 65, 67–68, 73, 145, 249–50
Morning-after brunch, 283
Mortgage registries, 164
Mothers of bride and groom
    corsages for, 138
    in receiving line, 245–46